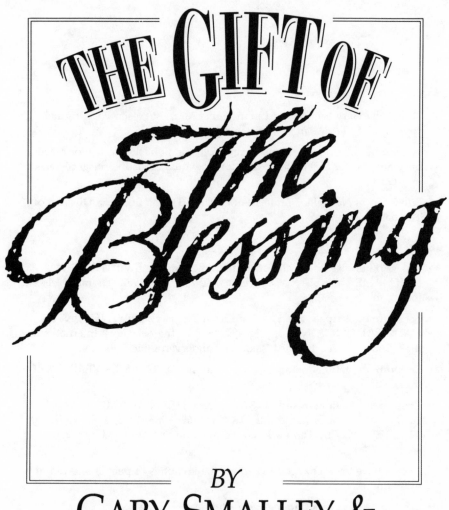

THE GIFT OF The Blessing

BY

GARY SMALLEY &
JOHN TRENT, PH.D.

A
JANET
THOMA
BOOK

THOMAS NELSON PUBLISHERS
Nashville

Published in Nashville, Tennessee, by Janet Thoma Books, a Division of Thomas Nelson Inc.

Unless otherwise noted all Scripture quotations are from THE NEW KING JAMES VERSION. Copyright © 1979, 1980, 1982, Thomas Nelson, Inc., Publishers.

Scripture quotations noted NIV are from The Holy Bible: NEW INTERNATIONAL VERSION. Copyright © 1978 by the New York International Bible Society. Used by permission of Zondervan Bible Publishers.

Scripture quotations noted KJV are from the KING JAMES VERSION of the Bible.

Scripture quotations noted NASB are from THE NEW AMERICAN STANDARD BIBLE, Copyright © 1960, 1962, 1963, 1968, 1971, 1972, 1973, 1975, 1977 by The Lockman Foundation and are used by permission.

Names have been changed to protect the identities of people referred to in this book.

Library of Congress Cataloging-in-Publication Data

Smalley, Gary.
　　The gift of the blessing / Gary Smalley, John Trent. — Rev. ed.
　　　　p.　　cm.
　　Rev. ed. of: The blessing. 1986.
　　Includes bibliographical references.
　　ISBN 0-8407-4849-3
　　1. Family—Religious life.　2. Parenting—Religious aspects—
Christianity.　3. Blessing and cursing.　4. Self-esteem—Religious
aspects—Christianity.　I. Trent, John T.　II. Smalley, Gary.
Blessing.　III. Title.
BV4526.2.S524　1993
249—dc20　　　　　　　　　　　　　　　　　　　　　　93-15277
　　　　　　　　　　　　　　　　　　　　　　　　　　　　CIP

Printed in the United States of America
16 17 18 19 20 – 01 00 99

Dedication

*T*his book is dedicated to our wives, Norma and Cynthia, for their loving support and encouragement, and to four couples who have been a tremendous source of blessing to us in making this book possible: David and Karen Cavan, Doug and Judie Childress, Jerry and Judy La-Brasca, and Steve and Barbara Uhlmann.

Contents

Acknowledgments

We would like to express our deepest thanks to the following people:

To the hundreds of people who have written and spoken to us over the years about the positive difference this book has made in their lives. This revised and expanded edition gratefully shares some of their insight, applications, and encouragement;

To Janet Thoma, Susan Salmon Trotman, and Laurie Clark, for their encouragement and hard work in this revision;

To Diana Trent, for the hours she put into proofreading the manuscript;

To Larry Weeden and Bruce Nygren, our editors at Thomas Nelson on the original version of *The Blessing*, for their encouragement and expertise;

To our teammate in ministry, Terry Brown, for his careful reading of the manuscript and helpful suggestions;

To the many individuals and small groups who were willing to offer their comments and suggestions to help us refine the concepts found in the book, especially to the following people: Randy Vogel, Pat Dixon, Richard and Donna Alverson, Chuck and Jane Beuerlein, Rick and Denita Ryan, Don and Nancy Schlander, and Rick and Angie Wonder.

THE BIRTH OF THE BLESSING

*T*he writing of every book has its own history.

Nearly fifteen years ago, God used two experiences to show me (John) the power of the blessing. I was leading a Bible study at Northwest Bible Church in Dallas, Texas, working through the book of Genesis. I was also completing my doctorate in counseling and working with many couples and individuals in therapy. Day after day, I saw people in deep depression and emotional distress over pain from their past. And, one day, while working on my Bible study, I ran into Genesis 27 and Esau's bitter cry, "Bless me, even me also, O my father"! (Gen. 27:34 NASB).

Suddenly, I saw echoed in the lives of those I counseled all the heartache and unfulfilled longing that Esau felt. What's more, stripped bare and laid before me was my own lack of receiving the blessing from my father.

Because of this profound revelation, the concept of the blessing became the subject of my doctoral dissertation. And then, several years after teaming up with Gary Smalley, we molded my research into an earlier version of the book you hold in your hand, *The Blessing* (Nashville: Thomas Nelson Publishers, 1986). Gary, too, missed receiving the blessing from his father. Together, in sharing and writing about the heartache we both felt, this book became our personal journey, not just an academic one.

Today, the blessing has become a life-message that I teach at "Blessing" seminars across North America and overseas, and at our "Love is a Decision" seminars. Each time I bring up Esau's lament, I look into the eyes of people who have felt that anguish. And I look into the eyes of people who want to make sure their own children never know that pain.

In this revised, expanded edition of *The Blessing* we have tried to maintain the basic content and structure of our first book. Yet after eight years we've gained new insights that we want to share with our readers.

While our original book focused on giving the blessing to young children, in this version you'll discover eight ways to give the blessing to your older children and grandchildren. You'll also learn more about the dark side of the blessing from those who have lived under a "curse." And you'll see how to personally deal with the loss of a parent who never blessed you.

We are convinced that the blessing is perhaps the most powerful parenting concept in the Scriptures. As you read this book (again, or for the first time), we hope it will be a source of great encouragement to you as a parent, and to you as an adult child. May it make your heavenly Father's love more real to you and within easier reach than ever before.

1

*I*N SEARCH OF THE BLESSING

All of us long to be accepted by others. While we may say out loud, "I don't care what other people think about me," on the inside we all yearn for intimacy and affection. This yearning is especially true in our relationship with our parents. Gaining or missing out on parental approval has a tremendous effect on us, even if it has been years since we have had any regular contact with them. In fact, what happens in our relationship with our parents can greatly affect all our present and future relationships. While this may sound like an exaggeration, our office has been filled with people struggling with this very issue, people just like Brian and Nancy.

THE CRUSHING OF BRIAN'S DREAM

"Please say that you love me, please!" Brian's words trailed off into tears as he leaned over the now still form of his father. It was late at night in a large metropolitan hospital. Only the cold, white walls and the humming of a heart monitor kept Brian company. His tears revealed a deep inner pain and sensitivity that had tormented him for years, emotional wounds that now seemed beyond repair.

Brian had flown nearly halfway across the country

to be at his father's side in one last attempt to try to reconcile years of misunderstanding and resentment. All his
life, Brian had been searching for his father's acceptance
and approval, but they always seemed just out of reach.

Brian's father had been a career Marine officer. His
sole desire for Brian was that when he grew up he would
follow in his father's footsteps. With that in mind, Brian's
father took every opportunity to instill in his son discipline and the backbone he would need when one day he
too was an officer.

Words of love or tenderness were forbidden in their
home. It was almost as if any slip into a display of
warmth might crack the tough exterior Brian's father was
trying to create in his son.

Brian's father drove him to participate in sports and
to take elective classes that would best equip him to be an
officer. Brian's only praise for scoring a touchdown or doing well in a class was a lecture on how he could and
should have done even better.

After graduating from high school, Brian did enlist
in the Marine Corps. It was the happiest day of his
father's life. However, his joy was short-lived. Cited for
attitude problems and a disrespect for orders, his son was
soon on report. After weeks of such reports (which included getting into a vicious fight with his drill instructor),
Brian was dishonorably discharged from the service as
incorrigible.

The news of Brian's dismissal from the Marines
dealt a death blow to his relationship with his father. He
was no longer welcome in his father's home, and for years
there was no contact between them.

During those years, Brian struggled with feelings
of inferiority and lacked self-confidence. Even though he
was above average in intelligence, he worked at various
jobs far below his abilities. Three times he had been
engaged—only to break the engagement just weeks before
the wedding. Somehow he just didn't believe that another
person could really love him.

Although Brian was unaware of it at the time, he

was experiencing common symptoms of growing up without a sense of the family blessing, a missing element in his life that finally led him to seek professional help.

We began counseling with Brian after he had broken his third engagement. As he peeled away the layers of his past, Brian began to see both his need for his family's blessing and his responsibility for dealing honestly with his parents. That is when the call came from his mother saying that his father was dying from a heart attack.

Brian went immediately to the hospital to see his father. The entire flight he was filled with hope that now, at long last, they could talk and reconcile their relationship. "I'm sure he'll listen to me. I've learned *so* much. I know things are going to change between us." Brian repeated these phrases over and over to himself during the flight. But it was not to be.

Brian's father slipped into a coma a few hours before he arrived. The words that Brian longed to hear for the first time—words of love and acceptance—now would never be spoken. Four hours after Brian arrived at the hospital, his father died without regaining consciousness.

"Dad, please wake up!" Brian's heartbreaking sobs echoed down the hospital corridor. His cries spoke of an incredible sense of loss: not only the physical loss of his father, but, like many others, also the emotional sense of losing any chance of his father's blessing.

Nancy Relives a Painful Past

Nancy's loss was a different sort, but the hurt and pain she received from missing out on the blessing stung her just as deeply. In fact, living apart from the blessing had caused problems not only with her parents, but with her husband and children as well.

Nancy grew up in an affluent suburb outside a major city. During Nancy's early years, her mother loved to socialize with other women at the club and at frequent civic activities. In fact, with a marriage that was less than fulfilling, these social gatherings became of paramount importance to Nancy's mother.

When Nancy was very young, her mother would dress her up in elegant clothes (the kind you had to sit still in, not play in) and take her and her older sister to the club. But as Nancy grew older, this practice began to change.

Unlike her mother and older sister, Nancy was not petite. In fact, she was quite large and big-boned. Nor was Nancy a model of tranquility. She was a tomboy who loved outdoor games, swinging on fences, and animals of all kinds.

As you might imagine, such behavior from a daughter who was being groomed to be a debutante caused real problems. Nancy's mother tried desperately to mend her daughter's erring ways. Nancy was constantly scolded about being "awkward" and "clumsy." During shopping sprees, Nancy was often subjected to verbal barbs designed to motivate her to lose weight. "All the really nice clothes are two sizes too small for you. They're your *sister's* size," her mother would taunt. Nancy was finally forced on a strict diet to try to make her physically presentable to others.

Nancy tried hard to stick to her diet and be all her mother wanted. However, more and more often Nancy's mother and sister would go to social events and leave Nancy at home. Soon all invitations to join these functions stopped. After all, her mother told her, "You don't want to be embarrassed because of the way you look with all the other children around, do you?"

When Nancy first came in for counseling, she was in her thirties, married, and the mother of two children. For years she had struggled with her weight and with feelings of inferiority. Her marriage had been a constant struggle for her as well.

Nancy's husband loved her and was deeply committed to her, but her inability to feel acceptable left her constantly insecure and defensive. As a result of this hypersensitivity, every time she and her husband began to draw close, Nancy would feel threatened. Invariably, some small thing her husband did would set her off, and her marriage was back at arm's length.

Frankly, because of her lack of acceptance in the past, being at arm's length was the only place Nancy felt comfortable in a relationship. Her marriage was certainly of concern to her. Yet where Nancy struggled most was with her children, and with one child in particular.

Nancy had two daughters. The older girl was big-boned and looked very much like Nancy, but the younger daughter was a beautiful, petite child. What was causing Nancy incredible pain was the relationship between her mother and this younger child and the effect of that relationship on Nancy's feelings and behavior.

Just as in Nancy's childhood, her mother catered to the younger "pretty" daughter, while the older daughter was left out and ignored. Old hurts and wounds that Nancy thought were hidden in her past were now being relived through watching her own children. The heartache and loneliness that her older daughter was feeling was an echo of Nancy's unhappiness.

In spite of herself, Nancy's attitude toward her younger daughter began to change. The slightest annoying thing this child did brought an explosion of anger. Bitterness and resentment began to replace genuine affection.

In her heart of hearts, Nancy was also angry at God. In spite of her prayers, she felt He had changed neither her relationship with her mother nor her present circumstances. She seemed doomed to repeat vicariously through her daughters her own painful past. As a result of this barrage of feelings, she stopped going to her Bible study group, calling Christian friends, and even praying to God.

For Nancy, her relationship with her husband, her children, and God had all been affected by missing out on the blessing that she had tried for years to grasp, but that never quite came within reach.

OUR NEED FOR ACCEPTANCE

For Brian and for Nancy, the absence of parental acceptance held serious consequences. For Brian, the lack of the blessing was a major reason for his broken engagements and for keeping him from getting close enough to another person to become genuinely committed. For Nancy, an inability to feel acceptable as a person was destroying her most important relationships. Without realizing it, Brian and Nancy were searching for the same thing—their family's blessing.

Brian and Nancy typify people who are searching for their family's blessing. For years after they had moved away from home *physically,* they still remained chained to the past *emotionally.* Their lack of approval from their parents in the past kept a feeling of genuine acceptance from others in the present from taking root in their lives. In Nancy's case, this lack of approval even kept her from believing that her heavenly Father truly accepted her.

Some people are driven toward workaholism as they search for the blessing they never received at home. Always striving for acceptance, they never feel satisfied that they are measuring up. Others get mired in withdrawal and apathy as they give up hope of ever truly being blessed. Unfortunately, this withdrawal can become so severe that it can lead to chronic depression and even suicide. For almost all children who miss out on their parents' blessing, at some level this lack of acceptance sets off a lifelong search.

This search for the blessing is not just a modern-day phenomenon. It is actually centuries old. In fact, we can find a graphic picture in the Old Testament of a person who missed out on his family's blessing. This person was a confused and angry man named Esau. As we look at this man's life, we will also begin to learn about the blessing and what it can mean to grow up with or without it.

"BLESS ME, EVEN ME ALSO, O MY FATHER!"
Esau was beside himself. *Could this really be happening?* he may have thought. Perhaps his mind went back to the events of that day. Just hours before, his father had called him to his side and made a special request. If Esau, the

older son, would go and bring in fresh game for a savory meal, his father's long-awaited blessing would be given to him.

What was this blessing that Esau had waited for over the years? For sons or daughters in biblical times, receiving their father's blessing was a momentous event. We will discover that it gave these children a tremendous sense of being highly valued by their parents and even pictured a special future for them. At a specific point in their lives they would hear words of encouragement, love, and acceptance from their parents.

We will see that some aspects of this Old Testament blessing were unique to that time. However, the *relationship elements* of this blessing are still applicable today. In Old Testament times, this blessing was primarily reserved for one special occasion. In contrast, parents today can decide to build these elements of blessing into their children's lives daily.

For Esau, his father, Isaac, followed the custom of waiting until a specific day to give his son the blessing. Now at long last, Esau's waiting was over. His time of blessing would begin as soon as he could catch and prepare a special meal.

With all the skill and abilities of an experienced hunter, Esau had quickly and efficiently gone about his work. In almost no time a delicious stew was prepared as only one familiar with the art of cooking in the field could do.

All had been done just as he was told. Why, then, had his father trembled so when Esau stood before him? As if in a dream, the scene played over and over in Esau's mind. He had just entered his father's tent and greeted him:

> "Let my father arise and eat of his son's game, that your soul may bless me." And his father Isaac said to him, "Who are you?" So he said, "I am your son, your first-born, Esau."
>
> Then Isaac trembled exceedingly, and said, "Who?

Where is the one who hunted game and brought it to me?
I ate all of it before you came, and I have blessed him—
and indeed he shall be blessed."

When Esau heard the words of his father, he cried with
an exceedingly great and bitter cry, and said to his father,
"Bless me—me also, O my father!" (Gen. 27:31-34, italics
added)

Little did Esau know that when his aged and
nearly blind father had called him to his side, another had
been listening. Rebekah, the mother of Esau and his twin
brother, Jacob, was also in the tent. As soon as Esau went
out into the fields to hunt fresh game, she ran to her favorite son, Jacob, with a cunning plan.

If they hurried, they could kill a young kid from
the flock and prepare a savory meal. What's more, they
could dress Jacob in his brother's clothing and put animal
skins on him to simulate Esau's rough and hairy arms,
hands, and neck.

Putting on Esau's clothes did not present a problem, but one thing they couldn't counterfeit was Esau's
voice. That almost blew the whistle on them (Gen. 27:22).
But even though Isaac was a little skeptical, ultimately
their plan worked just as they had hoped it would. We
read in Genesis 27:22-23, "So Jacob went near to Isaac his
father. . . . And he did not recognize him, because his
hands were hairy like his brother Esau's hands; so he
blessed him." The blessing meant for the older son went
to the younger.

Jacob should not have had to trick his way into receiving the blessing. God Himself had told Isaac that regarding his twin sons, the "older shall serve the younger"
(Gen. 25:23). Yet while Esau went out to hunt for food, an
even more cunning hunter stole into his father's tent, and
came out with a priceless treasure.

When Esau returned and discovered that he had
lost the blessing to his brother Jacob, he was devastated.
Was Esau crying over losing his inheritance? As we will
see later, the oldest son's inheritance was something that

came with his birthright, and entitled him to a double
share in his father's wealth. Yet years before, Esau had
already *sold* his birthright to his brother for a pot of red
stew! (Gen. 25:29–34)

Esau wasn't lamenting the fact that he lost the cat-
tle and sheep—he had already despised that gift. What
ripped at his heart was something much more
personal . . . his father's blessing. In Old Testament times
a father's blessing was irretrievable, and irretractable once
it was given, and now Isaac's blessing was forever outside
Esau's reach.

Filled with hurt, he cried out a *second* time, "Do
you have only one blessing, my father? Bless me, even me
also, O my father." So Esau lifted his voice and wept
(Gen. 27:38 NASB). In response to his pitiful cries, Esau
did receive a blessing of sorts from his father (Gen. 27:39–
40), but it was not the words of high value and acceptance
that he had longed to hear.

Can you feel the anguish in Esau's cry, "Bless me,
even me also, O my father"? This same painful cry and
unfulfilled longing is being echoed today by many people
who are searching for their family's blessing, men and
women whose parents, for whatever reason, have failed to
bless them with words of love and acceptance. People just
like Brian and Nancy. People you rub shoulders with
every day. Perhaps even you.

THE IMPORTANCE OF THE BLESSING TODAY

Genuine acceptance; an unmet need in Brian, Nancy, and
Esau's lives; a need that goes unmet in thousands of lives
today—perhaps you have this need or a loved one is
struggling with it, a need that the blessing helps to meet.
Yet, the family blessing not only provides people a much
needed sense of personal acceptance, it also plays an important part in protecting and even freeing them to develop intimate relationships.

Today, as in centuries past, orthodox Jewish homes
bestow a special family blessing on their children. This
blessing is much like the patriarchal blessing we were in-

troduced to in the story of Esau. This blessing has been an important part of providing a sense of acceptance for generations of children. But recently, it has also provided an important source of protection to those children.

All across the country, cults are holding out a counterfeit blessing to our children. Cult leaders have mastered the elements of the blessing we will describe in the pages that follow. Providing a sense of family and holding out (at least initially) the promise of personal attention, affection, and affirmation is an important drawing card for many of these cults.

Children who grow up without a sense of parental acceptance are especially susceptible to being drawn into cults. In fact, thousands are drawn in every year. However, like beckoning hungry children to an imaginary dinner, the smell and aroma may draw them to the table; but after eating they are left hungrier than before.

If you are a parent, learning about the family blessing can help you provide your child or children with a protective tool. The best defense against a child's longing for imaginary acceptance is to provide him or her with genuine acceptance. By providing a child with genuine acceptance and affirmation at home, you can greatly reduce the likelihood that he or she will seek acceptance in the arms of a cult member or with someone in an immoral relationship. Genuine acceptance radiates from the concept of the blessing.

However, the blessing is not just an important tool for parents to use. The blessing is also of critical importance for anyone who desires to cleave, or draw close, to another person in an intimate relationship. One of the most familiar verses in the Bible is Genesis 2:24: "For this cause a man shall leave his father and his mother, and shall cleave to his wife" (NASB).

Many books and tapes talk about the need to cleave to our spouse. However, very few talk about the tremendous need people have to "leave" home. Perhaps this is because people have often thought of leaving home as simply moving away physically.

In reality, leaving home has always meant much more than putting physical distance between our parents and ourselves. In the Old Testament, for example, the farthest most people would actually move away from their parents was across the campfire and into another tent! Leaving home carries with it not only the idea of physical separation but also of *emotional* separation.

The terrible fact is that most people who have missed out on their parents' blessing have great emotional difficulty leaving home. It may have been years since they have seen their parents, but unmet needs for personal acceptance can keep a person emotionally chained to his or her parents' home, unable to genuinely cleave to another person in a lasting relationship. For this reason many couples never get off the ground in terms of marital intimacy. This is what happened to Brian and Nancy. You or a loved one may be facing this problem. Understanding the concept of the blessing is crucial to defeating the problem and freeing people to build healthy relationships.

A JOURNEY OF HOPE AND HEALING

In a world awash with insecurity and in search of acceptance, we need biblical anchors to hold on to. The search for acceptance that Brian and Nancy and so many others go through often leads people to accept a cure that is worse than the problem itself. Finding oneself through traumatic re-creations of the past or losing oneself through hypnosis or a similar psychological technique seldom, if ever, offers lasting change. On the other hand, God's Word and His principles do offer a changeless blueprint for constructing or reconstructing relationships.

In the pages that follow, you will discover more about the blessing. If you are a parent, you will see how to give your children, young and old, the blessing and how to discern if they have it now. You can also evaluate whether your parents received the blessing and how that may have affected their attitudes toward you. For those of you who grew up with the blessing, you will see how

your parents communicated it to you and you will be encouraged to express your thanks to them.

We also offer help if you had to grow up without
your parents' blessing. You will gain insight into common
patterns of those who grow up without the blessing. You
can discover practical lessons on living apart from an
earthly family blessing. And you will be exposed to God's
spiritual family blessing that is offered to each of His children. There is hope for ending the search for personal
acceptance you may have been on for years.

If you are a teacher, discovering the blessing can
help you better understand your students. If you counsel
others, it can provide a helpful framework for understanding many problems and offering practical solutions. If you
are involved in ministering to others, it can help you understand a crucial need every person has and give you
resources to meet that need.

Our prayer is that in the pages that follow, you will
take the time and have the courage to journey into the
past, a journey that can lead to hope and healing. Even
more, we pray that you will be willing to look honestly at
the present and apply the things you will discover.

These pages may end a lifelong search for you or
begin a new relationship with your children, your spouse,
your parents, or a close friend. Our deepest desire is that
this book will enrich your relationship with your heavenly
Father as you learn more about the source of blessing He
is to each believer. All this as we look at the family
blessing—yesterday and today.

2

*T*HE BLESSING:
Yesterday and Today

*O*ver the years we have heard countless stories of people who have, and have not received their parents' blessing. Both of us have experienced the pain of living *without* all or part of our fathers' blessings. Though we understand, firsthand, all the difficulties missing our fathers' blessings has brought into our lives, it still amazes us to see the devastating effect on a child when the blessing is with-held. It also amazes us to see the immeasurable, invalu-able impact when a child truly receives the blessing. For me (John), I can still remember the effects of receiving the blessing from the most important man in my early life.

When I was young, my grandparents came to live with us for several years to "help out" with three very rambunctious boys! My grandfather was a wonderful man, but a stern disciplinarian. He had rules for everything—and swats to go along with all his rules! But there was one iron-clad rule that we hated because it car-ried two automatic swats. *"Be home before the street light comes on!"*

There was no "grading on the curve" in my home. With the street light planted right in our yard, all he had to do was look out the kitchen window and see if we'd made it home in time. And one night, my twin brother, Jeff, and I, didn't.

Never one to delay punishment, I shuffled down the hallway to Grandfather's room, and received my two swats. But little did I know that I was also about to receive one of the greatest blessings in my life.

After my spanking, my grandmother told me to go back down the hall and call my grandfather for dinner. I didn't feel much like being polite to him at the time, but I didn't want to risk another spanking either. So off I went to his room.

While many children grow up with open access to the grandparent or parent's room, we didn't. We were to knock on his door, ask for permission to enter, and call him "Grandfather" or "Sir" when we addressed him.

I meant to knock on the door, but I noticed it was already slightly ajar. That's when I broke the cardinal rule and gently pushed it open to look inside.

What I saw shocked me. My grandfather, a man who rarely showed any emotion, was sitting on the end of the bed, crying. I stood at the door in confusion. I had *never* seen him cry, and I didn't know what to say. Suddenly, he looked up and saw me, and I froze where I was. *I hope catching him crying isn't a 60 swat offense!* I thought to myself!

Yet instead of another spanking, my grandfather said to me, "Come here, John," his voice full of emotion.

When I reached him, he reached out and hugged me closely, and in tears, he told me how much he loved me, and how deeply it hurt for him to have to spank me. "John," he told me, seating me on the bed next to him and putting his big arms around me, "I want more than anything in life for you and your brothers to grow up to become godly young men. I hope you know how much I love you, and how proud I am of you."

I can't explain it, but when I left his room that night, I was a different person because of his blessing. As I look back today, that evening provided me with a meaningful rite of passage from childhood to young adulthood.

For years afterwards, recalling that clear picture of my grandfather's blessing helped to shape my attitudes and actions.

A few months later, in that same room, my grandfather died instantly and unexpectedly of a cerebral aneurysm. I know now that the Lord allowed me, for that one and only time, to hear and receive the blessing from him. While I would never receive the blessing from my own father, I did receive it that day from my grandfather.

Just what is this blessing that seems to be so important? Does it really apply to us today, or was it just something for Old Testament times? What are the elements of which it consists? How can I know whether I have received it or whether my children are experiencing it now?

These questions commonly surface when we introduce people to the blessing. In answering them, we will discover five powerful relationship elements that the Old Testament blessing contains. The presence or absence of these elements can help us determine whether our home is, or our parents' home was, a place of blessing. In this chapter, we will also look at how orthodox Jewish homes have bestowed a blessing on their children and why they have done so down through the centuries.

A study of the blessing always begins in the context of parental acceptance. However, in studying the blessing in the Scriptures, we found that its principles can be used in any intimate relationship.

Husbands can apply these principles in blessing their wives, and wives their husbands. Friendships can be deepened and strengthened by including each element of the blessing. These key ingredients when applied in a church family can bring warmth, healing, and hope to our brothers and sisters in Christ, many who never received an earthly blessing from their parents. As we will see in a later chapter, they are the very relationship elements God uses in blessing His children.

Is the blessing we build into a person's life today exactly like the blessing in the Old Testament? Certainly

not. While the basic relationship elements of blessing remain the same, the Scriptures contain several spiritual
aspects of the blessing that were unique to that time.

UNIQUE ASPECTS OF THE BLESSING
IN THE OLD TESTAMENT

The Hebrew word for *blessing* in the Old Testament is one
of the most important words in the Bible. It was used over
640 times in the Old Testament alone, and held four crucial functions.

First, the word for blessing pictured God's original
plan for mankind. Do you know the very first thing God
did after creating us? In Genesis 1:27–28, we read, "So
God created man in His own image; in the image of God
He created him; male and female He created them. *Then
God blessed them . . .*" (italics added).

What an encouraging truth to know that we were
created for blessing! That is God's design for us. Yet, as
we'll see later, some of us have grown up under a
"curse," not a blessing. In Old Testament thought, there
was nothing worse than being under a curse. But as powerful as a curse might be, there was one thing
stronger . . . *a blessing*.[1]

In Genesis 12:3 God tells Abraham that through
his descendants (pointing to Christ), ". . . All the families
of the earth shall be blessed." When we experience God's
blessing, and learn to bless others, we are connected to
the major purpose for our creation.

Second, the blessing was a time to pull together a
group. In the Old Testament, many examples exist of a
blessing being given to unite a group of people. Melchize-
dek has Abraham gather his family and blesses them as a
group (Gen. 14:19, 20); Moses assembles the entire Nation
of Israel in the wilderness to bless them (Deut. 33:1–5), as
do Aaron, David, and Solomon after him (Num. 6:23–27;
2 Sam. 8; 1 Kings 8:15–61).

There is tremendous strength and unity when we
gather people together for a blessing. Many pastors call
their congregations to rise, and bless them as a group. In

orthodox Jewish homes, every Friday night finds a father calling the entire family together for a time of blessing. We even know of one flight leader during Desert Storm who would gather the six pilots he led, and their ground crews, and pronounce a blessing on them before they headed out on a mission. Blessing a group can increase the unity each member feels for that group and it can do much more.

Third, the blessing was a time to call upon God's protection. For those living in the days of the patriarchs, the blessing was a time to call on God's protection for a loved one. So important was this blessing, that if a family member was to travel beyond the horizon, they received a blessing before they set out. (See Genesis 28:1 where Isaac blesses Jacob before sending him to seek a wife.)

Travel in Bible times was even more dangerous than today, and no one ever wanted a loved one to go "beyond their sight" without words of blessing resting upon the traveler.

And fourth, the blessing was used to mark an important rite of passage. Whether it was at a birth (Ruth 4:14–15), a marriage (Gen. 24:60), or on the passing of leadership from an older generation to a younger (Gen. 27:1; 48:1), a blessing was used to mark significant milestones in one's life.

The Rabbinic tradition remains today with the *Bar Mitsva* at the coming of age of a son, and the *Bat Mitsva* for a daughter. These milestones of physical maturity are times when specific blessings are given from a father and mother to their child. They almost always become treasured memories.

These four functions of the Old Testament blessing: tying us to God's creative purpose, uniting a group, invoking God's protection, and providing a rite of passage, were common practices in Bible times. Unfortunately, today they're absent in many homes and churches.

While there were unique spiritual and prophetic aspects of the blessing, which lay with the patriarchs alone, orthodox Jewish homes have continued to practice blessing children. The basic relational elements of the blessing provide powerful tools to communicate acceptance, protection, and affirmation that still apply to men and women today.

THE BASIC ELEMENTS OF THE BLESSING

What are these basic elements, and how do they work together? While neither of the authors admits to being an expert gardener, an elementary understanding of how a flower grows can help us picture the way the basic components of the blessing work together.

A flower cannot grow unless it has the necessary elements of life. Every flower needs soil, air, water, light, and a secure place to grow (one where its roots are not constantly being pulled out). When these five basic ingredients are present, it is almost impossible to keep a flower from growing. The same thing is true of the basic elements of the blessing.

Like the flower's basic needs, the blessing has five key elements. These five elements, blended together, can cause personal acceptance to blossom and grow in our homes today. Each individual part provides a unique contribution. Each is needed in giving the blessing.

In later chapters, we will look in detail at each of these five elements. But for now, we will introduce them briefly.

A definition of the family blessing that contains its five major elements reads:

> A family blessing begins with *meaningful touching*. It continues with a *spoken message* of *high value*, a message that pictures a *special future* for the individual being blessed, and one that is based on an *active commitment* to see the blessing come to pass.

Here is another way to look at the five basic parts of the blessing.

THE FAMILY BLESSING INCLUDES:
- Meaningful Touch
- A Spoken Message
- Attaching "High Value" to the One Being Blessed
- Picturing a Special Future for the One Being Blessed
- An Active Commitment to Fulfill the Blessing

Let's look a little closer at each of these.

MEANINGFUL TOUCH

Meaningful touch was an essential element in bestowing the blessing in Old Testament homes. So it was with Isaac when he went to bless his son. We read in Genesis 27:26 that Isaac said, "Come near now and kiss me, my son." This incident was not an isolated one. Each time the blessing was given in the Scriptures, meaningful touching provided a caring background to the words that would be spoken. Kissing, hugging, or the laying on of hands were all a part of bestowing the blessing.

Meaningful touch has many beneficial effects. As we will see in the next chapter, the act of touch is a key to communicating warmth, personal acceptance, affirmation—even physical health! For Isaac, as well as for any person who wishes to see the blessing grow and develop in a child, spouse, or friend, touch is an integral part of the blessing.

A SPOKEN MESSAGE

The second element of our definition is based on a spoken message. In many homes today, words of love and acceptance are seldom heard. A tragic misconception parents in these homes share is that simply being present communicates the blessing. Nothing could be further from the truth. A blessing becomes so only when it is spoken.

For a child in search of the blessing, the major thing silence communicates is confusion. Children who are left to fill in the blanks when it comes to what their parents think about them will often fail the test when it comes to feeling valuable and secure. Spoken words at least give the hearer an indication that he or she is worthy of some attention. I (John) learned this lesson on the football field.

When I began playing football in high school, one particular coach thought I was filled with raw talent (emphasis on "raw"!). He was constantly chewing me out. And he even took extra time after practice to point out mistakes I was making. After I missed an important block in practice one day (a frequent occurrence), this coach stood right in my face and chewed me out six ways from Sunday.

When he finally finished, he had me go over to the sidelines with the other players who were not a part of the scrimmage. Standing next to me was a third-string player who rarely got into the game. I can remember leaning over to him and saying, "Boy, I wish he would get off my case." "Don't say that," my teammate replied. "At least he's talking to you. If he ever *stops* talking to you, that means he's given up on you."

Many adults we see in counseling interpret their parents' silence in exactly the same way. They feel as though they are "third-string" children to their parents. Their parents may have provided a roof over their heads (or even a Porsche to drive), but without spoken words of blessing, they are left unsure of their personal worth and acceptance.

Abraham spoke his blessing to his son Isaac. Isaac spoke a blessing to his son Jacob. Jacob gave a verbal blessing to each of his twelve sons and to two of his grandchildren. When God blessed us with the gift of His Son, it was His *Word* that "became flesh and dwelt among us" (John 1:14). God has always been a God of the spoken word.

"But I don't yell at my children or cut them down like some parents," some may say. Unfortunately, even a lack of negative words does not translate into a spoken blessing. We will see this lack illustrated in several painful examples in a later chapter.

To see the blessing bloom and grow in the life of a child, spouse, or friend, we need to verbalize our message. Good intentions aside, good *words* are necessary to provide genuine acceptance.

ATTACHING HIGH VALUE

Meaningful touch and a spoken message. These first two elements lead up to the words of blessing themselves, words of high value.

To value something means to attach honor to it. In fact, this is the meaning of the verb "to bless." In Hebrew, the word *bless* literally means "to bow the knee."[2] This word was used in showing reverence, even awe, to an important person. Now, this doesn't mean that in order to bless a person we are to stand back, fall to our knees, and bow before that person in awe! Nonetheless, words of blessing should carry with them the recognition that this person is valuable and has redeeming qualities. In the Scriptures, recognition is based on who they are, not simply on their performance.

In blessing his son, Isaac says, "Surely, the smell of my son/Is like the smell of a field/Which the LORD has blessed. . . . Let peoples serve you,/And nations bow down to you" (Gen. 27:27–29). That pictures a very valuable person! Not just anybody merits having nations bow down to him!

As you may have noticed, Isaac uses a word picture to describe how valuable his son is to him. ("The smell of my son is like the smell of a field which the LORD has blessed.") Word pictures are a powerful way of communicating acceptance. Later, we will look not only at the use of these word pictures, but we will also learn how to use them in giving a blessing. In the Old Testament, they were a key to communicating to a child, a spouse, or a friend a message of high value—the third element of the family blessing.

PICTURING A SPECIAL FUTURE

A fourth element of the blessing is the way it pictures a special future for the person being blessed. Isaac says to his son Jacob, "May God give you/Of the dew of heaven,/Of the fatness of the earth. . . . Let peoples serve you,/And nations bow down to you" (Gen. 27:28–29). Even today, Jewish homes are noted for picturing a special future for their children. One story we heard illustrates this activity very well.

Sidel, a young Jewish mother, was proudly walking down the street pushing a stroller with her infant twins. As she rounded the corner, she saw her neighbor, Sarah. "My, what beautiful children," Sarah cooed. "What are their names?" Pointing to each child, Sidel replied, "This is Bennie, the doctor, and Reuben, the lawyer." This woman believed her children had a special future and great potential before them! Isaac believed that about his son, and we should communicate this message to those we seek to bless.

One distinction should be made between Isaac's blessing and picturing a special future for a person today. Because of Isaac's unique position as a patriarch (God's appointed leader and a father of the nation of Israel), his words to Jacob carried with them the weight of biblical prophecy. This position was also true of Jacob later in the book of Genesis. His blessing to each of his sons pictured their future exactly as it would unfold for them.

As parents or loved ones today, we cannot predict another person's future with biblical accuracy. We can, however, encourage and help them to set meaningful goals. We can also convey to them that the gifts and character traits they have right now are attributes that God can bless and use in the future.

Psychological visualization and picturing grandiose accomplishments in the future will not give a person the blessing. If anything, such practices pile up unattainable expectations that can move the person further away from genuine acceptance.[3] However, as we will see in a later chapter, our Lord Himself speaks quite often about our future. In fact, He goes to great lengths to assure us of our present relationship with Him and of the ocean full of blessings in store for us as His children in the future.

We can use a healthy, biblical way to picture a special future for our children. With this fourth element of the blessing, a child can gain a sense of security in the present and grow in confidence to serve God and others in the future.

AN ACTIVE COMMITMENT

The last element of the blessing pictures the *responsibility* that goes with giving the blessing. For the patriarchs, not only their words, but God Himself stood behind the blessing they bestowed on their children. Several times, God spoke directly through the angel of the Lord to the patriarchs confirming His active commitment to their family line.

Parents today, in particular, need to rely on the Lord to give them the strength and staying power to confirm their children's blessing. They too have God's Word through the Scriptures as a guide, plus the power of the indwelling Holy Spirit.

Why is active commitment so important when it comes to bestowing the blessing? Words alone cannot communicate the blessing; they need to be backed with a commitment to do everything possible to help the one blessed be successful. We can tell a child, "You have the talent to be a very good pianist." But, if we neglect to provide a piano for that child to practice on, our lack of commitment has undermined our message.

When it comes to spending time with our children or helping them develop a certain skill, some children hear, "Wait until the weekend." Then it becomes "wait until *another* weekend" so many times that they no longer believe our commitments match our words.

The fifth element of the blessing, an active commitment, is crucial to seeing the blessing communicated in our homes.

Provide a flower with the essential elements it needs, and watch it grow! Provide the five basic ingredients of the blessing—meaningful touch, a spoken message, attaching high value to the one being blessed, picturing a special future for them, and confirming the blessing by an active commitment—and personal acceptance can thrive and bloom in a home.

To further understand the blessing in the Scriptures, let's turn our attention to the way it has been used in Jewish homes. For centuries, the blessing of children has been an important part of Jewish family life. In terms of communicating acceptance and affirmation, they have much to teach us about providing a blessing for important people in our lives.

THE BLESSING AND JEWISH FAMILY LIFE

Before the children can walk, they should be carried on the Sabbath and on the Holy Days to their father and mother to receive their blessing.

After they are able to walk, they should go to them of their own accord, with body bent and with head bowed, to receive the blessing.

(From the *Brantshpiegal*, a book on Jewish family life and practices written in 1602.)

From Old Testament times to today, the blessing has been an important gift offered to Jewish children. In fact, it has been a *duty* of parents to their children.[4] It has also been a regular part of the rabbis' duties toward children on *Shabat* (the Sabbath) and on feast and holy days.[5]

The earliest Jewish families we see are, of course, recorded in the Scriptures. The practice of blessing children was probably familiar to Abraham, even before God called him out from Ur of the Chaldees. All across Egypt and the Middle East, the practice of giving a blessing to children was common.[6]

In Old Testament times, each child in the family was given a general blessing as well as a special blessing for the firstborn. Esau, whom we saw in the first chapter,

looked forward to receiving his blessing as the firstborn
son in his family. In Genesis 49, not only the oldest, but
also each of Jacob's twelve sons, received a blessing from
their father. While there were additional *privileges* that
went to the firstborn, the essential *elements* of both blessings were the same as those we listed above. What were
some of the special additional privileges the firstborn child
might enjoy?

Firstborn daughters had the right to be married
before a younger sister. Laban observed this custom in
arranging for Jacob to marry his older daughter, Leah.
Only after she was married was Jacob allowed to marry
Laban's younger daughter, Rachel (Gen. 29:21–30). (That
certainly wasn't the way Jacob had planned it, by the
way!) In addition, ancient tablets found in Syria spoke of
special rights of inheritance that belonged to the firstborn
daughter.[7]

Firstborn sons made out even better. For one thing,
their blessing bequeathed to them *twice* the inheritance of
any other brother (2 Kings 2:9). Now, perhaps you can see
how much Esau lost when he acted on impulse in selling
his birthright. By allowing hunger pangs to dictate his
actions, he became a negative example for all time. In the
book of Hebrews, God lists the greatest heroes of the faith
in Chapter 11. But in Chapter 12, in contrast to the heroes,
the writer says of Esau, "[See to it that . . .] . . . there be
no immoral or godless person like Esau, who sold his own
birthright for a single meal" (Heb. 12:16 NASB).

There were other aspects of the firstborn son's
blessing. The firstborn son was designated as the leader of
the family when the father died. It would become his responsibility to be the spiritual leader in the home. All in
all, firstborn children received many special privileges.

An Old Testament law prohibited arbitrarily by-
passing the eldest son to give the firstborn's blessing to
another child (Deut. 21:15–17), but it certainly could happen and was done. This even happened in Jacob's family.
Reuben was the firstborn son of twelve brothers, but it
was Joseph, the next to the youngest, who actually re-

ceived the firstborn's blessing (Gen. 48:22). Many ancient tablets mentioned that the shifting of the blessing from one child to the other—whether sons or daughters—was common during this period.[8]

As we have seen in our look at Old Testament times, parents gave a *general blessing* to each child and sometimes reserved a *special blessing* for the firstborn. While the firstborn could receive certain privileges a younger child did not, the basic elements of both blessings remained the same.

The next stop in our look at how Jewish families adopted the blessing comes during New Testament times, the time of the Pharisees. During this period there were rules and regulations for nearly every event—the blessing of children not excluded. Around the time of Christ's birth, Rabbi Jesus ben Sirach wrote, "The blessing of the father builds houses for the sons; the blessing of the mother fills them with good things."[9]

While there remained a general blessing for children during this time, a definite trend to favor blessing sons instead of daughters developed. This tendency is seen in many of the Hebrew commentaries on the law that sprang up during that day.

In an explanation of the priestly benediction, "The LORD bless thee, and keep thee" (Num. 6:24 KJV), one rabbi wrote, "May the Lord bless thee with sons, and keep thee from daughters because they need careful guarding!"[10] In even stronger language, another rabbi wrote, "What is the interpretation of the words 'all things' in the Scripture, 'The Lord blessed Abraham in all things'? That he had no daughter!"[11] His words may have been humorous—as long as you weren't a daughter.

While the tendency to bless only sons was present, exceptions to the rule were made in some Jewish homes with some religious leaders. In fact, another man some called rabbi during this same period welcomed both sons *and* daughters to receive His blessing. We read in Mark 10:13–16:

Then they brought little children to Him, that He might touch them; but the disciples rebuked those who brought them. But when Jesus saw it, He was greatly displeased and said to them, "Let the little children come to Me, and do not forbid them. . . ." And He took them up in His arms, laid His hands on them, and *blessed* them. (Mark 10:13–16, italics added)

Jesus knew that both little boys *and* little girls needed the elements of the blessing.[12] In a later chapter, we will see that in almost every detail, His blessing of children parallels the important elements of the family blessing.

Looking to modern-day Jewish homes and practices, the blessing is still an important concept in many orthodox families. At many Shabat (Sabbath) services, the parents are to bring their children for a special blessing. There the rabbi will call the children in the congregation forward to receive their blessing. Acting on behalf of the parents, the rabbi will lay his hand on the head of each child and recite words like these, "May God bless you and make you as Ephraim and Manasseh."

This blessing originally comes from Genesis 48:20, where Jacob was blessing Joseph's two sons—Jacob's *grandchildren*. Listen to the blessing this aging patriarch bestows on these two young boys: "So he blessed them that day, saying, 'By you Israel will bless, saying, "May God make you as Ephraim and as Manasseh!"' " What a blessing! Even today, centuries later, in synagogues and in Jewish homes, this blessing is a favorite for parents to use with their children.

While studying how the blessing is given in modern Jewish homes, I (John) had the privilege of speaking with several rabbis. In those interviews, I discovered that bestowing a family blessing was still very much alive. The family blessing is considered an important vehicle for communicating a sense of identity, meaning, love, and acceptance. In fact, in many orthodox homes, a weekly blessing is given by the father to each of his children. With the ceremonial candles lit, a time of blessing begins.

Sharing special meals; kissing, hugging, or the laying on of hands; creating a word picture or using one in the Scriptures to praise a child; even asking God to provide a special future for each child are common elements of blessing children in orthodox homes today.

While the blessing is an ancient practice, it still holds important keys to granting genuine acceptance. From a blessing to the firstborn to special words of love and acceptance for each child, the blessing remains a part of Jewish family life today. *For Christian parents who have the hope and reality of Jesus, the Messiah, and His love, their blessing can be even more powerful.*

AT HOME WITH THE FAMILY BLESSING

We have looked at the basic elements of the blessing and at how it has been carried on for centuries in Jewish homes. Our aim now is to become very practical as we look closely at each of the five key elements of the blessing. Learning more about these powerful tools for communicating personal and parental approval can help us become a source of blessing to our children, spouse, brothers and sisters in Christ, and others.

Some of you who are reading this book may already feel a little discouraged. In reading about the key elements of the blessing, perhaps you realized for the first time that you never got the blessing from your parents, or that it is not an active part of your relationship with your children. Please don't lose heart. As we look closely at the five basic elements of the blessing, you can gain practical skills to become a source of blessing to others. Later, you will also discover how to deal effectively with missing out on the blessing in your life.

Together, we will stop in several of the most common homes we see in counseling that *withhold* the blessing from their children. And we will look at God's provision for dealing with the loss of an earthly family blessing. We will also look at several modern-day homes that are models for bestowing the blessing on children, spouse, church family, and friends.

With that in mind, let's turn our attention to the first element of the blessing, meaningful touch. Harnessed within this first key to communicating personal acceptance is an incredible power to bless, right at our fingertips.

3

*T*HE FIRST ELEMENT OF THE BLESSING: *Meaningful Touch*

*I*sabel was a sensitive young woman, suffering greatly in a diabetic/medical-surgical unit. She was in so much pain, she would cry regularly to the nursing staff, pleading for pain killing injections. Yet the medicine therapy she was on and her own physical condition precluded her from receiving the shots in spite of her cries. The risk for infection and internal bleeding was simply too great.

Finally, after Isabel's continual badgering of the nurses on every shift, the senior nurse in charge went to talk to Isabel.

Nurse Heath was a thirty-year veteran of the wards and a reserved, capable teacher. She explained to Isabel, logically and practically, the potential dangers if they gave her a shot. She also assured Isabel that the other nurses were trying to protect her, rather than harm her, by administering the injections. Isabel listened intently, and even nodded understanding.

Her mission accomplished, Nurse Heath was preparing to leave when Isabel stopped her. "If I can't have my shot . . . *can you give me a hug?*"

Not thinking she had heard right, she asked, "Excuse me?"

Isabel repeated, "Could you give me a hug for the pain . . . *please?*"

Caught off guard, the stately nurse said, "Well, OK," and put her arm around Isabel's shoulder. But then, it was as if God spoke to her and said, "For goodness sake, Ida, that's not what she asked for!" Then Nurse Heath put her arms around Isabel and really gave her a hug.

Isabel burst into tears.

"All this time I thought the nurses hated me. I'm just hurting so badly. Whenever I need a pain shot, can I call you and get a hug instead?"

Nurse Heath assured Isabel that she could get her hug whenever she needed it, and even wrote it down on her medical Kardex under the medication section, "Pain hugs" for Isabel upon request.

Isabel died a few months later at the age of thirty-four. But before her death, whenever she was admitted to a different ward in the hospital, or when the nights became too long, she'd call Nurse Heath for her "pain hug."

A hug can't wipe away all our pain, but it can help. And while meaningful touch can't chase away all our fears, it can cure most of them.

A little four-year-old girl became frightened late one night during a thunderstorm. After one particularly loud clap of thunder, she jumped up from her bed, ran down the hall, and burst into her parents' room. Jumping right in the middle of the bed, she sought out her parents' arms for comfort and assurance. "Don't worry, Honey," her father said, trying to calm her fears. "The Lord will protect you." The little girl snuggled closer to her father and said, "I know that, Daddy, but right now I need someone with skin on!"

The honesty of some children! This little one did not doubt her heavenly Father's ability to protect her, but she was also aware that He had given her an earthly father she could run to: someone whom God had entrusted with a special gift that could bring her comfort, security, and personal acceptance—the blessing of meaningful touch.

This little girl was fortunate. Her father was willing to share this important aspect of the blessing with his daughter. Not all children are as fortunate. Even in caring homes, most parents (particularly fathers) will stop touching their children once the children reach the grade school years.[1] When they do stop touching them, an important part of giving their children the blessing stops as well.

For a four-year-old, being held and touched is permissible in most homes. But what about the need a fourteen-year-old has to be meaningfully touched by his mother or father? (Even if the teenager outwardly cringes every time he or she is hugged.) Or a thirty-four-year-old? Or your spouse or a close friend?

Your spouse and others need meaningful touch. However, children are particularly affected by touch deprivation. Sometimes the absence of touch can so affect a child that he or she spends a lifetime reaching out for arms that will never embrace him or her.

"I wish. . . . I wish. . . ." Lisa had slumped down in her chair, hugging herself and rocking backward and forward as she repeated these words. Lisa was a new adolescent patient in the psychiatric ward where I (John) was a seminary intern. Whenever she felt afraid or sad, she would wrap herself in her arms and rock back and forth.

We found that Lisa had behaved this way since she was seven years old. That was when her mother had abandoned her at an orphanage.

Lisa was trying to escape the hurt and pain she was feeling by holding herself. Lisa had no one else to hold her; all she had was the wish her mother would return. She needed meaningful touch so much that she would wrap her arms around *herself* and try to hug away the hurt.

THE BLESSING: MEANINGFUL TOUCH
In the Scriptures, touch played an important part in the

bestowal of the family blessing. When Isaac blessed Jacob, an embrace and a kiss were involved. We read, "Then his father Isaac said to him, 'Please come close and kiss me, my son'" (Gen. 27:26 NASB).

The Hebrew word for "come close" is very descriptive. It is used of armies drawn together in battle. It is even used to picture the overlapping scales on a crocodile's skin.[2] It may have been a while since you last saw a battle or a crocodile, but these word pictures still call up in our minds a picture of a very close connection.

Isaac wasn't asking his son to give him an "Aunt Ethel hug." (Remember Aunt Ethel—the one who pinched your cheek and then repeatedly patted you on the back when she hugged you like she was bringing up gas?) Free of the current taboos our culture sets on a man embracing his son, Isaac was calling Jacob close to give him a bear hug.

For fathers in North America, there is strong correlation between the age of a son, and whether his father will touch him.[3] Yet with Isaac, his grown son was at least forty years old when he said, "Come close and kiss me, my son."[4]

Children of all ages need meaningful touch, particularly from a father. Studies show that mothers touch their children in more nurturing ways, and fathers in more playful ways. But when the children were interviewed, perhaps because it didn't happen as often, they perceived their father's touch as more nurturing.[5]

As we have seen with Lisa, our need for meaningful touch does not go away when we enter grade school. Isaac modeled someone who didn't set up barriers around the need to be touched. He was a model that parents, husbands and wives, and even friends at church need to follow in giving the blessing.

I (John) deeply appreciated my mother's commitment to meaningfully touch us when we were children, even when we didn't show her how we appreciated it!

As a single parent, my mother had to work full-time to support three hungry, healthy boys. In the morning, she'd get us all up, get herself ready, and then we'd all pile in the car, us off to school and her to work.

While her driving saved us the long walk, there was one thing about the taxi service that my twin brother and I hated. Before we were allowed to get out of the car, we had to give Mom a hug.

As you can imagine, hugging your mom in front of all your school friends was not tops on the list of two aspiring football players. In fact, each year, we'd make our mother drop us further and further from school—just in case someone saw us hugging her!

Her pattern of hugging us was so regular, even when we'd say, "Oh, Mom!," or, "I can't stand it!" I can remember only one time when it didn't happen, and it got me in major trouble!

On one particular morning, we were all in a rush to get the day launched. We were anxious to get to school to shoot some hoops before the morning bell, and my mother had a major presentation at work. Distracted by her busy day, she let us out of the car without forcing us to give her a hug.

As she drove away, Jeff and I just looked at each other. She hadn't even *mentioned* hugging us—and I instantly thought the worse.

"She must know something," I told Jeff. "I *know* she knows something!"

Unfortunately, at the time there were a number of things she could have found out that could have resulted in our being grounded until we were in our mid-thirties.

All day, we brooded over "what" she'd discovered that caused her to be so angry that she'd chosen not to hug us. And finally, the day was over and we were all sitting around the dinner table—in silence. While dinner time was normally filled with enthusiastic conversation, that night there was dead silence as we waited for the storm to break. While Jeff could have waited all night, the silence quickly got to me and I broke down and blurted out, "OK, Mom. We're sorry. I can't believe you found

out, but we are *really* sorry." I wasn't ready for the confused look that came across my mother's face.

"What are you talking about John?" she asked.

"Well, this morning," I told her. "When we got out
of the car . . . You know . . . You didn't hug us!"

Laughing, she said, "Oh, I'm sorry. I guess I was
so busy thinking about the presentation I had to make, I
just forgot." But then her smile vanished, and she said,
"But what was it you were confessing to?"

As Jeff glared at me, I realized I had just gotten us
both in big trouble, all because I'd missed the hug I
always said I hated!

What a contrast with my father, however. If I could
count on my mother's touch, I could rely on his being off-
limits. When we finally began a relationship with our
father after nearly fifteen years of his absence, it was obvious that meaningful touch wasn't something he was comfortable with.

Of course, during my teenage years I didn't mind
the absence of public displays of touch. But as the years
went on, I found myself wishing that even once, my
father and I could stand and hug each other. At my wedding. Or when Kari was born. Or Laura. Or at Christmas
time, or anytime.

The handful of occasions when I held my father's
hand were when he was so seriously ill he couldn't object, and each time stands out like a beacon. A memory of
closeness that was pushed away from me any time he had
the strength.

In the Scriptures, we find another clear example of
including meaningful touch in bestowing the blessing.
This time the blessing involves a grandfather who wanted
to make sure his grandchildren received this special gift of
personal acceptance. Let's look in on this "touching"
scene:

> And Joseph said to his father, "They are my sons, whom
> God has given me in this place." And he said, "Please
> bring them to me, and I will bless them." Now the eyes of

> Israel were dim with age, so that he could not see. Then Joseph brought them near him, and he kissed them and embraced them.
>
> Then Israel stretched out his right hand and laid it on Ephraim's head . . . and his left hand on Manasseh's head. (Gen. 48:9-10, 14)

Jacob (whose name had now been changed to Israel) not only kissed them and held them close, but he also placed his hands on each grandson's head.[6] This practice of laying on of hands was an important part of many of the religious rituals for the patriarchs and for Israel. There are at least two important reasons why placing our hands on someone as a part of the blessing is so special. First, there is a symbolic meaning attached to touching, and, second, there are tremendous physical benefits to the laying on of hands.

THE SYMBOLIC MEANING PICTURED BY TOUCHING

In the Old Testament, the symbolic picture of the laying on of hands was important. In this touch was a graphic picture of transferring power or blessing from one person to another.[7] For example, in the Old Testament book of Leviticus Aaron was instructed to use this practice in his priestly duties. During the Day of Atonement, he was to place his hands on the head of a goat that was then sent into the wilderness. This picture is of Aaron symbolically transferring the sins of Israel onto that animal. (It is also a prophetic picture of how Christ, like that spotless animal, would take on our sins at the Cross.) In another example, Elijah passed along his role as God's prophet to Elisha by the laying on of hands.

Even today the symbolic meaning of touch is powerful. While we may not be consciously aware of it, the way we touch can carry tremendous symbolic meaning.

A young woman holding hands with a new boyfriend can signal "I'm taken" to other would-be suitors. Two men shaking hands can seal an important business transaction. A minister at a wedding says to a couple, "If you then have freely and lawfully chosen one another as husband and wife, please *join your hands* as you repeat these vows."

Near the end of the Desert Storm campaign, Gary and I witnessed an example of the symbolic meaning of touch at one of our favorite places to watch human behavior—the airport.

A young, Japanese-American soldier was on our plane coming into Ontario airport in Los Angeles. He was on his way home from almost six months in the Gulf, and had ridden a tank through the heaviest fighting. He told of firefights at night, burning oil wells, the jubilant Kuwaitis, and of missing home. Then our plane touched down.

At the Ontario airport, a glass wall separates the passengers who have cleared the metal detectors from family and friends who have come to meet them. As we rounded the corner, we heard cries of joy.

There, pounding on the glass wall were the soldier's wife, two sets of parents, and two young children. While many orientals may be characterized by their reserve, there was nothing reserved about this young hero's reception. He ran through the exit doors and into his family's arms to be smothered with hugs, kisses, smiles, and tears. All of us in the waiting area were caught up in this wonderful reunion. Total strangers spontaneously burst into applause, and many had tears in their eyes as we all shared in the happiness of this homecoming.

Just a few months later, I (John) saw a different type of homecoming, which captured many of those same powerful emotions. The network television program, "20/20" chronicled the story of two Vietnamese orphans who had been evacuated when Saigon fell. While they were too young to realize it at the time, their parents were alive! Shelling from the advancing North Vietnamese army had separated this five- and four-year-old boy and girl from their parents. But instead of being casualties, their mother and father were desperately searching for them as they feared the worst.

Now, twenty years later, "20/20" cameramen went

to Vietnam with two grown children. While each had grown up in loving American homes, with caring adoptive parents, now they were going to the home of their birth.

The orphaned boy was a United States Army second lieutenant, and his sister, a married mother of three. They had kept in touch with each other over the years, and in high school began the painstaking research and writing that would one day lead them to discover that their parents were alive.

With relationships beginning to soften between Vietnam and the United States, the two children were finally granted visas to return and be reunited with their parents and the brothers and sisters they had never seen.

The emotion captured by the cameramen was incredible. Half a world separated this family. So too, a terrible war, over twenty years, and even now, language. Yet they still had one thing in common. When they saw each other for the first time, they ran and fell into each other's arms with sobs, hugs, and kisses that said, in a language they all understood, "We love you. . . . We missed you. . . . We're so glad you're home."

They may have needed a translator to talk with each other in *words*, but as they sat and held hands, they clearly communicated the warmth and love that even a war couldn't kill.

While great symbolism accompanies our touch, this is not the only reason God made it a part of the blessing.

MEANINGFUL TOUCH BLESSES US PHYSICALLY

For one thing, over one-third of our five million touch receptors are centered in our hands![8] Our hands are so sensitive that some blind people are being taught to read without Braille, by seeing through their fingertips! At Princeton University's Cutaneous Communication Laboratory, "vibratese" is an experimental procedure through which blind people are able to read a printed page by translating the words into vibrations on their fingertips.[9]

Interestingly enough, the act of laying on of hands has become the focus of a great deal of modern-day interest and research. Dr. Dolores Krieger, professor of nursing at New York University, has made numerous studies on the effects of laying on of hands. What she found is that both the toucher and the one being touched receive a physiological benefit.[10] How is that possible?

Inside our bodies is hemoglobin, the pigment of the red blood cells, which carries oxygen to the tissues. Repeatedly, Dr. Krieger has found that hemoglobin levels in *both* people's bloodstreams go up during the act of the laying on of hands. As hemoglobin levels are invigorated, body tissues receive more oxygen. This increase of oxygen energizes a person and can even aid in the regenerative process if he or she is ill.

We are sure that Ephraim and Manasseh were not thinking, "Wow, our hemoglobin levels are going up!" when their grandfather laid his hands on them. However, one of the things that certainly stayed with them as they looked back on their day of blessing was the old patriarch's gentle touch.

Hugs and kisses were also a part of meaningful touching pictured in the Scriptures. So healthy is meaningful touch, we ought to listen to the words of Ralph Waldo Emerson: "I never like the giving of the hand, unless the entire body accompanies it!" Let's look further at the physical benefits of touching and the deep emotional needs that can be met by this first element of the family blessing.

How would you like to lower your husband's or wife's blood pressure? Protect your grade-school child from being involved in an immoral relationship later in life? Even add up to two years to your own life? (Almost sounds like an insurance commercial, doesn't it?) Actually, these are all findings in recent studies on the incredible power to bless found in meaningful touching.

MORE REASONS WHY MEANINGFUL TOUCH BLESSES US PHYSICALLY

Every day, researchers are discovering more and more information about the importance of touch. If we are serious about being a source of blessing to others, we must consider putting these important points into practice. As we saw in the studies of the laying on of hands, a number of physical changes take place when we reach out and touch. Let's look at a few recent examples:

In a study at UCLA, it was found that just to maintain emotional and physical health, men and women need eight to ten meaningful touches each day![11]

At a marriage seminar I (Gary) was conducting, I told the couples that an important part of the blessing was given through meaningful touch. When I cited this UCLA study, I noticed a man in the second row reach over and begin patting his wife on the shoulder and counting, "One, two, three . . ." That is not meaningful touching! These researchers defined meaningful touch as a gentle touch, stroke, kiss, or hug given by significant people in our lives (a husband or wife, parent, close friend, and so on).

This study estimated that if some "type A driven" men would hug their wives several times each day, it would increase their life span by almost two years! (Not to mention the way it would improve their marriages.) Obviously, we can physically bless those around us (and even ourselves) with meaningful touch. But touching does much more than that.

Do you have a newborn in your home? Newborns make tremendous gains if provided with meaningful touch—and may be at risk if they don't.

Researchers at the University of Miami Medical School's Touch Research Institute began giving premature babies forty-five minutes of massage each day. Within ten days, the massaged babies showed 47 percent greater weight gain than those children who were not regularly touched.[12] In a second study, actual bone growth of young children who had been deprived of parental touching was half that of the bone growth of children who received adequate physical attention.[13] And in ground-breaking studies, Drs. Schanberg and Butler at Duke University Medical School found that without maternal touch, rat pups do not produce a type of protein crucial to their growth and development. When these rat pups were separated and unable to feel their mother's touch, they responded by slowly shutting down production of an enzyme crucial to the development of major organs. As soon as the pups were reunited with their mother, however, enzyme production returned to normal.[14]

Even the smallest act of touch can help a child who is unable to move. One group of physically handicapped children were placed on a smooth surface (like smooth Naugahyde) and a second group on a highly textured surface (like a rubber floor mat). EMG studies showed marked differences between the two groups, including increases in muscle tone, simply by having them lie on a textured surface![15] You can't get away from it. Overwhelming evidence shows that physical touch benefits and blesses children. But how about adults?

Are your parents getting up in years? Meaningful touch can be an important part of maintaining health and positive attitude with older persons. In a practice that has become commonplace now, residents in nursing homes were brought together with pets from a neighboring animal shelter. At first it was thought to be just a good recreational activity. Upon further study more significant results began to surface. Those residents who had a pet to touch and hold not only lived longer than those without a pet, they also had a more positive attitude about life![16]

Elderly patients with more serious problems have also demonstrated a number of tremendous benefits from regular, meaningful touching. For those suffering with dementia, a regimen of regular meaningful touch significantly increased their nutritional intake, helping them gain needed weight.[17] In addition, with Alzheimer's patients, physical touch decreased strange movements, picking up things, and repetitive mannerisms.[18]

But perhaps the most powerful study to come out of aging research is how touch may actually help preserve a healthy person's brain as it ages! Robert M. Stapolsky of Stanford University found that with even a small amount of extra stimulation soon after birth, there was a lasting effect on rats' brains. Meaningful touch in infancy caused their brains to put a brake on the development of glucocorticoids, stress hormones that are "a disaster to have in the bloodstream." By limiting their action, over time when these rats became old, they didn't lose any of the 10-to-20 percent of memory-critical gray matter that older rats, monkeys, and humans normally tend to lose.[19]

While meaningful touch may not be the "fountain of youth," it certainly does provide a clear stream of physical benefits for young and old alike. And what's more, people who regularly give and receive meaningful touch consistently feel better about themselves and have higher self worth![20]

MEANINGFUL TOUCH BLESSES OUR RELATIONSHIPS

An interesting study done at Purdue University demonstrates how important touch is in determining how we view someone else. Librarians at the school were asked by researchers to alternately touch and not touch the hands of students as they handed back their library cards. The experimenters then interviewed the students. Do you know what they found? You guessed it. Those who had been touched reported far greater positive feelings about both the library and the librarian than those who were not touched![21]

A doctor we know, a noted neurosurgeon, did his own study on the effects of brief times of touch. With half his patients in the hospital, he would sit on their bed and touch them on the arm or leg when he came in to see how they were doing. With his remaining patients, he would simply stand near the bed to conduct his interview of how they were feeling.

Before the patients went home from the hospital, the nurses gave each patient a short questionnaire evaluating the treatment they received. They were especially asked to comment on the amount of time they felt the doctor had spent with them. While in actuality he had spent the same amount of time in each patient's room, those people he had sat down near and touched felt he had been in their room nearly twice as long as those he had not touched!

In similar studies, shoppers in a Kansas City, Missouri, supermarket were asked to sample a new brand of pizza. Those who were touched for only a fraction of a second during the sales pitch were more likely to buy the new product.[22] Even flight attendants who "accidentally" touched people on a long distance flight saw similar results. Those who were touched rated the attendant as more qualified, the airline as more professional, and the plane trip as *safer* than those who were not touched![23]

Come on, Trent. Get serious, Smalley, you may be thinking. Do we really mean that a touch lasting a few seconds or less can help build better relationships? Actually, we hope you touch your loved ones much more than that, but even small acts of touch can indeed leave a lasting memory.

Touching a child on the shoulder when he or she walks in front of you; holding hands with your spouse when you wait in line; stopping for a moment to ruffle someone's hair—all these small acts can change how you are viewed by others. A ten-minute bear hug is not the only way to give another person the blessing. At times, the *smallest* act of touch can be a vehicle to communicating love and personal acceptance.

A free-lance reporter from the *New York Times* was interviewing Marilyn Monroe years ago. She was aware of Marilyn's past and the fact that during her early years Marilyn had been shuffled from one foster home to another. The reporter asked Marilyn, "Did you ever feel loved by any of the foster families with whom you lived?"

"Once," Marilyn replied, "when I was about seven or eight. The woman I was living with was putting on makeup, and I was watching her. She was in a happy mood, so she reached over and patted my cheeks with her rouge puff. . . . For that moment, I felt loved by her."[24]

Marilyn Monroe had tears in her eyes when she remembered this event. Why? The touch lasted only a few seconds, and it happened years before. It was even done in a casual, playful way, not in an attempt to communicate great warmth or meaning. But as small an act as it was, it was like pouring buckets of love and security on the parched life of a little girl starved for affection.

Parents, in particular, need to know that neglecting to meaningfully touch their children starves them of genuine acceptance—so much so that it can drive them into the arms of someone else who is all too willing to touch them. Analyzing why some young people are drawn to cults, one author writes:

> Cults and related movements offer a new family. They provide the follower with new people to worry about him, to offer him advice, to cry with him, and importantly, to hold him and touch him. Those can be unbeatable attractions.[25]

They certainly can, especially if meaningful touch has not been a part of the blessing a child receives. Even if a child is not lured into a cult to make up for years of touch deprivation, he or she can be drawn into the arms of an immoral relationship.

Promiscuous men and women, women who work as prostitutes, and women who repeatedly have unwanted pregnancies have told researchers that their sexual activity is merely a way of satisfying yearnings to be touched and held. Dr. Marc Hollender, a noted psychiatrist, interviewed scores of women who have had three or more unwanted pregnancies. Overwhelmingly, these women said that they were "consciously aware that sexual activity was a price to be paid for being cuddled and held." Touching before intercourse was more pleasurable than intercourse itself, "which was merely something to be tolerated."[26]

In a similar study with homosexual men, a common characteristic they shared was the absence of meaningful touching by their fathers early in life.[27] Dr. Ross Campbell, in his excellent book, *How to Really Love Your Child,* comes to a similar conclusion. He writes, "In all my reading and experience, I have never known of one sexually disoriented person who had a warm, loving, and affectionate father."[28]

Touch from both a mother and father is important. In a later chapter, we will look at how a single parent can help to make up for the lack of touch from a missing spouse. However, in any case, meaningful touching can protect a child from looking to meet this need in all the wrong places.

If we ignore the physical and emotional needs our children, spouse, or close friends have for meaningful touch, we deny them an important part of the blessing. What's more, we shatter a biblical guideline that our Lord Jesus Himself set in blessing others.

JESUS AND THE BLESSING OF MEANINGFUL TOUCH

As we mentioned in an earlier chapter, Jesus was a model of someone who communicated the blessing to others. Let's look at these verses again that speak of His touching the children.

> Then they brought little children to Him, that He might touch them; but the disciples rebuked those who brought them. But when Jesus saw it, He was greatly displeased and said to them, "Let the little children come to Me, and do not forbid them; for of such is the kingdom of God. . . ." And He took them up in His arms, laid His hands on them, and blessed them (Mark 10:13–14, 16).

Meaningful touching was certainly a part of Christ's blessing children. Mobbed by onlookers and protected by His disciples, Jesus could have easily waved to the children from a distance or just ignored them altogether. But He did neither. Jesus would not even settle for the politicians' "chuck under the chin" routine; He "took them up in His arms, laid His hands on them, and blessed them."

Jesus was not simply communicating a spiritual lesson to the crowds. If He was, He could have done so by simply placing one child in the center of the group as He did on another occasion (Matt. 18:2). Jesus was demonstrating His knowledge of a child's genuine need.

For children, things become real when they are touched. Have you ever been to Disneyland and seen the look on a little child's face when he or she comes face to face with a person dressed like Goofy or Donald Duck? Even if the child is initially fearful, soon he or she will want to reach out and touch the Disney character. This same principle allows children to stand in line for hours to see Santa Claus (the same children who normally can't sit still for five minutes).

Jesus was a master of communicating love and personal acceptance. He did so when He blessed and held these little children. But another time His sensitivity to touch someone was even more graphic. This was when Jesus met a grown man's need for meaningful touch, a man who was barred by law from ever touching anyone again. We read about this in Mark 1:40–42:

> And a leper came to Him, beseeching Him and falling on his knees before Him, and saying to Him, "If You are willing, You can make me clean."
>
> And moved with compassion, *He stretched out His hand and touched him*, and said to him, "I am willing; be cleansed." And immediately the leprosy left him and he was cleansed (NASB, italics added).

To touch a leper was unthinkable. Banishing lepers from society, people would not get within a stone's throw of them. (In fact, they would throw stones at them if they did come close!29) In a parallel passage in Luke, we are told that this man was "covered with leprosy." With their open sores covered by dirty bandages, lepers were the last persons anyone would want to touch. Yet the first thing Christ did for this man was touch him.

Even before Jesus spoke to him, He reached out His hand and *touched* him. Can you imagine what that scene must have looked like? Think how this man must have longed for someone to touch him, not throw stones at him to drive him away. Jesus could have healed him first and then touched him. But recognizing his deepest need, Jesus stretched out His hand even before He spoke words of physical and spiritual healing.

We know of one person who could understand the pain of not being touched. Her name was Dorothy, and she spent years of her life longing for meaningful touch.

We learned about Dorothy through a speech teacher at a large, secular university, a man in his early sixties who is an outstanding Christian. For nearly twenty-five years, this man had been a source of encouragement to students inside and outside of class. Many young men and women have trusted Christ as their Savior through his quiet modeling of godly principles. However, what changed Dorothy's life was neither his ability to communicate nor his stirring class lectures, but one act of touch.

During the first day of an introductory speech class, this teacher was going around the room, having the students introduce themselves. Each student was to respond to the questions "What do I like about myself?" and "What don't I like about myself?"

Nearly hiding at the back of the room was Dorothy. Her long, red hair hung down around her face, almost obscuring it from view. When it was Dorothy's turn to introduce herself, there was only silence in the room. Thinking perhaps she had not heard the question, the teacher moved his chair over near hers and gently repeated the question. Again, there was only silence.

Finally, with a deep sigh, Dorothy sat up in her chair, pulled back her hair, and in the process revealed her face. Covering nearly all of one side of her face was a large, irregularly shaped birthmark—nearly as red as her hair. "That," she said, "should show you what I don't like about myself."

Moved with compassion, this godly professor did something he'd never done before in a classroom. Prompted by God's spirit, he leaned over and gave her a hug. Then he kissed her on her cheek where the birthmark was and said, "That's OK, Honey, God and I still think you're beautiful."

Dorothy cried uncontrollably for almost twenty minutes. Soon other students had gathered around her and were offering their comfort as well. When she finally could talk, dabbing the tears from her eyes she said to the professor, "I've wanted so much for someone to hug me and say what you said. Why couldn't my parents do that? My mother won't even touch my face."

Dorothy, just like the leper in Christ's time, had a layer of inner pain trapped beneath the outward scars. This one act of meaningful touching began to heal years of heartache and loneliness for Dorothy and opened the door that drew her to the Savior.

We know that for many people, meaningful touch simply wasn't a natural part of growing up. For me, (John), growing up in Arizona, the cultural norm was, "It's OK to hug your horse, but not your kids!"

Wherever you live across the United States, you may not come from a warm, affectionate background. Sociologist Sidney Jourand studied the touch behavior of pairs of people in coffee shops around the world. The difference between cultures was staggering. In San Juan, Puerto Rico, people touched on average 180 times per hour. In Paris, France, it was 110 times per hour. In Gainesville, Florida, 2 times per hour. And in London, England, 0 times per hour.[30]

We aren't known as a country of huggers, and with all the media reports of child abuse and inappropriate touching, we've backed away from touch even more. We need to realize, however, that avoiding healthy, appropriate, meaningful touch sacrifices physical and emotional health in our lives and the lives of our loved ones.

If we want to be people who give the blessing to others, one thing is clear. Just like Isaac, Jacob, Jesus, and even the professor, we must include meaningful touch in our contacts with loved ones. This element of the blessing can lay the groundwork for the second key aspect of the blessing—a spoken message.

4

THE SECOND ELEMENT OF THE BLESSING: *Spoken Words*

Most of us grew up reciting clever sayings like, "Early to bed, early to rise, makes a man healthy, wealthy, and wise." "A bird in the hand is worth two in the bush." And "A stitch in time saves nine." But unlike all these words of wisdom, one saying we memorized is an absolute lie.

Do you remember the lines, "Sticks and stones may break my bones, but words will never hurt me"? All too quickly we learn that words *do* hurt. They can cut a person deeply, destroy a friendship, or rip apart a home or marriage.

Words have incredible power to build us up or tear us down emotionally. This is particularly true when it comes to giving or gaining family approval. Many people can clearly remember words of praise their parents spoke years ago. Others can remember negative words they heard—and what their parents were wearing when they spoke them!

We should not be surprised, then, that the family blessing hinges on being a *spoken* message. Abraham *spoke* a blessing to Isaac. Isaac *spoke* it to his son Jacob. Jacob *spoke* it to each of his twelve sons and to two of his grandchildren. Esau was so excited when he was called in to receive his blessing because, after years of waiting, he would finally *hear* the blessing. In the Scriptures, a blessing is not a blessing unless it is spoken.

THE POWER OF SPOKEN WORDS

If you are a parent, your children desperately need to *hear* a spoken blessing from you. If you are married, your wife or husband needs to *hear* words of love and acceptance on a regular basis. This very week with a friend, a coworker, or someone at your church, you will rub shoulders with someone who needs to hear a word of encouragement.

Throughout the Scriptures, we find a keen recognition of the power and importance of spoken words. In the very beginning, God "spoke" and the world came into being (Gen. 1:3). When He sent us His Son to communicate His love and complete His plan of salvation, it was His Word which "became flesh and dwelt among us" (John 1:14). God has always been a God who communicates His blessings through spoken words.

In the book of James, three word pictures grab our attention and point out the power and importance of spoken words. All three illustrate the ability the tongue has to build up or break down relationships, the ability to bless or to curse.

First, our tongue is pictured as a "bit" used to direct a horse (James 3:3). If you control a horse's mouth by means of a small bit, the entire animal will move in the direction you choose. (We have ridden a few horses who seem to be exceptions, but the general rule is certainly true.) The second picture illustrates this same principle in a different way. Here a "small rudder" is used to turn a great ship (3:4). These analogies point out the way spoken words can direct and control a person or a relationship.

A parent, spouse, or friend can use this power of the tongue for good. He or she can steer a child away from trouble or provide guidance to a friend who is making an important decision. He or she can minister words of encouragement or lift up words of praise. But this power can also be misused, sometimes with tragic results.

That is what the third word picture shows us. It illustrates all too clearly that spoken words can burn deeply into a person's life, often setting the course that person's future will take. Listen to the awesome power a spoken message can have:

> The tongue is a small part of the body, and yet it boasts of great things. Behold, how great a forest is set aflame by such a small fire! And the tongue is a fire, the very world of iniquity; . . . and sets on fire the *course of our life*. (James 3:5-6 NASB, italics added)

Just like a forest fire, what we say to others can burn deeply into their hearts. In fact, I (John) saw a living picture of the darkness that can result from fiery words.

I first met Lynda on a blistering summer's day in Arizona. The temperature outside was over 105 degrees and most people wore shorts or cool cotton clothing—but not Lynda. A tall, attractive twenty-year-old, she had on a heavy, long-sleeve *black* dress. (In Arizona, people avoid wearing black during the summer because it soaks up the already scorching heat. Yet in talking with her in counseling over several weeks, I found out that summer or winter, day or night, black was the only color Lynda would wear.)

Lynda grew up with a cruel, abusive father, who was addicted to alcohol and watching horror movies. As early as age five, Lynda was forced to stay in the family room and watch gruesome films. Then her father would laugh hysterically when she cried in fear. As the years passed, he continued exposing her to other aspects of the occult. Finally, when Lynda was in high school, he died and the horror stopped, in part.

As we talked, it wasn't the pictures of terror that had covered Lynda's heart with such darkness. They were terrible without question. But it was his *words* that had done the most damage. For all the hurtful things he did, what haunted her most was his favorite nickname for her. It came right out of his horror films: "demon daughter."

That nickname burned its way into her heart, and even affected the way she dressed on a summer's day.

In the Scriptures, there is tremendous power in a name. Before Moses went to Egypt to confront Pharaoh, he asked to know God's "name." God changed Abram's name to Abraham, father of nations. Jesus changed Simon's name to Peter, His rock. But leave it to an angry, evil father to change Lynda's name to one that represented darkness and death.

Thankfully the ending to Lynda's story is one of great hope, not hurt. Through counseling and a loving church, she came to know Christ personally and traded in her old nickname for a new one "child of God." Like Jesus promised in the book of Revelation, "I will write on him [believers] the name of My God . . . My *new* name" (Rev. 3:12, italics added). God's love broke through to Lynda's heart in a dramatic way. Today, Lynda is married to an outstanding Christian man, wears a radiant smile, and has a wardrobe full of beautiful, pastel colored clothes.

Perhaps you still stumble over hurtful words your parents, spouse, or a close friend spoke to you (or negative words we have spoken to ourselves), words that come to memory time and again and point you in a direction in life you don't want to go. If so, don't lose hope. As you learn more about the blessing, you can begin to hear and speak words that can lead to a new course of life.

Each of us should be keenly aware of the power of spoken words. We should also be aware of how powerful the *absence* of spoken words can be.

"I'll Tell Them Tomorrow": Today's Most Common Choice

In homes like Lynda's, negative words can shatter children emotionally rather than shape them positively. But that is not the most common choice of parents. Most parents genuinely love their children and want the best for them. However, when it comes to speaking words of love and acceptance—words of blessing—they are up against an even more formidable foe than the temptation to speak negative words.

A thief is loose in many homes today who masquerades as "fulfillment," "accomplishment," and "success." Actually, this thief steals the precious gift of genuine acceptance from our children and leaves confusion and emptiness in its place. That villain's name is *overactivity,* and it can keep parents so busy that the blessing is never spoken. Even with parents who dearly love their children, as one woman we talked to said, "Who has time to stop and *tell* them?"

In many homes today, both parents are working overtime, and a "family night" makes an appearance about as often as Halley's comet. The result is that instead of Dad and Mom taking the time to communicate a spoken blessing, a babysitter named *silence* is left to mold a child's self-perception. Life is so hectic that for many parents, that "just right" time to communicate a spoken blessing never quite comes around. What is the result?

- A father tries to corner his son to communicate "how he feels about him" before he goes away to college, but now his son is too busy to listen.
- A mother tries to communicate a spoken blessing to her daughter in the bride's room just before the wedding, but the photographer has to take her away to get that "perfect" shot.

Spoken words of blessing should start in the delivery room and continue throughout life. Yet the "lack of time" and the thief's motto, "I'll have time to tell them tomorrow," rob children of a needed blessing today.

"Oh, it's not that big a deal," you may say. "They know I love them and that they're special *without* my having to say it." *Really?* We wish that explanation worked with many of the people we counsel. To them, their parents' silence has communicated something far different from love and acceptance.

Let's look at what commonly happens in homes

where spoken words of blessing are withheld. What we will see is that silence does communicate a message; and like an eloquent speech, silence too can set a course for a person's life. But it's not the path most parents would like their children to take. In fact, for many, silence affects their every relationship and leaves them wandering between workaholism and extreme withdrawal.

WHAT HAPPENS WHEN WE WITHHOLD WORDS OF BLESSING?

Both people and relationships suffer in the absence of spoken words of love, encouragement, and support—words of blessing. Take a marriage, for example.

Dr. Howard Hendricks, a noted Christian educator, is fond of telling the story of a couple he counseled several years ago. This couple had been married over twenty years, but their problems had become so acute they were now considering divorce. Dr. Hendricks asked the husband, "When was the last time you told your wife you loved her?" The man glared at him, crossed his arms, and said, "I told my wife I loved her on our wedding day, and it stands until I revoke it!"

Take a guess what was destroying their marriage. When a spoken blessing is withheld in a marriage, unmet needs for security and acceptance act like sulfuric acid and eat away at a relationship.

Not only marriages, but individuals—particularly children—suffer from the lack of a spoken blessing. Without words of love, acceptance, and encouragement, children often grow up traveling one of two roads that lead to unhealthy extremes. Take Dan, for example. He took the road marked, "Try a little harder, maybe that will get you the blessing."

TAKING THE ROAD TO WORKAHOLISM

Dan grew up in a home where nothing positive was ever said. In fact, little of *anything* was ever said. His parents seemed too busy with their careers or too preoccupied with constantly "remodeling" the house to do much talking. There came, however, an exception to the general rule of indifference when Dan was just a boy.

At the end of one semester in grade school, Dan received an excellent report card with nearly all *A*'s. For the first time in memory, his parents openly spoke words of praise. At last, he felt like a somebody.

Like a starving man who stumbles across a loaf of bread, Dan thought he had learned the key to hearing words of acceptance: *overachieve*. Acceptance was worth the hours spent inside studying (with the neighbor kids playing right outside his window) just to hear a few words of affirmation at the end of a semester. This working to overachieve lasted right through college.

The only problem Dan had was that his need for words of acceptance outlasted the years he spent in school. As a result, he took his motivation to "show them I'm somebody" right into the marketplace. Naturally, Dan became a "perfect" junior executive (which translated means he was a committed workaholic, always driven to achieve more and more regardless of the personal or relationship costs).

Why the intense drive and the insatiable need to achieve? Just look back at Dan's home, where no spoken blessing was given—except for some spectacular achievement. While Dan would never admit it (but inside he always knew it), pulling into his parents' driveway in a new car said he was still a somebody—didn't it? Getting that corner office would show them—wouldn't it?

Dan met every qualification of a "driven" man. He had fallen into the trap many men and women do who never received the blessing. Like Moses' fading glory, accomplishments could not sustain a missing sense of personal acceptance. Dan was forever having to make one more deal, sell one more product, attend one more motivational seminar. Spoken words of love and acceptance went unsaid early in Dan's life; as a result, his search for acceptance left him at the door of the driven.

Dan finally came to grips with missing out on the blessing. Until then, his search for personal acceptance kept him on the barren road to success and away from the pathway of life.

TAKING THE ROAD OF WITHDRAWAL

Many people who missed out on hearing words of blessing take another road. These people head in the opposite direction. Convinced they can do nothing to hear words of love and acceptance, they give up and travel down the road of apathy, depression, and withdrawal. At the end of the road of withdrawal can be a terrifying, yet beckoning, cliff.

A classic example of a child who took this road is found in a film that circulated several years ago. As the movie begins, we see several children waiting for their school bus. The sun is out on a cold January morning. Snow covers the rural countryside like a beautiful, white blanket.

All bundled up for winter weather, a few of the children are making snowballs and throwing them at a fence. Others laugh and talk and stomp their feet trying to stay warm. All except Roger.

Standing by himself at the edge of the group, Roger stares down at the ground. In the next few moments, you almost get the feeling that Roger is invisible. Several children run right by him in excited conversation; others crowd around him when the bus finally comes. But Roger never looks up, and the other children never speak to him or acknowledge his existence.

The children rush to see who gets on the school bus first. Glad to be in out of the cold, the children happily take their seats—that is, all except Roger. The last one on the bus, he wearily mounts the steps as if climbing each one requires a monumental effort. He stops briefly and looks up expectantly into the faces of the other children, but no one beckons him to join them. Heaving a sigh, he slumps into a seat behind the driver.

The sound of compressed air is heard being released from the bus's hydraulic system, and the door slams shut. With one look behind him to make sure everything is in order, the bus driver pulls slowly away from the curb and onto the country lane.

They have traveled only a few miles when suddenly Roger drops his books and staggers to his feet. Standing next to the bus driver, steadying himself on a metal pole, Roger has a wild and distant look in his eyes. Shocked by his sudden ill appearance, the bus driver asks, "Are you all right? Are you sick or something? *Kid, what's the matter?*" Roger never answers, and half out of frustration, half out of concern, the bus driver pulls over to the side of the road and opens the door.

As Roger begins to walk down the steps of the bus, he pitches forward and crumples into the snow. As the opening scene ends, we see the bus driver standing over Roger's body, trying to discover what has happened. As the camera pulls away, we hear an ambulance siren begin to whine in the distance, but somehow you know its coming will be too late.

This scene is from the excellent educational film *A Cipher in the Snow*, a film designed for teachers but that speaks to anyone concerned about giving the blessing to others. The movie is a true story of a young boy who actually died on the way to school one day and the resulting confusion over the reasons.

Medical records indicated no history of problems in either Roger or his family. Even the autopsy shed no light on his death. Only after an interested teacher looked into his school and family background were the reasons for his death discovered.

This teacher found that Roger's life had been systematically erased like a blackboard. In his first few years at school, he had done well, up until problems began at home. His parents' marriage had disintegrated, and a new, preoccupied stepfather never had time to fill any of the missing gaps. Resentful of any attention his new wife gave Roger, the stepfather would limit their time together. His mother loved Roger dearly, but soon she was either too busy or too intimidated by her new husband to give Roger any attention at all. Like being pushed away from a seat near the fireplace, Roger was now left with only the cold ache of indifference.

As a reaction to his home life, Roger's school work began to suffer. Homework assignments were either turned in late or not at all. Tired of his apparent apathy, his teachers gave up on him and left him to work alone. He also began to withdraw from the other children at school, and he lost the few friends he once had. Roger would not begin a conversation, and soon other children wouldn't bother to try. Slowly but surely he was retreating into a world of silence.

In only a few months, everything and everyone of value to Roger had either been lost or taken from him. With no place of shelter and no words of encouragement, he felt like a cipher—an empty zero. This sensitive child was unable to stand the pain for long.

Roger was not killed by an infirmity nor a wound. He was killed by a lack of words of love and acceptance. Roger withstood the painful silence as long as he could. Ultimately, however, the lack of a spoken blessing from family and friends acted like a deadly cancer. After months of pursuing its course, it finally ate away his will to live. He died a cipher in the snow, believing he was totally alone and unwanted.

Are words or their absence *really* that powerful? Solomon thought so. Like throwing ice water in our faces, he shocks us into reality with his words, "Death and life are in the power of the tongue" (Prov. 18:21).

If we struggle with speaking words of love and acceptance to our family or friends, another proverb should encourage us. Again, it is Solomon writing:

> Do not withhold good from those to whom it is due/ When it is in the power of your hand to do so./Do not say, . . . "Go, and come back,/And tomorrow I will give it,"/When you have it with you. (Prov. 3:27–28)

If we can open our mouths to talk, we have the ability to communicate the blessing by spoken words. By deciding to communicate words of love and acceptance verbally, we do not have to send away a child, spouse, or friend in need.

WHY IS IT SO HARD TO SPEAK WORDS OF BLESSING?

The damage of withholding words of blessing should be obvious in the examples of Mike, Dan, and Roger. But if spoken words of love and acceptance are so important, why are they offered so infrequently? Here are a few reasons we have gathered from people we have counseled:

"I don't want to inflate my child's ego."

"I'm afraid if I praise them, they'll take advantage of me and won't finish their work."

"Communication is too much like work. I work all day, then she expects me to work all night talking to her."

"I just don't know what to say."

"They know I love them without my having to say it."

"If I get started, I'll have to make a habit of it."

Our favorite reason is this one:

"Telling children their good points is like putting on perfume. A little is OK; but put on too much and it stinks."

If the truth be known, the reason many people hesitate to bless their children or others with spoken words of love and acceptance is that their parents never gave them this part of the blessing.

BEWARE OF SOME FAMILY RULES

Both praise and criticism seem to trickle down through generations. If you never heard words of love and acceptance, expect to struggle with speaking them yourself. Why? If your family had a "rule" that loving words were best left unsaid, you may find it very difficult to break this rule.

Every family operates by certain "rules." These rules make up "the way our family does things." Some families have a rule that "people who know anything about anything" open Christmas presents on *Christmas morning*. Other families follow the rule that "truly civilized people" open Christmas presents on *Christmas Eve*. (Both our wives, Cindy and Norma, just groaned when we wrote this!) Conflicting family rules often meet in a marriage. Many an argument has gone fifteen rounds to see whose family rule will win out in a new marriage.

Families set all kinds of rules: What we will eat in this family, and what we won't eat. What television programs we can watch, and which are dull or off limits. What is safe to talk about, and what subjects should never be brought up. Whom we invite over to the house, and who doesn't get an invitation.

In some cases family rules can be very helpful. For example, families can adopt biblical rules like "not letting the sun go down on our anger" and "being kind, one to another." Another way of setting positive family rules is by using "contracts" that can help build communication and encourage your children.[1] These types of family guidelines can be safely passed down generation after generation.

But not all family rules are worth retaining. Some family rules—written or unwritten—can devastate a family. Like words cast in steel, a destructive family rule can hammer away at a family, from parent to son or daughter, until at last someone breaks this painful pattern, someone like Cherryl.

When Cherryl was growing up, a simple plaque hung in the family room. The plaque had belonged to Cherryl's grandfather and had become a kind of unspoken "family motto." The plaque was not impressive looking, and it carried only two hand-painted words: STAND UP. Just two words—yet these two words had written volumes of hurt into three generations of Cherryl's family.

The words were originally part of a longer sentence, a motto that went something like this: "Don't take anything off anyone. Stand up and fight." This slogan may have been a helpful frontier slogan, but it did nothing but damage to personal relationships in Cherryl's family. Just look at Cherryl's father.

Cherryl's father had been infected with the "never give an inch" attitude of *his* father. "I'm sorry," or "You're right" were not in the vocabulary of someone who based his life on the words "Stand up and fight." Also absent were words that were not useful in a fight. Words like "I love you," "Will you forgive me?" and "You're important to me." While following this family rule of "never give an inch" pushed Cherryl's father ahead in business, it pushed him back into a corner with his wife and children.

Cherryl's mother and father fought constantly, each an expert on the other's faults, neither willing to give an inch in an argument. When each of Cherryl's four brothers and sisters grew old enough to dislike "taking orders" from their father, they joined the battle too. Soon there were seven people under the same roof following the family rule of "Stand up and fight" and its corollary principles, "Fight for my rights" and "Death before saying I'm sorry." This situation was true until Cherryl became a Christian.

Cherryl went away to a Young Life camp and trusted Christ as her Lord and Savior. The first thing Cherryl noticed when she came back home were those two words, "Stand Up." She thought about how Jesus had laid down His life and how tired she was of following this family rule. Little by little, and at the painful cost of constant ridicule from her brothers and sisters, Cherryl began to break several family rules.

Right in the middle of a fight, Cherryl would say, "I'm sorry; you're right. Would you forgive me?" and end the argument. She even began saying, "Love you, Mom, love you, Dad," and then giving them a hug as she left for school.

Cherryl's father had never gotten the blessing from his parents, only a plaque that almost destroyed his marriage and family. But over the next two years, he received the blessing from Cherryl. Meaningful touch, spoken words of high value, the picture of a future filled with hope, and the commitment to love him, no matter the cost—all these were relationship tools that chipped away at their existing family structure.

Family rules die hard, but they can be broken. Cherryl's younger sister was so taken with Cherryl's changed life that she also trusted Christ. Soon Cherryl's older brother followed, and the plaque on the wall was beginning to shake. Last Christmas, as a baby Christian, her father took down the plaque.

What a testimony to God's power to break even the most difficult family rule! And what a help to Cherryl's family to have a new family rule to follow! They are now free to "speak up" and share words of blessing with each other—because of one child's courage to go to battle with a hurtful rule of silence.

PUTTING WORDS OF BLESSING INTO PRACTICE

We put spoken words of blessing into practice in our homes and relationships by deciding to speak up rather than clam up. Good intentions aside, good words are needed to bestow the blessing on a child, spouse, or friend.

We are not simply saying talk more to your children or others. While that is normally a good idea, sometimes if you don't know how to communicate in a positive way, you can say less by saying more. As we will see in the next chapter, it is not just *any* words, but words of high value, that attach themselves to a person and communicate the blessing. These are the kinds of words you often hear in the final hours before a family reunion ends.

Almost all of us have had the opportunity to attend a family reunion. A common phenomenon at these gatherings is that during the first two days, everyone is busy talking up a storm about this recipe, that football team, this book they've read, or that movie to attend. But something happens the last afternoon of the reunion. Suddenly with only an hour left before family members say their good-byes, meaningful words will begin to be spoken.

A brother will say in private to his sister, "I know things will work out in your marriage. I'll be praying for you." An aunt will say to her niece, "You've always made me proud. I know school is hard, but I know you can do it. I believe in you." Or a daughter will say to a parent, "Look around you, Mom. We didn't turn out half bad, did we? We have you and Dad to thank."

Spoken words—many times we have to be facing the pressure of time before we say the things closest to our hearts. What we have tried to communicate in this chapter is that with your children, your spouse, your close friends, even with your parents, it's later than you think. In some relationships, it is already late afternoon in your opportunity to talk to them.

In 1986 a tragic airplane crash in Japan took the lives of over five hundred people. Four people survived the crash, and they told authorities and reporters the story of the tragic last half hour of their doomed flight. For thirty-four minutes, the plane was without a rear tail sta-bilizer to control their descent. As a result, the erratic de-scent of the airplane was a time of panic and horror for all on board. While some passengers cried in fear and others took the time to don life jackets, one middle-aged Japa-nese man, Hirotsugu Kawaguchi, took his last few mo-ments of life to write a note to his family. His note was found on his body by rescuers at the wreckage site, and it finally made its way to his wife and three children.

Listen to the last words of this man who deeply loved his family. They picture his desire for his wife and children to have a special future, even now that they would be physically separated in this life.

> I'm very sad, but I'm sure I won't make it. The plane is rolling around and descending rapidly. There was some-thing like an explosion that has triggered smoke. . . . Ysuyoshi [his oldest son], I'm counting on you. You and the other children be good to each other, and work hard. Remember to help your mother. . . . Keiko [his wife],

please take good care of yourself and the children. To think our dinner last night was our last. I am grateful for the truly happy life I have enjoyed. . . .[2]

This man's wife and children no longer have him to hold and love. Hirotsugu Kawaguchi died when the plane crashed. But they do have his final words to them, words that pictured his hopes for their future, and words that will echo in their lives in a positive way in the years to come.

In the next chapter, you can learn about the *kind* of words—words of high value—that can especially bless people, but don't delay. Time passes so quickly. Please don't let that important person leave your life without hearing the second element of the blessing—spoken words.

5

THE THIRD ELEMENT OF THE BLESSING: Expressing High Value

Diane's parents had tried unsuccessfully for years to have children. Perhaps that is one reason why their joy was unbounded when they learned that they were expecting their first child. Everything seemed normal during the pregnancy and delivery, until they saw the doctor's reactions. When Diane was given to them for the first time they saw that her left arm had never developed below the elbow.

There were tears in the delivery room and deep concern as test after test was performed on Diane. As doctors and specialists sought to determine the extent of her physical problems, Diane's parents didn't know how they should handle the anxious questions from relatives and friends.

Two days later, the doctors told Diane's parents some encouraging news. In all their tests, they had not picked up any other signs of medical or physical problems. Diane appeared to be a normal, healthy baby girl, with the exception of her left arm.

After the doctors had gone, Diane's parents bowed together in prayer. They thanked God that their daughter had no other serious problems. But they prayed something else that proved to be of tremendous benefit to their daughter. In that hospital room, with Diane nestled in her mother's arms, her parents prayed that their love for her would make up for any lack of physical abilities she possessed. They decided that morning that they would encourage Diane to become all that God would have her be, in spite of the problems they and Diane would have to face along the way.

Years have gone by since Diane's parents prayed for her in that hospital room. In fact, Diane is nineteen now and attending a major university. However, something special about Diane draws your attention away from her empty sleeve, particularly when you listen to her play a beautiful melody on the piano—with only one hand.

Diane has had to deal with tremendous obstacles in her nineteen years. The stares, giggles, and tactless questions of her peers in grade school; the fears and uncomfortable feelings of whether to go to a dance in junior high; the questions and worry that perhaps she would never date in high school, just to name a few. On the other hand, throughout the real-life struggles of being born handicapped, Diane received a precious and powerful gift from her parents—the security of knowing she was highly valued and unconditionally accepted.

"My parents didn't try to hide from me the fact that I was different," Diane told us. "They have been very realistic with me. But I always knew, and they have told me over and over that 'I am their greatest claim to fame.' Whether I was trying out for softball or my dad was teaching me how to drive, they have been my biggest fans. They have prayed for me and thought the best, even when I've pouted and gotten angry at God because of my handicap. Without question, my parents deserve a lot of credit for helping me accomplish the things I have."

They certainly do. Credit for deciding, in spite of a physical deformity, to value their daughter as whole and complete. Diane's parents are realists. They have not sugar-coated the very real problems their daughter has faced. But for nineteen years, they have communicated the blessing to her by showering her with meaningful touch and spoken words of high value and unconditional acceptance.

WORDS OF HIGH VALUE

What do we mean by "high value"? Let's look at the word *value* to see the part it plays in the blessing.

As we mentioned in an earlier chapter, to "value" something means to attach great importance to it.[1] This is at the very heart of the concept of "blessing." In Hebrew, to "bow the knee" is the root meaning of blessing.[2] This root word is used of a man who had his camel bend its knees so he could get on (Gen. 24:11). In relationship to God the word came to mean "to adore with bended knees."[3] Bowing before someone is a graphic picture of valuing that person. Notice the important principle here: Anytime we bless someone, we are attaching high value to him or her. Let's illustrate this by an example in my (Gary's) home.

In my life, I want God to be of utmost value to me. He is my best friend and the source of my life. If I were to chart this on a 1-to-10 scale, I would value the Lord at "10," of highest value. Right beneath my relationship with the Lord would come my relationship with Norma, my wife. Humanly speaking, she is my best friend, and I love and value her right beneath my love for the Lord, maybe a "9.5." Then come my children. I love each of them dearly, and while neither they nor Norma are aware that I love them at a different level, I would value them at about a "9.4," right behind Norma. I do not love them less; but in attaching value to them, they come right behind my relationship with my Lord and with my wife.

Now I need to be honest with you. Emotionally, there are times with the kids when my feelings for them might drop to a "6.4" or even a "4.2." Particularly if we are camping in our mini-mobile home, and it has been raining all week. But, because I want to love and value them at a "9.4," I continually try to push their value back where it belongs. The same thing is true with Norma. I don't want to hurt or devalue her in any way. That is why if I do offend her, I immediately decide to raise her value to just beneath where I value the Lord. How does this apply to the blessing?

This principle is so important, let's repeat it. When we bless someone, we are deciding that he or she is of high value. This is what the psalmist is telling us in Psalm 103 when he says, "Bless the LORD, O my soul;/And all that is within me, bless His holy name." When we "bless the Lord," we are actually recognizing God's intrinsic worth and attaching high value to Him. He is worthy of our "bowing the knee" to Him.[4]

In the Scriptures, we are often called on to bless or value the Lord; but the Scriptures also give many examples of men blessing other men (Deut. 33:1, 2; Josh. 14:13; 2 Sam. 6:18) and others. When they did, they were attaching high value to the person they were blessing. They were recognizing him or her as a very special individual.

This valuing is exactly what the patriarchs in the Old Testament did in blessing their children with the family blessing. They were attaching high value to them. We do the same thing when we bless our children, spouse, or friends, and every person today needs the blessing to feel truly loved and secure about himself or herself. This concept of valuing another person is so important that we believe it can be found at the heart of every healthy relationship.

WORDS OF HIGH VALUE IN OLD TESTAMENT HOMES

In the Old Testament, shining threads of love and value run throughout the fabric of the blessing. We can see this in the words Isaac spoke to Jacob: "Surely, the smell of my son/Is like the smell of a field/Which the LORD has blessed. . . . /Let peoples serve you,/And nations bow down to you" (Gen. 27:27–28).

Telling your children today that they "smell like a field" would probably not be seen as a compliment! But Jacob knew what his father meant. So can you if you remember driving through the country when hay or wheat has been harvested recently. Particularly with the morning dew on the ground, or after a rain shower, the smell of a newly cut field is as fresh and refreshing as a mountain spring.

Isaac also pictured his son as someone who other people, including his own family, should greatly respect. He was even someone who deserved to be "bowed down to" by nations because he was valuable.

In the United States, no premium is placed on bowing before dignitaries. About the only people who know how to bow anymore are orchestra conductors and high school debutantes. Most of us would have to practice for hours to properly bow if we were going to meet a visiting king or queen. In Isaac's day, to bow the knee was a mark of respect and honor, something that was expected in the presence of an important person.

We can't miss the idea in these two pictures of praise that Jacob's father thought he was very valuable, someone who had great worth. This message is exactly what modern-day children need to hear from their parents. This message is what Diane received and what caused her life to blossom and grow, in spite of her physical deformity.

WORD PICTURES: HELPFUL TOOLS FOR COMMUNICATING VALUES TO OTHERS

Telling children they are valuable can be difficult for many parents. As we saw in the last chapter, that just right time to say such important words can get crowded out by the urgent demands of a busy schedule. Some parents do struggle through the obligatory "I love you" during holidays or at the airport; but it seems stiff and out of place.

Other children may hear an occasional word of praise, but only if they perform well on a task (like Dan's story in the previous chapter). When words of value are only linked to a child's performance, they lose much of their impact. Children who have to perform to get a blessing retain a nagging uncertainty about whether they ever really received it. If their performance ever drops even a small amount, they can ask and re-ask, "Am I loved for 'who I am' or only for 'what I can do'?"

We need to find a better way to communicate a message of high value and acceptance, a way to picture a person's valuable qualities and character traits apart from his or her performance. Hidden inside the family blessing is a key to communicating such feelings to our children, spouse, friends, or church family, a key we can perfect with only a little practice, and one that even gets around the walls a defensive adult or child can set up. This key is found in the way word pictures are used throughout the Scriptures.

We may not be aware of it, but we use word pictures all the time. Let me give you one example of a word picture that I (John) remember vividly.

I was at lunch some time ago with a close friend in Dallas, Texas. We were eating at a quaint little basement restaurant where you walk down a steep flight of steps to reach the front door. The hostess seated us, and from our table we had a view of the stairs leading down to the restaurant. That is when it happened.

While we were waiting for our meal, we noticed at the top of the stairs a little girl of about two. She was holding on to someone's hand who as yet we could not completely see. In fact, all we could see were two huge tennis shoes and a massive hand holding on to this little girl. As these two came down the stairs, we were able to see more and more of this very large man helping his little daughter down the stairs.

When they reached the foot of the stairs and the door to the restaurant opened, in walked a football player for the Dallas Cowboys. At 6'4" and 265 pounds, this huge defensive tackle took up nearly the whole doorway! As he and his daughter walked by our table (the ground shaking and plates rattling on our table as he walked by), my friend leaned over to me and said, "Boy, what a moose!"

Calling this man a moose is using a word picture. Randy White does not have antlers and fur; and while he

is very large as far as human beings go, he does not out-
weigh even a baby moose. Yet by picturing him as a
moose (when he couldn't hear us do it of course), I instantly knew what my friend was talking about: a very
large individual was walking by our table!

Some men have called attractive women chicks
down through the years. Obviously, they do not refer to
the fact that they scratch around in the dirt. A junior high
school girl who tells her girlfriends that her latest boyfriend is a "dream" at a slumber party does not mean he
will evaporate when she wakes up (even if it frequently
happens!). Each of these "word pictures" captures an
emotional feeling apart from the literal meaning of the
words.

Now, let's look at the Scriptures and the blessing
Jacob used with three of his sons. Each is a beautiful example of how this communication tool can be used to
communicate high value to a child.

Jacob used a different word picture with each of his
sons to bestow the blessing. We read, "And this is what
their father said to them when he blessed them. He
blessed them, every one with the blessing appropriate to
him" (Gen. 49:28 NASB).

> Judah is a lion's [cub] . . ./And as a lion, who
> dares rouse him up? (Gen. 49:9 NASB)

Judah was depicted as a "lion's cub." In the Scriptures, a lion portrayed strength and was also a symbol of
royalty in the ancient Near East.[5] The leadership qualities
and strength of character Judah possessed were illustrated
by this word picture.

> Naphtali is a doe let loose,/He gives beautiful
> words. (Gen. 49:21 NASB)

Jacob pictured Naphtali as a "doe." The grace and
beauty of this gentle animal were used to show the artistic
qualities this son possessed. He was the one who spoke
and wrote beautiful words.

Joseph is a fruitful bough,/A fruitful bough by a
spring. (Gen. 49:22 NASB)

Joseph was called a "fruitful bough by a spring."
This word picture illustrated how Joseph's unfailing trust
in the Lord resulted in his providing a place of refuge for
his family. Jacob's word picture carries a similar message
to one used first of Jesus in Psalm 1:3: "And he will be
like a tree firmly planted by streams of water,/Which
yields its fruit in its season,/And its leaf does not wither;/
And in whatever he does, he prospers" (NASB).

Each of Jacob's sons was an individual, and each of
them received a blessing that depicted his value to his
father in the form of a word picture he could remember
always.

Before we rush off to call our child or spouse a
lion, doe, or someone filled with fruit, we need to learn a
little more about word pictures. To do so, let's turn to a
book in the Old Testament that is filled with them. Word
pictures can be used in any relationship to communicate
words of high value. While this book pictures a marriage
relationship, the same principles are used in giving children the blessing. Let's look in on how this couple communicated words of love, acceptance, and praise. In doing
so, we will discover four keys to communicating high
value.

WORD PICTURES: FOUR KEYS TO COMMUNICATING HIGH VALUE

In the Song of Solomon, God's picture of an ideal courtship and marriage, this loving couple praise each other
using word pictures over eighty times in eight short chapters. That's a lot! But they had a lot they wanted to communicate about how highly they valued each other and
their relationship.

Let's begin our look at how they used these descriptive words with each other by looking in on their
wedding night. Not often is someone's wedding night

written up for posterity, but this one is worth remembering. It is a loving record of a godly relationship.[6]

Seven times (the biblical number of perfection) Solomon praises his bride. She was altogether beautiful to him. He begins his praise of her by saying, "Behold, you are fair, my love!/Behold, you are fair!/You have dove's eyes behind your veil" (Song 4:1).

THE FIRST KEY: USE AN EVERYDAY OBJECT

What Solomon does with his word picture (and what a wise parent does in blessing his or her child) is to try to capture a character trait or physical attribute of his beloved in an everyday object. In this case, he pictures her eyes as dove's. The gentle, shy, and tender nature of these creatures would be familiar to his bride. By using a familiar object, Solomon is able to communicate far more meaning using a picture than he could by using mere words. Spoken words are often one-dimensional, but a word picture can be multidimensional. Plus, an added feature is that each time she saw a dove thereafter, it would remind her of how her husband viewed her and valued her.

Let's look at how one young woman's parents used an everyday object in a blessing to their daughter and how it ministered to her life. While Christmas doesn't come every day, their choice of an object was familiar to their loved one.

Nancy was born in late December, near Christmas day. As she grew older, her parents would repeatedly say to her, "Just remember, you're God's special Christmas gift to us, a gift of great price because you're so special to us." As a way of illustrating their feelings, each Christmas (now for almost thirty-five years), a small package is placed under the Christmas tree addressed from Jesus to Nancy's parents. Each year, Nancy is given the honor of opening this package. Inside the package is her baby picture! Listen to Nancy's thoughts about how being called a Christmas gift over the years has ministered to her.

"There have been many times when I haven't felt
very special. I can remember one time in particular. It was
my thirtieth birthday, and I was really struggling with
growing older. When I was at my lowest point, I received
a package in the mail from my parents. In the package
was a brightly wrapped box, and inside was my baby picture and a note from my parents. I've always known I
was special to them. But I *needed* to know I was special
that day. It wasn't even Christmas, but reading again that
I was their special 'Christmas gift' and very special to
them—even on my thirtieth birthday—filled my heart with
love and warmth."

THE SECOND KEY: MATCH THE EMOTIONAL MEANING OF THE TRAIT YOU ARE PRAISING WITH THE OBJECT YOU'VE PICKED

Over and over Solomon uses everyday objects that
capture the emotional meaning behind the trait he wants
to praise. These objects may not be familiar to us, but
they were familiar to his bride. Take, for example, his
praise for his beloved just a few verses later.

Solomon looks at his bride and says, "Your neck is
like the tower of David,/Built for an armory,/On which
hang a thousand bucklers,/All shields of mighty men"
(4:4). Was Solomon trying to end his marriage before it
began? Certainly not. Let's look at just how meaningful
this analogy would have been to an insecure, blushing
bride on her wedding night.

High above the old city of Jerusalem stood the
Tower of David. A farmer working outside the city walls
could look up from his work and see this imposing structure. However, what would impress him even more than
the height of this tower was what was hanging on it.

Hanging on this tower during times of peace were
the war shields of David's "mighty men." The mighty
men were King David's greatest warriors and the leaders
of his armies. Looking up at the sun shining off their
shields would be a reassuring sight for one outside the
protection of the city walls. By the same token, if that

farmer looked up and the shields of the mighty men had been taken off the tower, he would know it was time to hightail it inside the city walls! Danger was in the land.

Solomon's comparing David's tower to his bride's neck now begins to make more sense. In Old Testament times a person's neck stood for his or her appearance *and* attitude. That is why the Lord would call a disobedient Israel a "stiff-necked people" (Ex. 33:5). For Solomon, the peace and security represented in David's tower provided a powerful illustration to express his love for his bride. He was praising the way she carried herself; with serenity and security.[7]

Let's give a modern-day example to reinforce what we have discovered about word pictures, something that took place right in my (John's) home.

For four years before her sister was born, our oldest daughter, Kari, had our undivided attention. So it's understandable that there were adjustments for all of us when a precious baby named Laura came home with Cindy from the hospital.

With all the demands of a newborn, Kari was trying her best to be the perfect big sister. She'd run to get a diaper for Mommy; or tiptoe down the hall on those rare occasions when the baby was napping; or she'd simply sit next to Cindy when she was feeding the baby, stroking Laura's little head or holding her dainty little fingers.

While there were times when she felt envious of all the attention Laura demanded, her love and care for her sister didn't go unnoticed by Cindy. So Cindy decided to think of a creative way to communicate words of high value to our daughter. She looked around for an object that represented some of the same characteristics that Kari displayed. She found that object one day while they were watching television.

While feeding the baby, Cindy and Kari were watching a National Geographic afternoon special on the educational channel, a program about eagles in Alaska. The footage was breathtaking! During the show, there was a long scene where a beautiful mother eagle helped to feed, protect, and shelter her young. There was the picture that Cindy had been looking for. On a trip by a local toy store, she bought a small, inexpensive stuffed eagle and waited for a quiet time to talk with Kari.

"Sweetheart," she said. "Do you remember watching that television program about the eagles?"

Instantly Kari recalled many of the details and talked about how much she'd liked the program.

"Well, Honey, I want you to know that you remind me of that mommy eagle. You've helped take such good care of your little sister since she's come home—even when it hasn't been easy—and I want you to know how proud I am of you."

For *days*, Kari never let that stuffed eagle out of her arms. It was the first thing I saw when I got home that night, and the only stuffed animal she allowed to sleep with her at bedtime.

By using an object familiar to Kari to praise her, Cindy wisely communicated much more than a simple compliment. She gave our daughter a living (or at least a stuffed) illustration of one way she was so valuable to her mother.

A THIRD KEY: WORD PICTURES
UNRAVEL OUR DEFENSES

Solomon gained a third thing by using word pictures that a parent, spouse, or friend can also use today. What he gained is the ability word pictures have to get around the defenses of insecure or defensive people and to get across a message of high value. Let's look first at how a word picture can encourage an insecure person. We can see this with Solomon's bride herself, and it can be a valuable lesson to anyone who has a loved one who struggles with accepting herself or himself.

Like most young women who would unexpectedly meet a dashing young king, the Shulamite woman was insecure about her appearance. When she first meets Solomon she says, "Do not look upon me, because I am dark,/Because the sun has tanned me" (1:6). But after she had been around Solomon for only a short time, she calls herself, "The rose of Sharon,/And the lily of the valleys" (2:1). That is quite a change of perspective! How did it happen?

In spite of herself, Solomon's word pictures made their way around his bride's defenses. If Solomon had simply said, "You're cute," her insecurity could have thrown up a dozen reasons why this matter-of-fact statement could not be true: "Maybe his eyesight is bad." "I bet he's been hunting for three months, and I'm the first woman he's seen." "Maybe my father paid him to say that." These same kinds of reasons are used by insecure people today to ward off any compliments they hear about themselves. But word pictures capture our attention in spite of our defenses.

We will listen to praise more intently when it comes packaged in a word picture. That is one reason why our Lord used word pictures to communicate both praise and condemnation through the parables. These extended object lessons kept his audience's attention, even if, like the Pharisees, they really didn't want to hear what He was saying!

Jesus knew the importance of using word pictures with those who were timid of heart. He would talk about being the Good Shepherd who watched over the flock; the true vine that could bring spiritual sustenance; and the bread of life that would provide spiritual nourishment. By using everyday objects, He was able to penetrate the walls of insecurity and mistrust these people had put up, because stories hold a key to our hearts that simple words do not.

How do we know word pictures really got through to Solomon's bride in their marriage? Just look at how her attitude changed over the course of their married life.

During their courtship, she viewed their relationship with a certain insecurity and possessiveness. These feelings are evident in the way she talks about their relationship saying, *"My beloved is mine, and I am his"* (2:16, italics added).

As their story continues after their wedding—and as she grows more secure in his love—watch the subtle but powerful change in how she views their relationship. Once they are married, in speaking to the ladies of the court she says, *"I am my beloved's,/And my beloved is mine"* (6:3, italics added). This statement shows a little more security.

Then, as their story draws to a close, she even says, *"I am my beloved's,/And his desire is toward me"* (7:10, italics added). This final statement shows a lot more security than her view of their relationship just before their wedding night. Why? The major reason is the way word pictures of praise and great value have brought security to an insecure woman's heart. Repeatedly (over fifty times), Solomon expressed his high value for his bride by using word pictures, something parents and even friends can effectively use today in praising an insecure person.

As we mentioned above, word pictures can also be used with people who may not be insecure, but are defensive when it comes to what we want to tell them. Let us illustrate how one word picture got around the defenses of a couple that was struggling in their marriage and literally changed their relationship for the better.

I (Gary) was counseling a young couple who had been having heated arguments for a long period of time. Things had become so strained between Bill and Barb that they had even considered separating. They were angry and defensive when they walked into the office. Sitting with their arms crossed looking straight ahead, each of their nonverbals was saying "You just try and say something to change my mind. I'm walking out of this marriage."

Bill was a rugged outdoorsman who had moved his family outside the city limits so he would be closer to the hunting and fishing he loved. He didn't mind the thirty-five-mile drive to work each day as long as he could live in the wilderness. At first, his wife had liked joining him on his backpacking trips; but with two young children, now he did all his camping alone.

Barb was a petite, city girl who enjoyed socializing. With the move out of town, she was now an hour from her closest friend. The only socializing she did during the day was with two toddlers. While Barb loved her children deeply, being isolated from her friends and having a husband who hunted or fished every spare minute was leading her to become bitter and resentful.

After listening to them talk for more than an hour about how insensitive the other person was, I shared with them this word picture that opened their eyes to a completely new way of viewing each other.

"Let me close our time together by telling you two a word picture that comes to my mind as I have listened to you talk. Bill, I could see you as a picture, hanging on a wall, of a mighty stag with a huge rack of antlers. You are standing proudly near a mountain stream, looking over the forest, with your doe and newborn fawns in the background. The square frame around the picture is heavy and made out of antique wood.

"Barb, I see you as a picture of a delicate, beautiful wildflower with dazzling colors and fine brush strokes. Your picture has a lovely matting around the oval picture, and the frame is narrow and classy looking with white glossy paint.

"Both of you are beautiful pictures even though you look so different. However, you're not seeing the beauty in the other person's picture. In fact, you keep trying to repaint the picture to make it look more like your own. This week I'd like you to look for the beauty that is a part of each of your pictures, just the way you are. And let's get back together next week and talk about it."

What a difference a week can make. Using that one word picture communicated volumes to this couple. Instead of trying to change each other into their own image, they actually began looking at the beauty in each other's life and rediscovered the attraction that had drawn them together in the first place. Instead of dishonoring each other in anger, they began to be more patient with each other by recognizing the other person's uniqueness.

Whether we are dealing with defensive people, or those who battle with insecurity, using a word picture can help us get around their defenses and help us attach high value to them.

THE FOURTH KEY: WORD PICTURES POINT OUT A PERSON'S POTENTIAL

A fourth reason for using word pictures is to illustrate the undeveloped traits of a person. Jesus did this in changing Simon's name to Peter (literally "rock" in Greek). Peter certainly didn't act like a rock of strength and stability when he tried to talk Jesus out of going to the cross, when he went to sleep in the garden, or when he denied Jesus three times. But Jesus knew Peter's heart; and after the Resurrection, Peter became the rock he was pictured to be. In a modern-day instance, we saw this happen with a young lady in our church.

Several years ago, this young woman's husband divorced her to pursue an immoral relationship. Left with two young children under three, and no marketable skills or experience in the work force, she faced one struggle after another. Today, six years later, she has a good job that allows her time to spend with her children and still to provide for their basic financial needs. When we asked her what was the greatest source of help to her during those first, difficult years, she said:

"The Lord was certainly the greatest source of help to us when Jack first left; but from a human perspective, I would have to point to my father. Every time I wanted to quit school or just give up, he would say to me, 'You'll make it, Jenny. You're my rock of Gibraltar. I know you'll make it.' I didn't feel like a rock at the time. My whole world seemed to be caving in. But it helped me so much to know that he pictured me this way. It gave me the hope that maybe I could make it." We can give this same hope to others when we use a word picture to describe their abilities, abilities they might not acknowledge or even be aware of.

To review, we have discovered four keys to using word pictures in communicating words of high value:

- Use an everyday object.
- Match the emotional meaning of the trait you are praising with the object you've picked.
- Word pictures unravel our defenses.
- Word pictures can point out a person's potential.

A well-known saying tells us that one picture is worth a thousand words. When we link a word picture with a message of high value, we multiply our message a thousand times.

In the next chapter, we will look at the fourth major element of the blessing. Closely tied with words of high value is a message of a special future in store for the person being blessed.

6

THE FOURTH ELEMENT OF THE BLESSING: Picturing a Special Future

~~~~~~

*H*ow could anyone as dumb and ugly as you have such a good-looking child?" Mark's mother was grinning as she cuddled her grandson in her arms. To most observers, her words might have been brushed aside as a bad joke; but almost instantly, they brought tears to Mark's eyes.

"Stop it!" Mark said emphatically. "That's all I've ever heard from you. It's taken me years to believe I'm not ugly and dumb. Why do you think I haven't been home in so long? I don't ever want you to call me dumb again."

Mark's mother sat in stunned silence. Tears came to her eyes. After all, she really had meant her words as a joke. But for the first time, one of her children had had the courage to confront her. For years, without realizing the impact of her words, this mother had constantly kidded her children about being stupid, fat, or ugly. After all, she had been kidded unmercifully by *her* mother when she was growing up. . . .

WHAT KIND OF FUTURE DO OUR WORDS PICTURE?

When it comes to predictions about their future, children are literalists—particularly when they hear predictions from their parents, the most important people from an earthly perspective, in their lives. For this reason, communicating a special future to a child is such an important part of giving the blessing. When a person feels in his or her heart that the future is hopeful and something to look forward to, it can greatly affect his or her attitude on life. In this way we are providing our children, spouse, or friends with a clear light for their path in life.

Have you ever been camping in the woods on a dark night? If you have, you probably remember what it's like to walk away from your campfire into the night. In only a few steps, darkness can seem to swallow you up. Turning around and walking back toward the fire is a great deal more reassuring than groping around in the dark.

Words that picture a special future act like a campfire on a dark night. They can draw a person toward the warmth of genuine concern and fulfilled potential. Instead of leaving a child to head into a dark unknown, they can illuminate a pathway lined with hope and purpose.

Children begin to take steps down the positive pathway pictured for them when they hear words like these: "God has given you such a sensitive heart. I wouldn't be surprised if you end up helping a great many people when you grow older," or "You are such a good helper. When you grow up and marry someday, you're going to be such a help to your wife (or husband) and family." On the other hand, just the opposite is true as well.

If children hear only words that predict relationship problems or personal inadequacies, they can turn and travel down a hurtful path that has been pictured for them. This can happen if they hear statements like: "You'd better hope you can find someone who can take care of you when you're older. You're so irresponsible you'll never be able to do anything for yourself," or "Why bother to study so much? You'll just get married and drop out of school anyway." Let's look back at Mark's family to see how this happened in his home.

Over the years, Mark's mother had repeatedly given her children a negative picture of their future. "Nobody's going to want to date a fat mess like you!" she would say with a resounding laugh (and her daughter would ache inside). "You might as well drop geometry now; that's for smart kids," she would remark (and her youngest son would throw down his pencil and quit trying to understand the math problem in front of him, hating himself for giving up).

These were just playful words from the mother's perspective. Unfortunately, for her children, these words robbed them of an important part of the blessing, the critical need every child has to have a special future pictured for him or her.

In Mark's family, facing the future as dumb, ugly, or unappealing—even if such words were spoken in jest—eroded each child's self-confidence. The youngest son dropped out of high school after flunking his junior year. After all, he "never was intelligent" anyway. Mark's older sister neglected her appearance so much that no boys were interested in dating her. After all, she knew she was "ugly" anyway.

Mark had taken just the opposite approach to the negative future pictured for him. He became the family "overachiever." His entire lifestyle bordered on extreme workaholism in his need to be successful—all in an attempt to try to prove to his mother that her predictions were wrong.

If you add up the incredible costs exacted from the children in this family, you can see how devastating picturing a negative future can be. You can also see why the blessing in the Scriptures puts such a high priority on providing a special future for each child.

PICTURING A SPECIAL FUTURE IN PATRIARCHAL HOMES

In the Old Testament, the fourth element of the blessing pictured a special future for children. We can see this by looking at the words Isaac spoke to Jacob.

"Therefore may God give you
Of the dew of heaven,
Of the fatness of the earth,
And plenty of grain and wine.
Let peoples serve you,
And nations bow down to you.
Be master over your brethren,
And let your mother's sons bow down to you.
Cursed be everyone who curses you,
And blessed be those who bless you!" (Gen. 27:28–29)

When Isaac spoke these words, much of his son's blessing lay in the future. Jacob was not swamped with people wanting to bow down to him, and he had no land or flocks of his own that God could bless. Yet the picture of a fulfilling future was a powerful gift. The picture gave him the security of knowing he had something to look forward to.

One generation later, Jacob's son, Judah, received a blessing that pictured a special future for him. Jacob blessed him with these words: "Judah, you are he whom your brothers shall praise;/Your hand shall be on the neck of your enemies;/Your father's children shall bow down before you" (Gen. 49:8).

Like father, like son—Jacob passed down this part of the blessing. This blessing pictured a special future that would take years to become reality, but offered Judah a special hope as each year unfolded.

As we noted in Chapter Two, these patriarchs' words had a prophetic nature that is not a part of the blessing today. We as parents cannot predict our children's future with biblical accuracy, but we can provide them with the hope and direction that is part of picturing mean-ingful goals. Our children can begin to live up to these goals and so will gain added security in an insecure world, the kind of personal goals still pictured in many Jewish homes.

In orthodox Jewish homes and services, the wish

for a special future for each child is constantly present. At the synagogue, the rabbi often says to young boys:

> May this little child grow to manhood. Even as he has entered into the Covenant, so may he enter into the study of Torah, into the wedding-canopy and into a life of good deeds.[1]

In orthodox Jewish homes, blessing children is also interlaced with words that picture a special future. I (John) saw this blessing with a special future in a Jewish home I was invited to visit one Thanksgiving. By the time I arrived, almost forty people were preparing or waiting patiently for a scrumptious dinner. With the grandparents, parents, and their children, three generations had assembled for this special occasion.

When the meal was prepared and before it could be served, the patriarch of the family (the grandfather in this case) gathered all the family together. He had all the men and their sons stand on one side of the living room, and all the women and their daughters stand on the other side. He then went around, placing his hands on the head of every person in the room saying to each man, "May God richly bless you, and may He make thee as Ephraim and Manasseh" and to each woman, "May God richly bless you, and may you grow to be like Rebekah and Sarah."

From the oldest child, to the youngest grandchild, this time of blessing pictured a special future for each person in the room—even me, a stranger to him. Far from being a meaningless ritual, the blessing provided everyone with a warm wish for a fulfilling life in the years to come.

BRINGING OUT THE BEST IN THOSE WE BLESS

Picturing a special future for a child, spouse, or friend can help bring out the best in their lives. It gives them a positive direction to strive toward and surrounds them with hope. We can see this very thing in our relationship with the Lord. Listen to the beautiful way in which the prophet Jeremiah assures us of the special future we have in our relationship with the Lord: "For I know the thoughts that I think toward you, says the LORD, thoughts of peace and not of evil, to give you a future and a hope" (29:11).

Jesus also went to great lengths to assure His insecure disciples that they had a special future with Him. During their last Passover meal together, Jesus made sure they knew their future together would not end at His death. In John 14:2–3 we read:

> "In My Father's house are many mansions; if it were not so, I would have told you. I go to prepare a place for you. And if I go and prepare a place for you, I will come again and receive you to Myself; that where I am, there you may be also."

Time and time again, God gives us a picture of our special future with Him in His Word. However, His written Word is not the only way God communicates this message to us. Scattered throughout nature are a number of physical pictures of spiritual truths, pictures that illustrate the importance of providing a special future for the ones we love.

Anyone who has ever watched a caterpillar emerge from its cocoon as a butterfly has seen such a picture. The caterpillar is probably not on anyone's list of the world's "ten most beautiful creatures." Yet a caterpillar has the potential to be transformed into a list-topping, beautiful butterfly. What does this have to do with the blessing? Words that picture a special future for a child, spouse, or friend can act as agents of transformation in their lives.

Words really do have that kind of transforming power. The apostle Paul certainly thought so.

The actual term for the transformation of a caterpillar to a butterfly is the Greek word *metamorphosis*. Paul used this same Greek word in the book of Romans, which we translate as "transformed." In writing to the church in Rome, Paul was aware that the world had tremendous power to squeeze and mold these saints into a godless image. To counter this, he tells these young believers to "be transformed by the renewing of your mind, that you may prove what is that good and acceptable and perfect will of God" (Rom. 12:2).

What does it mean to be "transformed by the renewing of your mind"? One excellent New Testament commentator explains the concept this way: "Since men are transformed by the action of the mind, transformed by what they think, how important to have the organ of thought renewed!"[2] In other words, godly thoughts and thinking patterns have the ability to transform us into godly men or women, rather than leaving us to be squeezed into the imperfect mold of the world. Let's see how this works with regard to the blessing.

Children are filled with the potential to be all God intended them to be. It is as if the Lord places them on our doorstep one day, and we as parents are left as stewards of their abilities. During the years we have children in our home, the words we speak to them can wrap themselves around them like a cocoon. What we say shapes and develops their thoughts and thinking patterns. Loving words that picture a special future help children change and develop in a positive way. In the previous chapter we saw how this picture of the future helped Diane.

In spite of her physical handicap, Diane's parents provided emotional support and words of a special future that lay before her. When she "emerged from the cocoon" of her parents' home and went off into the world, her love for the Lord and other people shone as brightly as the colors on a Monarch butterfly's wings.

In other homes, the words that wrap around developing children actually restrict growth and positive change, rather than promote it. This restriction was true in Barry's home.

"You're a bum. You'll always be a bum." Barry's father said these words to him on his way to his college graduation—a ceremony his father did not even attend. This was not the first time, nor the last, that Barry would hear these words. In fact, up until his father's death, they were the only comments Barry received about his future.

When we saw Barry in counseling, he had just lost an important position in a major insurance company. At first glance, it seemed hard to believe. Barry was extremely intelligent and gifted. He was an eloquent speaker and had that charisma that marks many successful businessmen. However, in less than a year after he had been given an important position in this company he had self-destructed.

Barry demonstrated all the motivation in the world in the way he worked to land his job; but all that motivation seemed to evaporate once he was hired. He became irresponsible in handling projects and people, and within six months he was looking for work.

What was it that acted like an anchor in holding Barry back from reaching his God-given potential? Three words: "You're a bum." Repeated over and over in Barry's mind (even eight years after his father's death), they wrapped themselves around him like a cocoon; and he emerged an insecure, irresponsible, and defeated man. Barry was searching for the acceptance found in the blessing he missed.

A law of physics says that water cannot rise above its source. A similar principle could be applied to Barry and many people like him. If a parent pictures for a child that his or her value in life is low, that child will find it difficult to rise above these words. In one insightful study of fathers and their daughters, it was found that these women's achievements in life were directly related to the level of their father's acceptance of them.[3] Those who truly desire to give their children the blessing will provide the room for these boys and girls to grow by encouraging their potential and by picturing a special future for them.

Let's look at another important picture in nature that mirrors what happens when we bless our children with words of a special future. This picture, explained to me (John) by my twin brother Jeff, a medical scientist, is of something that happens in every cell in our body.[4]

Imagine a typical cell in our body by thinking of a circle. Attached to the outside of this circle are a number of receptor points. We could picture these receptor points as little squares that almost look like gears on a wheel. To make things easier for us to understand, let's picture these receptor sites as little square people.

Floating around near the cell are "Harry" hormone and "Ethyl" enzyme. They would each love to shake hands with (or activate) these little receptor sites. In fact a great number of these hormones and enzymes could grasp hold of a receptor site, but some have a special ability to stimulate a cell's activity. We can picture this special ability as someone coming up to you and shaking your hand up and down so vigorously that your whole body shakes! This stimulation is called "positive cooperativity"; and not only does this one receptor site get to shaking (and working harder as a result), but all the other receptor sites around it get to shaking and working harder as well!

Other hormones and enzymes act in a negative way when they "shake hands" with a receptor site (called "negative cooperativity"). Have you ever had your hand squeezed so hard that you almost crumpled over in pain? That's the kind of thing that happens when these hormones and enzymes grab hold of a receptor site. In fact, not only does this one receptor site shut down and stop working because its "hand" is being squeezed, but all the receptor sites around it stop too.

Words that picture a special future for a child act like positive hormones that attach themselves to a child. In fact, they stimulate all kinds of positive feelings and decisions within a child that can help him or her grow and develop. With words of a special future, a child can begin to work on a particular talent, have the confidence to try out for a school office, or even share his or her faith with other children. But just like the negative hormones that shut down cell activity, a critical, negative picture of the future can pinch off healthy growth in a child. Emotional, physical, and even spiritual growth in a child can be stunted because of the stifling effect of a negative picture of the future.

PUTTING WORDS OF A
SPECIAL FUTURE INTO PRACTICE

No more pictures of butterflies or cells shaking hands! Now we *know* how important it is to provide our children with words that point out a special future for them. However, to make sure we not only understand this principle, but also know how to apply it in our homes, let's look at two practical ways to make sure our message gets across to those we want to bless. We'll begin by taking two steps back to make sure our past actions do not undermine our words about the future.

CONSISTENCY IN THE PAST

Inconsistency in the past can make a person unwilling to believe our words in the present. If we are serious about offering a message of a special future to our children, we need to follow the example the Lord sets. His consistency in the past acts like a solid footing on which words of a special future can stand.

Throughout the Scriptures, the basis for believing God's Word in the future lies in His consistency in fulfilling His Word in the past. In Psalm 105:5 we read: "Remember His marvelous works which He has done,/His wonders, and the judgments of His mouth." And in Psalm 33:9 the psalmist wrote: "He spoke, and it was done;/He commanded, and it stood fast."

Because God has been reliable in the past, His words of a special future for us in the present have credence. The same principle is true in our desire to provide a special future for those we wish to bless. Our credibility in the past will directly affect how our words are received in the present. Just as it did for Ted.

Ted was a sales manager for a national marketing chain. His job responsibilities meant that he was in town one week and out the next. In an average year (adding in an occasional "back to back" trip and sales conferences and subtracting major holidays), Ted was gone thirty-one weeks a year. His schedule ate away at the credibility of his words that his children had a special future.

Ted had two young children at home, and they loved their daddy dearly. All week they would besiege their mother with the question, "Is Daddy coming home today?" When Daddy finally did come home, he was so tired from "jet-lag" and his demanding schedule that he didn't have the energy to spend meaningful time with the children.

Ted did a good job of "picturing" a special future for his children. The only problem was that he never followed through on his word. He had noticed his daughter's deep love for animals, and he would say, "Samantha, we're going to get a horse for you so you can ride it and take care of it. You might even become a veterinarian someday." His son was very athletic for his age, and he would say to him, "Bobby, you're pro shortstop material. Just give me a little time to rest up, and we'll go down to the park and I'll hit you some grounders." However, a few days would pass and then it was time for Ted to go back on the road. Somehow there was never enough time to settle all the details on what kind of pony Sam should get and where they would stable it; nor a free afternoon to hit grounders to Bobby, a potential shortstop.

After nine years of being on the road, Ted finally realized that he needed to greatly reduce his traveling schedule if he was ever going to build a secure marriage and family life.

Ted even took a cut in pay to move to a position in the company where he could stay at home. One of the first things he did was to surprise his daughter with a new pony—only now, nine years later, Samantha wasn't interested in horses anymore. Neither was Bobby interested in going with his father to a pro baseball game. His children had listened to the empty promise of a special future for them so long that Ted's words carried as much weight as the air used to speak them. They had their friends, their relationship with their mother, a new set of interests, and a deep-set impression that any future they had would not include their father's being involved in it.

This story has a happy ending, however. Ted truly loved his wife and children, and he persevered in trying to regain lost ground with his family. As the weeks turned into months, Ted was beginning to build up a track record of honored commitments. It took nearly two years, but Ted finally built up a "past" with his children that assured them he really did want the best for their future. Interestingly, Samantha even began to rekindle an interest in animals, and Bobby dug his baseball glove out of the bottom of the closet.

Perhaps your past has been anything but consistent with those you want to bless. Today really *is* the first day of the rest of your life. And you can begin to build the kind of "past" that words of a special future need to rest on by honoring commitments to your children today. Remember, there is no such thing as inconsistent "quality" time that makes up for consistency in our relationships. We need to have a track record of daily decisions that demonstrate our commitment to our children, our spouse, or anyone we would bless. Only then will our words of a special future really find their mark.

COMMITMENT IN THE PRESENT

As we mentioned above, if our words of a special future are to take hold and grow, we need to demonstrate commitment in the present. This idea of commitment is so important, we will spend the entire next chapter looking at it. Commitment is the fifth element of the blessing. However, one aspect of a present commitment applies directly to our look at picturing a special future. That aspect is the degree of certainty our children have in whether we will be around long enough to see our predictions come to pass. I (Gary) saw this clearly one night at the dinner table in something my grade-school daughter said.

We were all sitting around the table, enjoying a

meal my wife, Norma, had prepared. We were all talking about our day and having a nice conversation, when out of the blue Kari turned to her mother and said, "Mom, do you think you'll ever divorce Dad?" Everyone got quiet the moment she asked the question, and Norma nearly choked on her dinner. "Kari!" she said in shock, "you know that I would never divorce your dad." Then stopping to think about it a little more, Norma added with a twinkle in her eye, "Murder maybe, but never divorce!"

After we stopped laughing, we found out why Kari had asked her question. We were only two months into the school year, and already the parents of two of her classmates had gotten a divorce. What Kari was asking that night was the same thing every child asks (whether out loud to parents or in the silence of his or her heart) about his parents: "Will you be here in the future as I grow up, or will one of you leave me?"

Recently, I (John) counseled a husband and wife who were constantly fighting. I had asked the entire family to come in to try to get a better picture of what was happening with the couple. That meant that I had an eleven-year-old boy and a six-year-old girl join us for our counseling session. I began the session by addressing my first question to this six-year-old young lady (children are *soooooo* honest, even when their parents hesitate to be too specific).

"What bothers you the most about your parents' arguing?" I asked. What was causing her the greatest pain and insecurity wasn't their loud voices or even what they said. What concerned her most was the surprising answer she gave me. "Every time my daddy gets mad at my mom, he takes off his wedding ring and throws it away."

Children are incredibly perceptive, and this little girl was no exception. While her father said it was "no big deal," his habit of pulling his wedding ring off his finger and throwing it somewhere in the house sent out a message loud and clear. Every time he "threw away" his wedding ring, this little girl saw her future with her parents (the greatest source of security a child has) go sailing right along with it.

Words of a special future for a child can dissolve into ashes when a husband or wife walks out on a relationship. In a later chapter, we will see just how difficult it is for some children to feel blessed who have lost a parent due to divorce or death (and also how a single parent can help correct this). For those of you who are married, an important part of picturing a special future for your children is keeping your present commitment to your spouse strong and intact.

A GUIDING LIGHT TO FOLLOW

Thankfully, many people realize the importance of providing their children, spouse, or friends with a picture of a special future. These people know how to use words of blessing to help mold, shape, and guide others into the full potential God has in store for them. Even when that person was labeled a "slow learner" like Marcia.

Marcia struggled throughout her years in school. If it took her classmates a half hour to do an assignment, you can bet Marcia would only be halfway through the same project an hour later. Her parents even received the disturbing news from her teacher that she was being placed in the "slow learners" group. However even this news did not discourage Marcia's parents from picturing a special future for her. While they knew she was struggling in school, they also knew that their daughter had many positive characteristics.

Rather than pushing Marcia to "hurry up" or read faster, her parents would praise her for being methodical and for staying with an assignment until she finished it. They also noticed that Marcia had an obvious gift for verbally encouraging her younger sisters and the neighbor children and for explaining things to them in a way they could understand. They began to encourage her to use these talents by letting her help them teach the young

children in Sunday school and use her gifts in serving
these little ones.

After Sunday school one morning, Marcia an-
nounced to her parents that she wanted to be a teacher
when she grew up. Her comments could have been met
with a chuckle, a "What'll you want to be next week," or
even the pious words, "Now Marcia, let's be realistic"
(particularly when the quarter's grades had just come out
and Marcia was still at the bottom of her class). However,
Marcia's parents looked beyond her sagging test scores
and saw the God-given talents Marcia had.

Instead of laughing at her, they pointed out these
gifts and encouraged her. They said that if she was willing
to stay with it, one day she could become a teacher. This
picture is of a future few "slow learners" would ever
dream of painting for themselves or ever hear pictured for
them by their parents.

Marcia struggled through every year of school. Her
parents had to provide and pay for tutors in grade school
and special reading classes in high school. When Marcia
decided to go to college, it took her six and a half years to
graduate from a four-year program because she could not
handle taking a full load of classes. Nonetheless, on a
beautiful Saturday afternoon in May, Marcia graduated
from college with an elementary education teaching degree.

While graduation day meant that many of her
classmates were just beginning to look for a job, Marcia
already had one. She had done such a magnificent job of
student-teaching at an elementary school in a fine school
district that the principal had asked her to return the next
year and take over a first grade teaching position.

Actually, three people deserved to be honored that
graduation day. Marcia certainly deserved a great deal of
credit for plodding forward day by day to reach her goal of
being an elementary school teacher. Yet her parents also
deserved high praise for encouraging her to reach her
dream. Even more, they deserved acclaim for encouraging
their daughter's dream by picturing a special future for

her—even when years' worth of grade school report cards had branded Marcia a "slow learner."

Are you providing your children, spouse, or intimate friends with a blessing that pictures a special future for them? Did your parents take the time and effort to provide you with the hope of a bright tomorrow as you grew up? Wherever the blessing is given or received words that picture a special future are always spoken, words that represent the fourth element of the blessing.

7

THE FIFTH ELEMENT OF THE BLESSING: *An Active Commitment*

Most children have at least one subject in school that they particularly dread. Whether it is history, English, geography, or in my (Gary's) case, geometry, that course represents the worst hour of their school day.

Mathematics was always the subject I dreaded the most. In grade school it was my poorest subject, and that continued to be true during my first two years of high school. In fact, when I had to repeat geometry my senior year I was sure after only a month that I was going to flunk the course. One reason I had such a difficult time getting into the subject was because my teacher felt sure I was going to flunk the course. My only solace was the fact that more than half the class was flunking with me. Our teacher would constantly remind us of this fact by arranging our chairs according to our current grade. Those of us who were failing lined the back wall.

One Monday morning when we dragged ourselves into the classroom all that changed. Sitting behind the teacher's desk was a substitute teacher. That was good news in itself! Then when we found out that our regular teacher had been reassigned to a different district, we felt like the people in Paris during World War II who had just been liberated! The only problem that remained was that half of us were still failing the course. I was particularly discouraged. A new teacher might bring some relief, I reasoned, but I still felt I was below average when it came to mathematics.

Something that teacher said that morning literally changed my life. In fact, it motivated me so much that I ended up minoring in mathematics in college! While I didn't realize it at the time, he actually blessed me and the other students in the class. He did this by providing us with a clear picture of an active commitment—the fifth element of the blessing.

Standing before the class that morning, our new teacher told us, "If anyone fails this class, then I have failed." He made a commitment that morning to do whatever it took to see that we all passed the course. He pledged himself to see that we learned and enjoyed the subject to the best of our abilities. Whether that meant his staying after school to tutor us or even coming in for a special session on the weekend, he dedicated himself to seeing that each of us made it through the course. Nearly every Saturday morning he would help several of us with our homework, and then he played a little volleyball with us for fun.

Imagine the turnaround that took place in that class. Where once we dreaded coming, now it became something we looked forward to. Even better was what happened at the end of the school year. When our teacher posted our grades the last day of class, we all passed! I even received my first *A* in math! You should have seen it. We were all jumping around and hugging each other. All because one man committed himself to a struggling bunch of students.

In the school of life, children desperately need parents who will make that same type of active commitment to them. In the area in which they are weak, they need to be encouraged and built up. They need to be hugged and verbally praised for their strengths. When they are hurting, their parents' arms need to be around them giving them assurance and helping them back on their feet. Undeveloped potential needs to be brought out into the open and developed—even if it takes our weekends. These actions and attitudes are a part of bestowing the blessing.

In the past four chapters we have looked at the first four elements of the blessing.

- Meaningful touch
- Spoken words
- Expressing high value
- Picturing a special future

These four elements are the building blocks of the blessing. But the mortar that holds them together is an active commitment—the fifth element of the blessing.

TWO WAYS TO EXPRESS AN ACTIVE COMMITMENT

What do we mean by "active commitment," and why is it such an important part of the blessing? Commitment is important because as we have seen in earlier chapters, words of blessing alone are not enough. They need to be backed by the commitment of a person to see the blessing come to pass. This principle is what the apostle James wants us to understand in his letter. There we read:

> If a brother or sister is naked and destitute of daily food, and one of you says to them, "Depart in peace, be warmed and filled," but you do not give them the things which are needed for the body, what does it profit? (James 2:15–16)

To answer his question, such words are about as useful as a crooked politician's shouting promises on election eve. Children of all ages need the daily "food and clothing" of love and acceptance that the blessing can provide. Yet like the verse we have just read, mere words of blessing are not enough.

We need to take action if we are to give the blessing. If we "talk the talk" but then fail to put the elements of the blessing into practice in our home, we leave our children undernourished and ill-clothed in their need for love and acceptance.

In strong contrast to speaking empty words to our loved ones is the blessing in the Scriptures. It pictures two ways we can make sure we have an active commitment to our children, spouse, or others. These steps begin by asking the Lord to be the one who confirms their blessing.

THE FIRST STEP: COMMIT THE PERSON BEING BLESSED TO THE LORD

When you look at the blessing in the Old Testament, something that stands out is the way the patriarchs committed their children to the Lord. When Isaac blessed Jacob, we read: "May *God* give you/Of the dew of heaven,/Of the fatness of the earth" (Gen. 27:28, italics added). Years later, when Jacob blessed his sons and grandchildren, he began by saying, "The *God* who has been my shepherd all my life to this day/ . . . Bless these lads" (Gen. 48:15–16 NASB, italics added). One reason why they called on God to confirm their child's blessing was because they were sure of His commitment to them. We can see this clearly with Isaac and Jacob.

In Genesis 26, Isaac was facing real problems. Living in the desert, he knew that his most precious commodities were the wells he dug for fresh water. Twice Isaac had been driven from wells his father had dug. Finally, he had to dig a third well to provide water for his flocks and his family. As if to assure Isaac of his future in this land, we read: "And the Lord appeared to him the same night and said, 'I am the *God* of your father Abraham; do not fear, for I am with you. I will bless you and multiply your descendants'" (Gen. 26:24, italics added).

Isaac had been driven away from two wells that rightfully belonged to him. Hearing his heavenly Father declare His commitment to him must have been like drinking cool refreshing water on a hot summer's day.

God echoed His words of commitment to Jacob at a difficult time in his life. Fleeing his brother Esau's anger, he stopped one night to sleep out in the desert. It was there that God spoke to him and said:

> "I am the LORD God of Abraham your father and the God
> of Isaac. . . . Behold, I am with you and will keep you
> wherever you go, and will bring you back to this land; for
> I will not leave you until I have done what I have spoken
> to you." (Gen. 28:13–15)

Isaac and Jacob were sure of their relationship with God. A natural extension of that certainty was to ask the Lord to bless their children through them. This is something we frequently see in churches today.

This past Sunday, in churches all across the country, the pastor closed the service with the words, "May the Lord bless you, and keep you." By linking God's name to the blessing he spoke, the pastor was asking God Himself to be the one to confirm it with His power and might, the very thing Isaac and Jacob did with their children.

We also see this in a "children's dedication" at the church. Often the pastor will lay his hands on a child and bless the child, a picture of the desire the parents and the entire congregation have in asking God to bless this little one.

Wise parents will model this practice in bestowing the blessing on their children. When they say, "May the Lord bless you," they are first recognizing and acknowledging that any strength they have to bestow the blessing comes from an all-powerful God. Even the very breath of life they have to speak words of blessing comes from Him.

We are all prone to be inconsistent, and we stumble occasionally in providing the elements of the blessing for our children. In contrast, God remains changeless in His ability to give us strength to love our spouse and children in the way we should.

A second important reason to commit our children to the Lord when we bless them is that this teaches them that God is personally concerned with their life and welfare. Stressing the fact that the Lord is interested in their being blessed is like introducing them to someone who can be their best friend, a personal encourager they can draw close to throughout their lives.

When the Lord is brought into our words of blessing, it provides a sense of security for a child that we as frail humans cannot convey. We saw this in the way the children in one family reacted after the unexpected death of their father.

Karen and Nichole were still in grade school when their father died. He was only forty-one years old when he died of a massive heart attack. These children no longer had his arms to comfort them or his encouraging words to bless them. But they did have a certain knowledge that Papa was with the Lord, and that Jesus would confirm their blessing. Why such certainty? Because a wise father and mother had reassured them of this fact over and over. Listen to the words of his widow, Lisa, who also could draw comfort from her husband's words.

"Before Ray died, he used to gather us all together right before dinner. We would all get in a little circle, holding each other's hands. Then Papa would pray and thank the Lord for our day and for the food. He would end each prayer by squeezing my hand and saying, 'Lord Jesus, thank You that You are Karen's, and Nichole's, and Lisa's, and my shepherd. Thank You that You will never leave us or forsake us. Amen.' It's been rough this past year without Ray, but it has helped so much to be able to remind the children that Jesus is still their shepherd as well as their father's."

Children need the certainty and security that comes from our committing them and their blessing to the Lord. That does not mean that we do not participate in the blessing. Rather, it means that we recognize and acknowledge that only by God's strength and might will we ever be able to truly bless our children.

THE SECOND STEP: COMMIT OUR LIVES TO THEIR BEST INTERESTS

How do we begin committing ourselves to our children's best interest? First, as we have noted throughout the book, it takes a commitment of our time, energy, and resources. However, Jacob observed another important principle in blessing his children. He recognized that every one of his children was unique.

In Genesis 48 and 49, Jacob (now called Israel) pronounced a blessing for each of his twelve sons and two of his grandchildren. After he had finished blessing each child, we read: "This is what their father [Jacob] said to them when he blessed them. He blessed them, *every one* with the blessing appropriate to him" (Gen. 49:28 NASB, italics added).

In Hebrew, the end of this verse reads, "He blessed them, every one with his own blessing." While the elements of the blessing might remain the same, how they are applied in blessing a child is an individual concern. One daughter might need a dozen "hugs and kisses" at night before going to bed, while her sister does well with two. One son might feel secure with hearing encouraging words only once, while his brother may need to hear "You can do it" over and over again in approaching the same activity.

Wise parents will realize that each child has his or her own unique set of needs. The book of Proverbs shows us this.

Most of us are familiar with the verse, "Train up a child in the way he should go,/And when he is old he will not depart from it" (Prov. 22:6). However, another helpful way to view this verse would be to translate it, "Train up a child according to his bent. . . ."[1] In training (or blessing) a child, we need to take a personal interest in each child. The better we know our children and their unique set of needs, the better we will be able to give them their own unique blessing.

Please pay close attention to this next statement: Physical proximity does not equal personal knowledge. We can spend years under the same roof with our spouse and children and still be intimate strangers. Many people feel as though they "know" another person's interests and opinions because they took an active interest in their lives in the past. However, people's thoughts, dreams, and desires can change over the years. Doctors tell us that every cell in our body wears out and is replaced by new cells within a few years. We are constantly changing physically and emotionally.

In our homes, we can be people who are close in terms of proximity to each other, but far away in terms of understanding the other person's real desires, needs, goals, hopes, and fears. However, we can combat this by taking the time to understand the unique aspects of those we wish to bless.

Blessing our children involves understanding their unique bent. In addition, it means being willing to do what is best for that person—even if it means having to correct them when they are wrong.

BLESSING OUR CHILDREN ALSO INVOLVES DISCIPLINING THEM

We want to show you a second way we can actively commit ourselves to our children's best interest. While it may seem the very opposite of "blessing" another person, in actuality we bless our children by providing them with appropriate discipline. We see this when we look back at the individual blessings Jacob gave to each of his children.

Genesis 49 records a blessing for each son. We are told this very clearly in verse 28, "He [Jacob] blessed them, every one with the blessing appropriate to him" (NASB). However, at first glance the blessing that Reuben, the oldest son, received looks more like a curse than a blessing. However, Jacob dealt with each son individually, and in Reuben's case his blessing included discipline as well as praise:

> "Reuben, you are my firstborn,
> My might and the beginning of my strength,
> The excellency of dignity and the excellency of power.
> Unstable as water, you shall not excel,
> Because you went up to your father's bed;
> Then you defiled it." (Gen. 49:3-4)

If we look closely at these verses, Jacob balances words of praise with words of correction. Reuben had several positive qualities his father praised (his might, strength, dignity, and power). However he also had a glaring lack of discipline in his life. His unbridled passions led him to the bed of one of his father's concubines. As a result he now was being disciplined for his actions.

It should not surprise us that blessing and discipline go hand in hand. If we genuinely love someone, we will not allow him or her to stray into sin or be hurt in some way without trying to correct our loved one. This lesson the writer of Hebrews explains to us when he says, "My son, do not regard lightly the discipline of the Lord/. . . for those whom the Lord loves He disciplines" (Heb. 12:5-6 NASB).

God actively deals with us as children rather than merely ignoring our wrong behavior. With other people's children, many earthly parents couldn't care less about their actions. However, like a loving parent with a highly valued child, God does care about our behavior.

Our sons' and daughters' actions will also concern us if we are going to be a person who truly blesses them. We should not shy away from including loving discipline when it is appropriate and in their best interest.[2]

Initially, disciplining another person can seem painful for both parties. Yet being willing to take that risk can help bring out the best in that person's life by training that person and guiding him or her to a place of peace and righteousness (Heb. 12:11). Discipline is an important way of actively committing ourselves to a person's best interest.

We have already looked at two ways in which we can demonstrate an active commitment in blessing others. We can commit them to the Lord and we can seek their best interest. A third way we can demonstrate an active commitment to them is to become a student of those we wish to bless. This is something I (John) have seen modeled before me all my life.

THIRD STEP: BECOME A STUDENT
OF THOSE WE WISH TO BLESS

Nestled away in a modest condominium in southern Arizona lives a seventy-two-year-old woman. Seven major operations due to rheumatoid arthritis have slowed her down a bit; but she is still busy, active, and lots of fun to visit.

If you were to drop in on her some day, you would see something in her home that pictures what it means to be a "student of your children." While it might not catch your eye right off, whenever I walk into my mother's home, it flashes at me like a neon light. What is it? It is a nondescript-looking bookshelf, but it carries special meaning for my two brothers and me.

One rack of the bookshelf is filled with theology and psychology books, and a second is filled with medical journals and books on genetics. The third shelf seems even more out of place for a seventy-two-year-old, arthritic woman. Lining this shelf are past issues of *Heavy Equipment Digest* and "How to" books on driving heavy equipment.

These seemingly unrelated books and magazines might lead a person to think this woman is an "eccentric" who reads anything, or perhaps even has a touch of schizophrenia that causes her to jump from one topic to the next. Neither of these explanations would be close to the truth. This collection is actually a beautiful picture of the active commitment our mother has made in giving us the blessing.

Over the years, in my studies in seminary and in my doctoral program, my mother has asked for and read numerous popular books and textbooks on theology and psychology. They are in her bookcase because she has taken an interest in my interests.

My twin brother, Jeff, is a medical doctor who specializes in genetic research in the battle against cancer. To try to understand his field of interest and to be able to converse with him about it, she has read (or tried to read) medical and genetics books. At the age of sixty, she even enrolled in a beginning genetics class at a local university!

To be truthful, she ended up dropping the course after failing the first two major exams. However, sitting proudly on the shelf with other highly technical books is the slightly worn textbook she struggled to understand. Each book is a trophy of her willingness to learn and her desire to communicate with my brother in his areas of interest.

What about the magazines and books on operating road construction equipment? My older brother, Joe, is now Director for Dealer Support for a national company; but for several years he excelled as a heavy equipment operator. Because my mother was also interested in what this son was involved in, she subscribed to *Heavy Equipment Digest* just so she would know about the latest bulldozer or earth mover.

This magazine does not get many subscription requests from seventy-two-year-old, grey-haired, arthritic women—but they did from this one. All because she made a commitment to become a student of each son and of his individual interests.

FIRST STEPS TOWARD BECOMING A STUDENT OF YOUR CHILDREN

We would like to give you some practical help in how you can become a student of your children, spouse, or others. One thing that can greatly help is to be lovingly persistent in communicating with them. I (Gary) learned this lesson from my oldest son, Greg, when we were both on a television talk show.

We were on a talk show discussing my parenting book, *The Key to Your Child's Heart*. Because my children actually helped me write the book, I had brought Greg on the show with me to share his perspective on parent/child communication. I learned a great deal about my son, and about children in general, by listening to one of his answers to a question.

The show's host asked Greg what one thing he would urge parents to do to communicate with their children. Without hesitation Greg said, "Don't believe it when your son or daughter tells you they 'Don't want to talk.' Sometimes I'll say that to my dad and mom when they ask me how I'm doing, but I don't mean it. I'm really hoping they will be persistent and help me talk about it."

Particularly if we have struggled in our relationships with our children or we haven't been close to them in the past we must be lovingly persistent in encouraging them to talk. That doesn't mean badgering them or trying to pry the words out of their mouths. We must consistently set up times with them when meaningful communication can develop.

In our parenting book, we talk about a second step toward becoming a student of those we wish to bless—the importance of sharing activities.[3] Not only do they draw us closer together, but sharing activities with our children offers tremendous opportunities to learn about our children.

My younger son, Mike, and I went hunting together recently. With deadlines to face in writing books and with a busy traveling schedule, I was not too thrilled about taking a week to walk up and down steep mountains. However, I knew it would be a tremendous time to spend with my son.

Sitting next to each other on the flight, walking in the woods, sitting by the campfire—these are the kinds of "unguarded" moments when meaningful conversation can take place. Without having to "manufacture" conversation, we ended up talking about some of his dreams, his girlfriend situation, and on and on. In some ways, I felt as though I had been re-introduced to my son.

"But I don't know what to ask them about themselves or how to get started!" For those parents who want to become a student of their children, but need some questions to get them started in conversation, here are several that you can begin to ask in those unguarded times at the hamburger place, at the ball game, or just taking a walk. Taking the initiative in asking questions can be a third important way to become a student of our children.

DO I KNOW THE FOLLOWING THINGS ABOUT MY CHILDREN?

1. What do they most often daydream about?

2. When they think of their years as a young adult (twenty to thirty), what would they really enjoy doing?

3. Of all the people they have studied in the Bible, who is the person they would most like to be like, and why?

4. What do they believe God wants them to do for humankind?

5. What type of boyfriend or girlfriend are they most attracted to, and why?

6. What is the best part of their school day, and what is the worst?

Let's look a little closer at each of these.

These are just a few questions that can help us become a student of our children. We can and should ask our children many more to help us learn about them and so to value them for who they really are.

A fourth practical way to get started in becoming a student of those we wish to bless is to listen to them with our full attention. We actually bless our children by being emotionally present when they talk to us rather than by being preoccupied with something else.

Many of us at some time or another have carried on an entire conversation with our children while we were absorbed in the evening news or in reading the paper. "Uh, huh" and "That sounds good, Honey" uttered with our head in the newspaper does not communicate acceptance to our children; nor does it help us become a student of what they want to share.

One way to remind ourselves to actively listen to

our children, spouse, or others is found in the book of Proverbs: "Bright eyes gladden the heart" (Prov. 15:30 NASB).

Most of us have had the experience of walking into a room and seeing somebody's eyes "light up" when he or she sees us. That sparkle in another person's eyes communicates to us that that person is really interested in us and in what we have to say. An interesting research study was done based on this very verse.

In this study, a number of college men were given ten pictures of college-aged women who were nearly equally attractive. Each student was then asked to rate the pictures from "most attractive" to "least attractive."

What these young men did not know was that five of the women had been given an eye-drop solution just before their picture was taken. This solution dilated the pupils in their eyes, the same thing that happens naturally when we are really glad to see someone! The results of the study were just as we might expect. The girls with "bright eyes" were chosen hands down as the five most attractive women in the pictures!

Do our eyes "light up" when we listen to those we wish to bless? Our children or our spouse will notice if they do or don't. We can decide to put down the newspaper or turn off the television to talk to our loved ones as we take an active interest in their interests. Active listening is an important part of communicating acceptance and blessing to our loved ones.

Those of us who are parents need to realize that our children are incredibly complicated people. So are our wives or husbands. If we would begin today to list all their wishes, opinions, goals, and dreams, it would take us a lifetime to complete the task. That is just the right amount of time needed to finish the course entitled, "Becoming a Student of Your Loved Ones," a class men and women will enroll in if they are serious about bestowing an appropriate blessing to each person in their life. All it takes to register is a decision to actively commit ourselves to others and a pair of "bright eyes."

A KEY TO CONTINUED COMMITMENT

Many of us have shelves of notebooks from various marriage or parenting seminars, and pages of notes from the pastor's sermons. Typically, we will get excited about a certain principle we have read or a tape we have listened to, and it can make a dramatic difference in our lives. However, let a few weeks go by, and that book or tape usually finds its way to a dusty bookshelf with the other inspirational material.

In teaching people about blessing their children, we have seen dramatic changes in their lives. For the first time many people have come to grips with whether they ever received the blessing themselves and with how well they are doing in providing it for their children. We hope you have already seen your parents' home and your own in a new and challenging light. Yet like any other call to commitment, that inner voice that encourages us to bless our children can be heard less and less as time wears on.

How can we establish a pattern of commitment that can make each element of the blessing a permanent resident in our homes? The best thing we know of is found in a single word—accountability.

For some reason we don't fully understand, genuine commitment to provide the blessing for our loved ones grows best in small groups. When three or four couples take the time, week by week, to go through a book or tape series together, lasting changes can take place.

Imagine someone asking us how we did in terms of providing meaningful touching for our spouse or children that week; what encouraging words we spoke that attached high value to a son or daughter; or even asking on a "one-to-ten" scale, how high was our commitment to bless our family this week?

Even better, imagine a place where you can admit your struggles and learn from other people's insights (and mistakes). Does this description sound challenging and inspiring? It can happen during Sunday school at your church or in your home on a weeknight. All it takes is the courage to ask honest questions and a loving spirit to share God's truth and your own personal insights. And you need one more thing: the nerve to pick up the phone and call three or four other couples.

Even if you are not part of a small group, you can stop right now and ask your spouse or a close friend how well you are doing in being a source of blessing to them. If your children are old enough, you can even ask them how they think you're doing in terms of giving them the blessing. Children will usually be honest with you, and you can learn valuable lessons from them—if you will take the time to talk and listen to them. On the next page we have included an evaluation sheet that you can photocopy and use with your children, with your spouse, or in a group to help you get started in the accountability process.

We know that asking questions, and even more, being willing to answer them, can be threatening to some people. Even so, small groups or one-on-one conversations are a tremendous way to evaluate where we are at the present. These meetings also give us an added incentive to work on an area we are struggling with. Left on our own, most of us will tend to forget or sidestep these important areas. Faithful friends can help us face things and help us grow as a result. Their love and emotional support can share our sorrow and double our joy.

Accountability can help train us in how we can become even better vessels of blessing for those we love. It can also give us an edge in developing continued commitment as we seek to bestow the blessing.

ONE FINAL LOOK AT THE COST OF COMMITMENT

No doubt about it, commitment is costly. If you are serious about committing yourself to blessing those you love, expect to pay a price. Not in monetary terms necessarily. A spouse and even small children are far too wise to be bought off with presents for very long. Rather think in terms of the time, energy, and effort you will need to in-

Personal Evaluation Sheet

On a scale of 1-to-10, how well am I doing in bestowing the blessing on my loved ones?

Circle your response.

1. **Do I meaningfully touch them?**

   1   2   3   4   5   6   7   8   9   10

   RARELY   FREQUENTLY

2. **Do I verbally speak words of blessing?**

   1   2   3   4   5   6   7   8   9   10

   SELDOM   OFTEN

3. **Am I attaching "high value" to the people I'm blessing?**

   1   2   3   4   5   6   7   8   9   10

   LOW VALUE   HIGH VALUE

4. **Have I pictured a special future for their life?**

   1   2   3   4   5   6   7   8   9   10

   SELDOM   OFTEN

5. **Overall, my commitment level to fulfill my words of blessing is:**

   1   2   3   4   5   6   7   8   9   10

   VERY LOW   VERY HIGH

vest to see the blessing become a reality in their lives. Is the price worth it? The book of Proverbs certainly seems to show us that it is.

The final chapter of Proverbs describes a woman who blesses her family in many ways. She is industrious and loving, has a positive outlook on the future, and is committed to her husband and children. Of equal importance are her words to her family that are filled with wisdom and kindness.

Did she just happen to be born this way? Certainly not. Each of these qualities was developed at a price. What is often skipped over when this passage is taught is how often this woman was up at dawn and how hard she worked to bless her family with her actions and words. She used the same kind of energy that gets parents out of bed on the weekend to take their children camping or that is needed to stay up late helping a husband or wife complete a project.

Was it really worth all that effort? It was for this woman. Read what her family has to say about her and her decision to make a genuine commitment to them; "Her children rise up and call her blessed;/Her husband also, and he praises her:/'Many daughters have done well, /But you excel them all'" (Prov. 31:28–29).

It takes hard work, wrapped in the words "active commitment," to provide the blessing to another person. It takes time to meaningfully touch and hug our children when they come home from school or before they go to bed. It takes courage to put into a spoken message those words of love for our spouse that have been on the tip of our tongue. It takes wisdom and boldness to "bow our knees" to highly value those we love. It takes creativity to picture a future for them filled with hope and with God's best for their lives. But all this effort is worthwhile.

One day, perhaps years later, that blessing will return. Your children will rise up and bless you. What's more, your joy at seeing another person's life bloom and grow because you have been committed to their best is a blessing in itself. Just ask one couple who took the time early in their only son's life to provide him with the blessing. When he grew up, he would provide words of blessing to his parents—in a most unusual way.

"Bubs" Roussel was only seventeen on that infamous Sunday morning in 1941 when Pearl Harbor was bombed. Later that day, he told his father and mother the shocking news of the Japanese attack.

Not long after, Bubs was called into the Army and

ended up serving in the Army Air Corps (now called the
Air Force). After special training in communications in
Kansas, he was assigned as a radio operator in a B-29
bomber. The youngest in his crew, Bubs and many young
men like him had to grow up fast. In only a few months
he was stationed on the island of Saipan in the western
Pacific.

From this tiny island, B-29s were making bomber
runs on Japan. The work was dangerous and deadly. On
the morning of December 13, 1944, eighteen bombers
soared out over the Pacific to make a bomb run on facto-
ries at Nagoya, Japan. Four of the planes that left Saipan
that morning never returned. Bubs's plane was among
them.

Official word came from the War Department saying their son had been killed in action. Family members of
each of Bubs's crew received along with the telegram a
small white flag, bordered with red and trimmed with
blue and gold. The flag had one small gold star in the
middle—the symbol of a son who has fallen in battle.

Bubs's parents received something else. Almost a
month after his plane went down, they received a letter
Bubs had placed on his pillow before his last mission.

> Dear Folks:
> I have left this with instructions to send it on to
> you if anything happens to me. I send you my love and
> blessings. My life has been a full one. I have been loved
> like very few persons ever. I love you all with the best that
> is in me. It hasn't been hard for me, knowing you believe
> in me, trust me, and stand behind me in fair or foul.
> Knowing this has made me strong.[4]

Would our children be able to write a letter like this
to us? They could in homes committed to being a source
of blessing, homes like the one in which Bubs grew up.
The words might be different, but the sentiment would be
the same. Giving our children the blessing is like casting
bread upon the waters. In years to come, they too will rise
up and bless us.

Our prayer for every person who reads this book is that you will become a person of blessing. The cost is genuine commitment, but the rewards can last a lifetime and beyond.

For five chapters we have looked at homes that bestow that blessing on children. Unfortunately, not all children receive a blessing they can give back to their parents. Let's look now at the homes we see most commonly in counseling that withhold the blessing—and the consequences on their children and later generations as a result.

8

HOMES THAT WITHHOLD THE BLESSING: Part 1

*F*ew people see themselves as struggling with missing out on their family's blessing, but people around them see it. Whether it is reflected in an underlying sense of insecurity, or, more blatantly obvious, in an angry, hostile spirit, we can hide very little from those who know us well.

As we have noted all along in looking at the blessing, living for years with our family leaves a profound mark on us. In most cases, this mark is a positive one, issuing from a family that deeply cares for us. Yet some have struggled in homes where the blessing was never given. Often, the parents who withhold the blessing lack the knowledge or skill to pass on the blessing. But some homes have serious problems that can deeply scar a man or woman. These homes can cause an individual to wear the mark of his or her family like the mark of shame God put on Cain.

Such people can spend years struggling to free themselves from their past and as a result are never free to enjoy a commitment relationship in the present. If hurtful patterns from the past are not broken, they are likely to repeat themselves in the next generation. Unfortunately, this is where the terrible truth found in Exodus 20:5

comes true, a home where "the iniquity of the fathers" is passed down to the third and fourth generations.

In a later chapter, we will look at how these hurtful patterns from the past can be broken. We will also discover God's spiritual family blessing that can provide healing to those living apart from their parents' blessing. However in the next two chapters, we want to introduce you to the six most common homes we see in counseling that withhold the blessing.

We recognize that there may be more homes than these; but in counseling couples and individuals all over the country, these six patterns have continued to surface time and time again. We also want to share with you seven characteristics of those we see who have never come to grips with living apart from the blessing. These characteristics will help us identify and better understand someone who has grown up apart from the blessing.

Before we begin our tour of these homes and common characteristics, we want to make one thing clear. In no way do we want this chapter to become ammunition to dishonor a parent or to become an excuse to blame all present problems on the past. In fact, just the opposite is true. We hope that speaking truthfully and honestly about these homes and patterns will lead us to honor our parents (perhaps for the first time) and take responsibility for how we behave today.

Only when we can honestly look at our parents and our past are we ever truly free to "leave" them in a healthy way and "cleave" to others in present relationships (Gen. 2:24). If we are carrying around anger or resentment from the past, we are not free to "leave." Rather, we are chained to the past and are likely to repeat it.

In gaining a better understanding of these homes that withhold the blessing and the characteristics they produce, we may also find we better understand our parents' backgrounds. Our parents were greatly influenced by growing up with their parents, and that experience reflects on us. By looking at the type of home our parents grew up in, we can often find answers to difficult questions about our parents that may have plagued us for years.

Our aim in the pages that follow is to inspire comparison, not heap criticism on horrible parents. Most horrible parents are people who truly love their children (even if they do not know how to show it) and have tried their best with the information they had. Even with those who have not, we can still decide to value them and forgive them just as God, in Christ, has forgiven us. To reinforce this desire, we will share in the pages that follow the stories of people who have actually worked through having missed out on the blessing—by applying the information we will make available in a later chapter.

God's Word gives help and hope to deal with the lack of the family blessing, hope that doesn't come from dishonoring our parents or burying our heads in the sand and ignoring the past. Yet before we can look at a remedy, we need to understand the problems that exist. Only then can we be free to move forward in the present and to receive help not to repeat a painful past.

With this important caution in mind, let's look at the first home that commonly withholds the blessing. In our first example, one child is showered with the blessing and the other children are not.

THE FIRST HOME: FACING A FLOOD
OR A DROUGHT

In the springtime, the Seattle area is particularly beautiful, lush, and green. Almost every day, clouds will roll in and drench the land with refreshing rain showers. However, if you leave the city and travel only a few hours east, up and over the mountains that are set in from the coastline, you will see a far different scene. These mountains do such an effective job in halting the rains that very few clouds get past them. As a result, the land on the east side of the mountains is actually semi-arid.

We can see a picture of a similar phenomenon in many homes today. One child, for what can be a number of reasons, will be drenched with lush showers of blessing

from his or her parents. As a result, outwardly this child
thrives and grows.

Unfortunately, sitting "just east" of him or her at
the dinner table can be one or more siblings whose emotional lives are like parched ground. So few drops of
blessing have fallen on the soil of their lives that emotional
cracks begin to form. This very thing happened in one
Old Testament patriarch's home.

We are already familiar with the patriarch Jacob
and the fact that at the end of his life he gave each son a
special blessing. However, the Scriptures paint real life,
not Hollywood fiction; and the facts are that Jacob showered only one son with the blessing when his children
were young. We read about this in Genesis 37:3–4:

> Now Israel loved Joseph more than all his children, be-
> cause he was the son of his old age. Also he made him a
> tunic of many colors. But when his brothers saw that
> their father loved him more than all his brothers, they
> hated him and could not speak peaceably to him (Gen.
> 37:3–4).

That beautiful tunic may have spelled special acceptance to one son, but it brought out hatred from eleven
brothers. Each one knew at that time that he was living
apart from the blessing. This anger reached such propor-
tions that Joseph's brothers came close to putting him to
death (Gen. 37:18–22).

Anger, resentment, and insecurity are often emotions that children carry who grow up without the blessing. Particularly when that blessing was so close, yet so
far away. Like a thirsty man looking at rain falling at a
distance, discouragement and depression can well up inside a child who is left out of the blessing. In such people's lives, emotional cracks and pain can result in
persistent anger or resentment.

We normally think that only Joseph's brothers, or
those like them, face all the problems in this type of
home; but that is far from the truth. Both the children
who miss out on the blessing and the one being showered

with it can experience significant problems. We have seen this regularly in the one child who gained the blessing in a family but who feels guilty and defensive about receiving it.

Pro athletes commonly have this feeling. Often, because of their outstanding physical abilities, they are singled out for special praise far beyond any brother or sister. We talked to one athlete who feels this extra attention was a curse, not a blessing! He desperately wanted to have a close relationship with his brothers, but his parents' excessive attention to him kept his brothers at arm's length and left him aching with loneliness and feeling rejected inside.

Please don't misunderstand. Each child needs to be singled out sometimes for special praise or recognition. But if the elements of the blessing fall exclusively on one child, serious problems can develop for each child in the family. Just ask Joyce. Her story is perhaps the most dramatic we've ever heard when it comes to the damage that favoritism can wreak on a home and it clearly shows the potential damage that can be done in this all-too-common home.

Joyce's parents were well-to-do educators at an outstanding university. After growing their careers for years, they finally decided that they had room in their lives to grow a family as well. That is, a home for *one* child.

When Joyce's mother became pregnant, ultrasound technology or heartbeat "microphones" weren't as popular as they are today. And that's why her parents were so shocked when several months into the pregnancy, the two heartbeats that had been linked as one finally separated. Joyce wasn't alone! There would be a surprise guest, a twin sister, on the day Joyce was born. Double the joy? Not for this couple. In their well ordered, well coordinated lives, there wasn't room for *two*. They only wanted one child, and they would express their disappointment and anger in subtle and obvious ways throughout the girls' growing up years.

Twins are difficult. As a twin, I (John) can attest to

that fact personally! But to have one twin, Joyce, come into the world and be verbally praised and appreciated by her parents, and the younger twin, Janice, to be scorned, brought resounding heartache to both children.

When children don't receive positive attention, they'll look for it any way they can. And so Janice began, even in early grade school, to live up to her "unwanted" label. She did poorly in school, received even worse marks in conduct, and brought home the kind of notes and comments from her teachers that made her "educator" parents livid.

Things deteriorated until finally, at age seventeen, Janice ran away from home with her latest boyfriend. "Good riddance!" were her parents' only publicly printable comments, and they went back to "blessing" their oldest daughter. Little did they know that it would be over twelve years before they saw their daughter again. Neither could they guess the circumstances that would lead to that reunion.

I (John) first met Joyce at a conference on the Blessing I did at a large, metropolitan church. For two days, I had taught on this subject, and during each break I talked and counseled with many people who came from homes that withheld the blessing. It was then that Joyce came up and told me her story—and how it ended.

Joyce had gone on to college, and her parents had even paid for her to complete a two-year master's degree in music. She then married, and two beautiful grandchildren sported their mother's and grandparents' red hair. But a terrible sorrow and sadness lay behind all the joy in Joyce's life. All because of her sister.

The hurts the neglected child faced in a home with extreme favoritism, are obvious. But for Joyce, the pain of being the one who received the blessing had been magnified 100 times. That happened on the day that her parents received a call from an AIDS clinic in New York. Her sister had just died there—a prostitute who had contracted the deadly disease. After several days the clinic had finally traced her back to her hometown through old letters, and confirmed her identity through dental records. Janice was so hurt and alienated from her family, that even in her dying days, she would not pick up the phone and call home.

Her parents refuse to talk about what happened, but Joyce can't forget it. The joy of watching her own children grow up, the education she received that her sister never did, the husband who loves her, and the church she enjoys so much—suddenly all those positive things seemed to be a product of a terrible home, not gifts from a loving God. And all because she'd been born 7½ minutes before Janice.

While this story is the most dramatic we've heard, we've seen literally hundreds of examples of people who have suffered in a home that plays unfair favorites. Yet as we'll see, honestly coming to grips with this fact can be the first step towards freeing us from a home where the blessing falls on only one side of the mountain.

THE SECOND HOME: WHERE THE BLESSING IS PLACED JUST OUT OF REACH

Craig looked strangely out of place in the psychiatric ward where I (John) was a seminary intern. He was tall, athletic looking, and quite handsome. With his preppie clothes, he looked as if he belonged back on his university campus, not in the hospital; that is, until you looked at his wrists and saw the thick bandages wrapped around them.

Craig had been admitted to the hospital for attempting suicide. If his roommate had not unexpectedly come back to the dorm and found him, Craig would have succeeded. What was it that caused this young man so much pain that he felt he could no longer face the future? He grew up in a home where the blessing was always placed just out of reach.

Craig's father was a petroleum engineer who was considered a genius in his field. He demanded excellence from himself and expected nothing less from his family. As a result of his critical attitude and incredibly high expectations from his son, his blessing became like the mechanical rabbit at a dog race—running slow enough to excite the chase, but fast enough not to be caught.

Nothing Craig accomplished ever quite measured up to his father's standards. That was particularly true when it came to Craig's academic abilities. Craig had done well in school. He even received a partial scholarship to a good engineering school in the state. His father's only remark on this achievement was that it "wasn't a full scholarship" and that there were "better schools out of state he didn't hear from." What finally caused Craig to attempt to take his life was that for the first time in his three years at college, he was going to receive a *B* in a class.

Craig wanted his father's blessing so badly that he had studied diligently to be an *A* student, just like his father. And receiving his first *B* meant more to him than losing a perfect grade point. That *B* meant losing any chance at his father's blessing. This "failure" discouraged Craig so badly that the future was not worth facing.

When the blessing is held just out of reach, it can create tremendous problems for a child. While most people will not come to the point of trying to take their lives as Craig did, almost every child who grows up in this type of home will be lured into a futile chase for his or her parents' blessing.

Robin was an example of someone who spent her life in pursuit of her parents' love and acceptance.

Robin's parents were both demanding. Her father was a successful businessman, and her mother was a leader in social circles. "Success" was a motto in their home and had something to do with every magazine they subscribed to. They demanded excellence from Robin and would only award praise or hugs upon a spectacular achievement. What these parents didn't realize by placing the blessing way up on the top shelf was that their daughter grew up in a terrible "double bind."

To try to please her father, Robin had majored in marketing in college, just as he had. She did quite well in school and landed a job with prestige and the chance for further advancement. Robin spent many extra hours at her

job, and her father was quite pleased with her achievements.

Then Robin fell in love and married a junior partner in the company. After a few years, children were born
to the couple. Immediately their two boys became the apple of their grandmother's eye. Robin's mother expected
her daughter to do all the things with the children that she
had done (forgetting that she had never worked during
her marriage) and told Robin this constantly.

Soon Robin was being mercilessly pulled in two
directions. To try to capture her father's blessing, she tried
to keep the same pace at work that had won his praise in
the past. But she didn't have two preschool children then.
To try to reach her mother's blessing, Robin tried to be
"supermom" and do everything with her children that a
nonworking mother could do. After several years of a killing schedule, one day the pressure became too much.
Like pressing too hard against a glass window, her emotional life shattered around her.

In the United States we live in a culture that is so
"fast paced" that it makes it easy to be "driven" to the
breaking point. Unfortunately, people who have missed
out on the blessing are often susceptible to this kind of
frenzied activity. In reaching for parental acceptance, they
can become workaholics.

Workaholics seeking the blessing are found in the
Christian community, and not just among those sitting in
the pews. Many church leaders today are driven to do
more and more to serve others. However, what is really
driving them may be an attempt to gain acceptance from
other people that they never received at home from their
parents.

Forgetting about God's sovereignty and biblical
passages concerning our need for a "Sabbath rest,"[1] many
modern-day pastors will work themselves until they drop.
In the process of helping so many people, they often receive "buckets" of praise and appreciation that are poured
on their lives. However, instead of this praise fulfilling
their missing blessing from the past, it actually creates the

need to help even more people in order to somehow feel
acceptable. This is exactly what happened to a friend of
ours in the ministry who never received the blessing from
his parents.

Pastor Rick was what many considered a model
pastor. He had majored in Hebrew and theology in seminary and had still managed to win the preaching award
for his class. He began his pastoral ministry working at a
small church that had not grown at all in over fifteen
years. Within two years he had tripled the attendance and
had moved on to another church. Great success followed
this move up the church growth ladder, and he was
pushed even further into the Christian limelight. After
four years at his second church, working day and night to
minister to the congregation, he was offered the senior
pastorate at a "mega-church" with a membership of several thousand people. For a pastor in his denomination,
he was on top of the mountain of success looking down.

Everywhere Pastor Rick went, more and more people would tell him how great he was. And he would feel
more and more empty when they did. Television appear-
ances and making the "conference circuit" could not fill
his real needs, though. At the peak of his profession, at
only forty-six years of age, he had a nervous breakdown
and had to leave his church.

One major reason this happened was that crowds
of people could never fill the lack of acceptance this man
felt from his parents. His parents were not believers, and
nothing he ever accomplished brought words of blessing
from their lips. He had tried harder and harder to be the
perfect minister, trying to prove to his parents that he was
worth blessing; but their blessing never quite came within
reach. His drive to fill that missing blessing with the
praise of others left him emotionally broken and his life in
ruins.

This man needed to deal honestly with the underlying forces that shaped him. Fortunately, he did. After
four months of honestly looking at his life and of taking
the time to re-introduce himself to the God who says,

"My yoke is easy, and my burden is light," he was able to go back into the ministry with a whole new perspective. Because he was no longer driven to try to fill this need for personal acceptance through other people, for the first time in his years of ministry he was truly free to serve his congregation. He could finally enjoy God's acceptance for just breathing, not for trying to meet all the thousands of needs around him. His ministry, his wife, and his family blossomed as a result.

Through applying the same principles we will discover in a later chapter, this pastor discovered how to live a fulfilling life apart from his parents' blessing. He learned to drink from his heavenly Father's overflowing cup of blessing, rather than from his parents' empty cup. But he only did this by honestly coming to grips with his past, a past that included growing up in a home where the blessing was always just out of reach.

THE THIRD HOME: WHERE THE BLESSING IS EXCHANGED FOR A BURDEN

In some homes, a form of the blessing is given to a child, but at a terrible price. Read the words of one woman who wrote a letter to a national columnist. Her words speak of an incredible cost associated with gaining only a small part of the blessing:

> Ever since I was a little girl, my mother made me feel guilty if I did not do exactly as she wanted. Dozens of times she has said, "You will be sorry when I am in my coffin." I was never a bad girl! I always did everything she requested me to do. . . .
>
> Both my parents are eighty-two. One of these days my mother will die, and I am terrified of what it will do to me.[2]

This poor woman has paid a tremendous price for her blessing—her very life. A blessing she is not even sure she has received. One certainly can't say she didn't try hard enough. Did you catch her words? "I was never a

bad girl. I always did everything she requested me to do."
In spite of all her efforts, she received a burden instead of
a blessing.

In this third home that withholds the blessing, a
terrible transaction takes place. A child is coaxed by guilt
or fear into giving up all rights to his or her goals and desires. In return, the child gets a blessing that lasts only
until the parent's next selfish desire beckons to be met. So
it was with Nicole, a woman who had to carry around a
terrible secret in order to keep her blessing.

When Nicole was only nine years old, her parents
divorced. After a whirlwind romance, her mother remar-
ried in less than six months; and a stepfather moved into
the house. While Nicole's mother was away at work one
evening, her stepfather came into her room. What started
out in his words to be "playing" became an evening of
shame and horror for Nicole. Like thousands of young
girls her age, she became the victim of sexual abuse.

The next morning, her stepfather pulled Nicole
aside and told her that if she ever mentioned what had
happened to anyone, he would divorce her mother, beat
her within an inch of her life, and leave her and her
mother to "starve on the street." On the other hand, if she
told no one, he would accept her and be nice to her and
her mother.

The fear of what would happen to her mother,
added to her own feelings of shame, kept her quiet. Because Nicole never mentioned to her mother what happened, her stepfather kept his part of the bargain. He
went on with his life and marriage as though nothing had
ever happened. He even treated her decently after that
one event.

In remaining quiet to keep her stepfather's favor,
Nicole paid a terrible price. Over the years, she was emotionally held hostage in her own home. In error, she believed her silence would buy her stepfather's blessing for
her and her mother. Only later did she realize a man like
her stepfather gives only a curse.

When we first met Nicole, she was married and the mother of three children. For years she had been living in another state and only infrequently saw her mother and stepfather. To keep her parents together, she had paid a terrible price. Unable to share her deepest hurt and pain out loud, her painful memories shouted to her day and night to right this wrong. Only when she broke down and shared her secret with her loving husband did she begin to find freedom from this past burden.

Parents who hold out the elements of the blessing to their child with such strings attached do them a grave disservice. They are using one of the most powerful needs in the human heart to lure a child to the web of their own selfish needs.

Nicole and others like her can receive a genuine blessing. Nicole first saw this in the patient, loving attitude of her husband. Then she believed it when she discovered for the first time her heavenly Father's love, with no strings attached.

If we are carrying a great burden to gain our parents' blessing, or if we are expecting it of our children, we need to understand that we are giving or receiving a counterfeit blessing. The blessing we saw in the Old Testament was not purchased at such a terrible cost. The blessing was a gift that was given, not something that was earned. Like God's love, it is an act of unmerited favor and unconditional acceptance and is bestowed upon a person of high value.

In spite of the problems that were a part of their homes, Joyce, Jim, Craig, Robin, Pastor Rick, and even Nicole were able to work through missing out on the blessing. They discovered, as we all will in a later chapter, that help and hope are available for anyone who grew up in a similar situation. However, we still need to visit three more homes that commonly withhold the blessing. Then we will look at the help these people discovered. In our first stop, we will see a home that is more like a "minefield" than a place of rest and safety.

9

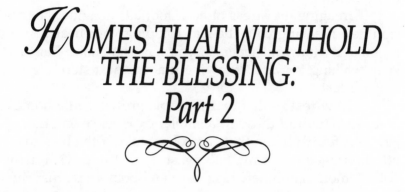

HOMES THAT WITHHOLD THE BLESSING:
Part 2

*I*t was 1969, and my twin brother and I (John) were sitting down with my father for lunch. This was a first! My father left home when my twin and I were just three months old. We rarely spent time with him and we had *never* been asked by our father to go to lunch.

But Jeff and I were facing something the next day, that my father had gone through himself when he was our age—the draft. So he called and asked to take us to lunch. "If your draft number is picked tomorrow," he said with deep concern, "you've got to know what you're going to face if you must go and fight." So for the next two hours, for the first and only time, I heard my father speak in detail about his war experiences.

A young marine with the Third Division, he fought and was wounded on an island called Guadalcanal. I still vividly remember many of the stories he shared that day, but in particular I remember his talking about the one thing he hated most about that campaign: "having to walk on point."

Picture the scene. You're deep in the jungle, on patrol with a squad of soldiers. You're the "point man," the first one in line, and it's your job to scout for enemy soldiers and snipers—and to watch for any booby-traps they left behind. You never know if your foot will come down on a camouflaged mine or if you'll trip over a wire that sets off an explosion that could cripple or kill you and those behind you.

Imagine the stress of each footfall. Imagine the tension never leaving you, the fear gripping your heart. And no matter what your feelings, you have no choice but to keep walking forward, knowing that the next step might be your last.

Now realize that many people grow up in a home that puts children through a similar experience emotionally. The fourth home that can rob a child of the blessing often reminds me of my father's story that day. It's a home with "emotional minefields," unseen booby-traps that can blow up in a child's face, and leave him or her with an inner tension, stress, and fear that runs counter to healthy relationships.

THE FOURTH HOME: A PLACE WHERE THERE ARE "EMOTIONAL MINEFIELDS"

Growing up in an explosive, emotional environment can leave a child openly fearful of connecting with others, or inwardly afraid of genuine commitment. In 1 John 4:18, we read that "perfect love casts out fear." Yet for children who grow up in an emotional minefield their fear can reverse the equation and make them *less* loving. Often these are ACA (Adult Children of Alcoholics) homes, and they commonly leave scars that are felt for a lifetime, just like they did for Steven.

Steven considered himself a typical teenage boy. When he got home from school, the first door he'd hit (after the front door) was the refrigerator door! In counseling, Steven recounted a typical occurrence in his minefield home.

On most days, his father would be sitting at the kitchen table when he walked in. One day, Steven could open the refrigerator and eat or drink anything he wanted. (Even drink right from the milk carton!) But then the next

day, if he even *reached* to open the refrigerator door, there
was an explosion of anger! His father would rant and rave
about "eating him out of house and home," and slam shut
the door, pushing Steven out of the way.

Steven learned that home was never safe. You
never knew *when*. You could never be sure what would set
it off. In a home with such explosions, you don't invite
friends over—because of the minefield. And you don't
walk into the house with an unguarded heart—because on
the day you do, all the mines explode. Such homes be-
queath an unsettling legacy, leaving children confused,
fearful, and often feeling powerless.

It's not only a father who can create such a home.
In his inspiring, and very honest autobiography, General
H. Norman Schwarzkopf tells of what it was like growing
up in a home with an alcoholic mother. While he avoided
many of his mother's "explosions," his sisters walked into
an emotional minefield almost every night.

> I used to dread coming home at night. I'd go
> around the side of the house, where there was a window
> that looked into the kitchen. I'd stand in the dark and
> look inside and try to judge what kind of night it was
> going to be. Mom had a Jekyll and Hyde personality.
> When she was sober, she was the sweetest, most sensi-
> tive, loving and intelligent person you ever met. But
> when she was drunk she was a holy terror.

That terror was often vented on General Schwarzkopf's sisters.

> When Mom was drunk, a terrible meanness
> would come out, mostly in the form of personal attacks
> on my sisters. She might look at Sally and say, "Sit up
> straight! Why are you always slouching? Why don't you
> sit up straight at the table?" Then it would be "Just look
> at you. You're such a mess. Look at that hair." The small
> jabs would go on until she sensed she'd hit on something
> my sister was particularly sensitive about, and then
> she'd bore in until my sister broke down in tears.[1]

There is an innate unfairness in homes like this that withhold the blessing. A mixed message that can say to a child one day, "I love you. I care. I'm sorry." And the next day those words are blown away with explosive actions that say, "I hate you. You're ruining my life. You're the reason for my unhappiness."

While growing up in an emotional minefield can cause lasting scars, these homes are in neck-to-neck competition with a fifth home that also robs a child of the blessing.

THE FIFTH HOME: WHERE UNFAIR
FAMILY "ROLES" RULE

Jim was confused and brokenhearted. At nineteen he had been ordered out of his parents' home by his father, and he didn't know where to turn. What was the problem? Was it open rebellion? Lying? Stealing?

Actually, for Jim's father, it was something even worse. Jim had a role he was expected to fulfill in his family, and Jim had decided it was a mold he did not fit. Such an attitude is an unpardonable sin in homes that fly the banner, "Unyielding Traditions Live Here." In this home the blessing is only given when these traditions are met.

Jim's father was a minister. His grandfather was a minister. Even his great-grandfather was a minister! Three generations of Smiths had heard the call to the ministry early in life and unquestioningly responded to it. Now it was the fourth generation's turn. Jim's older brother had decided to go into the ministry and was attending the seminary his father had attended. However, with Jim the pattern was about to be broken.

Jim had trusted Christ as his Lord and Savior early in life, and he had grown in his love for the Lord over the years. He was attending a Christian college in his hometown and dating another minister's daughter. Up to this point, Jim had fulfilled the prescribed plan for a Smith. Seminary would certainly be right around the corner, and then a small pastorate to continue his family's tradition.

Then Jim told his parents of a decision that left them angry and upset. When Jim had to declare his major in college, he had chosen marketing over missions.

Jim's father was mortified. Having three generations of Smiths in the ministry and both his sons in seminary or pre-seminary training had been such a good illustration in sermons and at conferences. Now he was in jeopardy of losing his bragging rights. All because a rebellious son dared to question the unquestionable, something that Smiths could not do.

At first, his girlfriend was suspected of luring Jim away from his calling; but that proved to be false. His closest friends were all believers, and little evidence could be amassed that a conspiracy had been launched from that direction. No, it came down to Jim himself. In an angry session in the living room after dinner one night, he and his father exchanged angry words. When Jim would not admit that it was sin in his life that had led him astray, his father "invoked discipline" on his erring son. Jim was ordered to separate himself from his family until he had repented of the error of his ways.

Sound incredible? This separation happens every day to a son or daughter who breaks an unbreakable family tradition. We have seen it with a son who refused to take over his father's garage and with a daughter who didn't marry into the right social class. This type of separation has surfaced with someone else's son who dared to vote Republican and with another daughter who turned down a bid to join her mother's sorority.

In each of the examples above, the parents felt cheated out of something they expected from their children. As a result, they have withheld or taken back their blessing from that child as punishment.

This fifth home that withholds the blessing, like the other homes we have looked at, causes problems for each child in the family. This home can force a brother to "choose sides" with his parents against another brother and force one sister to sneak out at night to visit another.

For erring sons or daughters, it can ruin every holiday and special family event because of the layer of ice that forms the moment they walk in the door.

We need to be clear about what kind of parents we are looking at who foster such actions. We are not talking about the kind of parents who grieve over a son or daughter who has strayed into legitimate error and who are, for that reason, forced to keep the child at arm's length—parents like Eddie and Belle.

Eddie and Belle's oldest son, Don, was an alcoholic. He had started drinking in Vietnam by turning to the bottle to try to deaden the horrors of war. When he returned home, he had continued to drink as an escape from facing the struggles of re-entry into civilian life.

Don met and married a young lady in less than four months, and within a year she had given birth to their first child. Unable to keep a decent job over the years and drinking more than ever, Don began to take out his frustrations on his wife and children. At one point things became so bad that his wife had to get a restraining order against him to protect herself and the children.

Don's destructive behavior broke his parents' hearts. They prayed for him daily and tried to be both counselors and encouragers. They had bailed him out financially innumerable times, and they had even bailed him out of jail on two occasions.

Throughout his struggles, Don's parents had never withheld their blessing. They never approved of his behavior, and they had told him so; but he was their son, and they loved him deeply. Yet when he began physically abusing his family, they made the painful decision to withhold financial support from Don, unless he attended an alcoholic treatment program.

Eddie and Belle shared their decision with their son in love, and he exploded in anger. Calling them every name under the sun, he said they had betrayed him. He threatened to get even and stormed out of the house.

Don's parents did not stop loving their son. Yet because they loved him and wanted the best for him as a

person even more than they loved their relationship with
him, they were willing to confront him and risk losing
him for a season. They withheld one aspect of the blessing from their son because of the destructive problems he
faced. Both biblically and relationally they were on firm
ground to withhold that portion of their blessing from
their son.

Such parents do not qualify to have the banner
"Unyielding Family Traditions" raised over their home.
Their tough love displays too much maturity, personal
integrity, and courage. The kind of house that deserves
this banner is reserved for people like Jerry and Helen
who withheld every bit of their blessing from their daughter for reasons as solid as quicksand.

Brenda was a charming, intelligent young lady who
deeply loved her parents. They cared for her too and had
the material resources to express that affection in tangible
ways—new clothes, new cars, the finest schools. These
were hers until she met and fell in love with Brent.

Brent was attending the same distinguished school
that Brenda was. But Brent was paying his own way. He
was doing extremely well and had a bright future ahead of
him.

Brent and Brenda met the first day of school at the
sorority house where Brent was "hashing" (cooking and
cleaning up) to pay for his meals. Both Brenda and Brent
were new believers in Christ, and they found out they had
many interests in common. Their relationship began as a
close friendship, but by the end of school it had developed into a deep love for each other.

They were each sure that a summer off from dating
would end their infatuation with each other; but after
dozens of letters back and forth and phone bills so high
that they could have provided the money to add two new
stories to the Southwestern Bell office, they knew they
had been smitten with the real thing. By December of the
next year they were talking engagement, and it was time
for Brent to meet Brenda's parents.

Brent's mother lived near the college, and Brenda

had seen her numerous times. Already, a deep affection was growing between these two. Brent's father had died in an automobile accident when Brent was just a boy, and his mother had raised him by working in a local grade school cafeteria. Brenda felt at home with Brent's mother, and she just knew her parents would welcome Brent with open arms. Nothing could have been further from the truth.

Brenda was so in love with Brent that she had failed to see the hardening attitude of her parents regarding their relationship. Not wanting to push her further into the relationship by forbidding it, they had hoped by hosting parties and taking her to the club where all the "nice boys" were she would break off the relationship on her own. The little they had heard about Brent's background had been more than enough. He would never, under any circumstances, enter their home much less become their son-in-law. Her parents had too much at stake when it came to their daughter's social standing, and their own.

Brenda was shattered when she received this message. Brent was sitting right in the room with her when she called her parents. She and Brent had been so excited to "break the news" that he was coming home with her to ask for her hand in marriage. However, in only a few minutes this couple's hopes had turned to ashes. Brenda could *not* bring him home, and she was to stop seeing him or lose her parents' financial backing at school.

Brent and Brenda tried to pick up the pieces of their shattered dreams. Brenda made a trip home to see if she could change her parents' attitude. She could not. They only repeated the firm warning that too much was at stake for her to throw it all away on someone who "didn't deserve" her or her family.

Brent and Brenda sought counsel from their pastor and close friends, and even called on Brenda's family's pastor to ask his advice. Yet heaven and earth were not sufficient to move her parents' ultimatum one inch.

Brenda explained to her parents that she felt the Lord had brought Brent and her together. Like everyone at the club, Brenda's parents went to church; but the God they knew would never approve of such a social outcast. If being poor were not enough, he was even a Yankee to top it off. In their minds, God's blessing, as well as their own, would never rest on such a person.

To try to honor Brenda's parents, Brent and Brenda put off their engagement and marriage for a year and a half. Still, any attempt for Brent to meet her parents face to face or to discuss the issue was stopped before it began.

With a semester of school left, Brenda made the most difficult decision in her life, a decision she is still paying for almost seven years later. She and Brent were married at a lovely service in a small university chapel, with only Brent's mother representing their parents. Brenda took a part-time job at the school bookstore to help pay for her final semester and graduation.

Brenda's parents have been out to see Brenda and Brent two times over the past seven years. Each time they have come to see a new grandchild for a few days. Yet their bitter rejection has never let up. By withholding their blessing on Brenda's marriage—even years after the wedding itself—they have won a hollow victory. They lost the battle when it came to whom their daughter married, but they win the war every lonely day and unhappy holiday that Brenda faces without their love and support.

It could be debated that Brent and Brenda should never have married in the first place, especially without her parents' blessing. However, to remain bitter, resentful, and unwilling to make contact with their daughter or her husband—even seven years after their wedding—shows a desire to punish, not to stand on principle.

Without question, one of the greatest gifts parents can give their child is their blessing when it comes to that child's marriage. When parents withhold the blessing from their children for cheating them out of a "high church" wedding, or for marrying a Greek instead of a Czech, a German instead of an Italian, or for choosing to attend First Presbyterian rather than Second Baptist, they hit below the belt.

We are not talking about parents who agonize over their believing son who is set on marrying an unbelieving woman or the parents who face the possibility that their never-married daughter may marry a man fresh from his fifth divorce. Yet even in these situations parents can still demonstrate love for their child in spite of disapproving his or her actions.

Homes that wave the banner "Unyielding Traditions Live Here" do not consider right and wrong—only tradition. They know full well the impact of their punitive decision to withhold their blessing—and that is exactly why they do it. Their pride has been hurt, now their children will hurt as well. As the years go by, the parents' position can harden. They are unwilling to give an inch, as if doing so meant giving a mile. They can sit through sermon after sermon about forgiveness in church, never once misunderstanding what the pastor says, but still refuse to put their son's or daughter's picture back on the mantle.

In these homes, fulfill every expectation, and the blessing will be given. Travel a different road, and expect to wander far from the shelter of acceptance. This is the fifth home that commonly withholds the blessing, and it can leave a child emotionally in a place where it is always winter, never spring.

THE SIXTH HOME: RECEIVING ONLY
A PART OF THE BLESSING

In this final home, a child does receive the blessing, but only in part. There are several ways in which this can happen, and each has the power to leave a child feeling only half-blessed. We will look at three common situations where a part of the blessing can be withheld: divorce, desertion, and adoption.

WHEN PARENTS DIVORCE

In previous chapters, we have discussed the effects that an "emotional divorce" can have on a child. This situation happens when one parent withholds the blessing from a child or spouse, yet the marriage stays together. It is equally difficult for children to handle when the parents actually do divorce, regardless of the age of the children when the divorce takes place.

In the typical scenario that surrounds a divorce, the wife will retain custody of the children and the father will move out. Studies have shown that during the first year following a divorce, many fathers see their children on a regular schedule. In fact, the "Sugardaddy" syndrome appears quite frequently.

This syndrome occurs when the father smothers the children with gifts and attention right after the divorce. As a result, the children may feel closer to him than they have in years. (The one who usually has difficulty during this time is the mother who is struggling to make ends meet and has to compete with lavish gifts and trips for the children, which she cannot afford.)

Unfortunately, such attention is usually temporary, and typically after one year the contact between father and child will begin to decrease. By the time three years have gone by, many fathers will see their son or daughter once a month or less.

Many of these children grow up experiencing only part of the blessing. They have the consistency of their mother's blessing and also the constant longing for the missing blessing of their father. When the flood of initial attention from their father slows down to only a trickle, anger, insecurity, and misbehavior can often result.

The blessing a father gives his child is just as important as the blessing the child's mother extends. When it is absent, there is going to be a vacuum present in that child's life, a vacuum that needs to be filled.

We want to stress one important point to the parent remaining at home who consistently gives his or her child the blessing. (This point is also important to consider for parents of children who were deserted or adopted.) Children will naturally long for the blessing of the absent parent, regardless of the situation surrounding the divorce. Their desire for that missing element does not negate or point out any flaws in the way they are loved by their custodial parent. Almost all children have an emotional need to re-establish connection with the other person responsible for their birth.

I (John) found this to be true in my life. My mother and father divorced when I was a little over thirteen months old. My mother retained custody of my older brother, my twin brother, and me, which gave her three children under three years of age to raise.

As I have had the opportunity later in life to look through "How to" books on single parenting, I discovered that my mother could have been on the cover. To this day, I cannot remember her running down my father verbally or erecting walls that would keep us from contacting him. This was true even in the first years after the divorce when she had to go to work.

My mother worked full time as an executive at a major savings and loan, yet her nights and weekends reflected her commitment to us children. On dozens of Friday nights, she would stuff us all in her car, hook on our little "teardrop" trailer, and off we would go to the mountains in northern Arizona or to the beach in Mexico to camp out with other families.

Camping was an acquired interest for my mother. Coming from an affluent home in Indiana, her only camping had been at Holiday Inns next to a campsite. Yet she knew that three growing boys needed the rigors of outdoor life and the male companionship of several married friends who treated each child in the "camping club" as their own.

I can say without question that my brothers and I learned about the blessing long before we could read about it in the Scriptures. From meaningful touching to attaching high value to us, to picturing a special future for each son—we learned the elements of the blessing by experiencing them. My mother is a very loving person; but she is also very wise. Wise enough not to question how adequate her love was, when after several years, my father sought to re-establish contact with us.

Today, my brothers and I enjoy a growing relationship with our father and still are very close to our mother. We have these good relations in large part because the natural desire to make contact with our father was not held against us. The blessing of both of my parents has never been used as a bargaining chip to play one against the other. Even in a home situation that is less than God's ideal, we have found help to make up for missing a part of the blessing.

We realize that not all divorces and parental relationships end up like the story described above. In part, that is why we will spend an entire chapter talking about how we deal with the lack of a blessing. However, we would like to share two other avenues for helping single-parent families in particular.

Two programs at our church have proved particularly helpful for single-parent families. The first is a "Big Brother/Little Brother, Big Sister/Little Sister" program designed to provide for the needs of boys and girls who are missing the elements of the blessing from a mother or father. By matching an adult male with a young boy and an adult female with a young girl, gaping holes caused by a missing parental blessing can begin to be filled.

The second program is an "Adopt a Grandparent" program that matches a single-parent child (or even children whose grandparents live out of state), with a member of the seniors' department. Often, these godly, older saints can provide a little boy or girl a precious commodity. As one little six-year-old commented, "Grandparents are the only adults who have time to listen." Match these children with a senior who needs to be needed, and each can become a source of blessing to the other.

Any parents who are considering divorce need to

face facts squarely. Splitting apart a marriage can severely affect each child in a negative way. While these children can learn to live without the blessing of both parents, a growing marriage is the best place for it to be given and developed.

WHEN ONE PARENT DESERTS THE FAMILY

Desertion by a parent can be harder on a child than losing him or her to death. When a parent dies, a child knows that in this life the opportunity to regain a missing part of the blessing from that parent is gone. When a parent deserts his or her children, they know that "out there somewhere" is a living person who still has the power to bless. Some children can catch a glimpse of that missing person's face in an airport or on a crowded street. But when they run to get a closer look, the likeness disappears, and they are left face to face with a stranger.

When a father or mother suddenly, unexpectedly, deserts the family, it can have serious effects on a child. In a seminar we attended on the effects on "displaced" children, one of the speakers used this quotation:

> The father who deserts his family suddenly and never sees them again can leave a daughter forever afraid to allow herself to be vulnerable to a man, sure that he too will leave her. . . . His daughter's resulting anger may give her trouble with men all her life. She may totally avoid men, or keep seeking the father she never had.[2]

With the Lord's help, such a prediction does not have to become a reality. However, nagging questions can remain in the mind of a child whose parents just walk out, questions Laurie asked herself for years.

Laurie's mother had walked out on her family. Surprisingly, wives leaving their families is not an uncommon occurrence any more. One popular secular book that noted this fact was even titled *The Runaway Wives*.

Laurie's mother was having an affair with her supervisor at work. When he was transferred across the country, she packed her bags one day when the rest of the family was gone and went with him. She did not leave a note written to Laurie, or even call to talk to her. Her mother just sent a certified letter that arrived addressed to Laurie's father, delivering notice of a pending divorce.

Laurie and her father did very well together through the grade school and high school years. She even went to secretarial school and landed a nice job as an executive assistant. Yet lurking in the shadows every time Laurie became serious in a dating relationship was a nagging fear deep inside.

Every time Laurie would think seriously about marriage or having a family, a little voice would say, "Don't do it. You'll be just like your mother and leave them too." The counsel of a helpful pastor and learning about how God could meet the missing part of her blessing finally helped her be able to marry and set up a happy family.

Desertion leaves so many important questions unanswered. It is a cruel dealer who passes out only half the cards a child needs to gain the blessing.

DEALING WITH THE QUESTIONS RAISED BY ADOPTION

We see yet another group of children in counseling who commonly struggle with gaining only part of the blessing. These are adopted children who struggle with the question, "Why did my natural parents leave me?"

We know many parents of adopted children who do a tremendous job of giving them the blessing. These parents more than make up for any loss a child might feel by being separated from his or her natural parents, especially if the child was adopted quite young. However, in even the best of homes where a child is totally secure in his adoptive parents' love, the question can still arise: "Why did my natural parents leave me?"

Sometimes this questioning comes in the form of misbehaving to see if his or her adoptive parents will "leave me like my natural parents did." These children will test the limits of their adoptive parents' commitment in an attempt to reassure themselves that they really are loved. Other children will join clubs or pay organizations to find their natural parents, all in an attempt to regain that part of the blessing they lost in years past or to hear it one last time.

Adoptive parents should expect some behavior of this sort, especially when the child gets old enough to ask such questions for himself or herself. However, by providing the five elements of the blessing, backed by God's unchanging love, adopted children can have the security and self-confidence to face these questions in a healthy way. They may still ask the questions, but they are not dependent on their natural parents' blessing to lay the foundation for their lives. God's love, demonstrated through providing them the blessing, can bring them the certainty they need about themselves and the certainty that they belong to a family that truly loves them.

WHEN BLENDED FAMILIES FAIL TO "BLEND"

As we travel across the country, we are constantly asked how remarriage affects the blessing. While many, many blended families do a wonderful job of giving the blessing to "yours," "mine," and "ours," children in these homes can still bear significant hurts. For younger children especially, three reactions to this new family can lead a son or daughter to actually work to see that a blended family doesn't blend, thus blocking the giving or receiving of the blessing.

First, almost all children will generate tremendous *expectations* concerning the possibility of remarriage, either negative or positive. Some children will look at a "new father or mother" as an idealized person, particularly if there have been fights between the husband and wife prior to the divorce. Someone who won't argue, someone who won't disappoint them or their custodial parent *ever*, or someone who will make up for hurts in the past. When the child learns that like anyone else, the new parent isn't perfect, anger and resentment can follow, sometimes blocking a parent's blessing.

Second, they often *fear* that accepting a new person into their lives is a form of betrayal of their natural, non-custodial father or mother. Family loyalties that go unaddressed can act like invisible stumbling blocks, making it difficult for a child to receive a new parent's blessing.

And finally, there can even be *panic* in the heart of a child who fears that this new person will crowd out his or her place in Mom or Dad's heart. If several years pass before a remarriage, a child can feel terribly threatened by a new person who is now competing for Mom or Dad's time.

It's important to realize that you will never be able to outlogic the emotions of these children. Lecturing a child that he has no reason to be fearful, shouldn't panic, or feel disappointed doesn't erase his feelings. Patience and understanding are needed to draw these deep-felt issues out of a child's heart.

Helping a child receive and accept the blessing from a blended family takes a concerted effort from both parents. We'd like to recommend a book to you! It's by our friend, Dr. Robert Barnes, and is called, *"You're not my Daddy! Winning the heart of your stepchild."*[3]

WITHOUT THE BLESSING, CHILDREN CAN BECOME . . .

THE SEEKERS

We have looked at several examples where children have reacted to missing the blessing by beginning a life-long search. Seekers are people who are always searching for intimacy, but are seldom able to tolerate it. These are the people who feel tremendous fulfillment in the thrill of courtship. But after marriage, their lack of acceptance from their parents leaves them uncomfortable in receiving it from a spouse. Never sure of how acceptance "feels," they are never satisfied with wearing it too long in a relationship. They may even struggle with believing in God's unchanging love for them because of the lack of permanence in the blessing in their early lives.

THE SHATTERED

These are the people whose lives are deeply troubled over the loss of their parents' love and acceptance. Fear, anxiety, depression, and emotional withdrawal many times can be traced to a person's missing out on his or her family's blessing. Their unhappy road can even lead them to the terrifying cliffs of suicide, convinced they are destined to be a "Cipher in the Snow."

THE SMOTHERERS

Like a two-thousand-pound sponge, these people react to missing their parents' blessing by sucking every bit of life and energy from a spouse, child, friend, or entire congregation. They are left so emotionally empty from their past that they smother other persons with their unmet needs and, like a parasite, drain these others of their desire to listen or help.

Unfortunately, when the other persons trying to make up for years of unmet needs finally tire of carrying these smothering persons' entire emotional weight, the message the smothering persons receive is that they are being rejected. Deeply hurt once again, they never realize that they have brought this pain upon themselves. They end up pushing away the blessing other people offer when actually they desperately need it.

THE ANGRY

As long as people are angry at each other, they are chained to each other. Many adults are still emotionally chained to their parents because they are angry over missing the blessing. They have never forgiven or forgotten. As a result, the rattle and chafing of emotional chains distract them from intimacy in other relationships. Many children thus go into life with a chip on their shoulders put there early in life when they believed they could never experience love and acceptance in their homes.

THE DETACHED

An old proverb says, "Once burned, twice shy." This motto is used by some children who have missed out

on the blessing. After losing the blessing from an important person in their lives *once,* they spend a lifetime protecting themselves from its ever happening again. Keeping
a spouse, children, or a close friend at arm's length, they
protect themselves all right—at the price of inviting loneliness to take up residence in their lives.

THE DRIVEN

In this category line up extreme perfectionists,
workaholics, notoriously picky housecleaners, and gener-
ally demanding people who go after getting their blessing
the old-fashioned way: they try to "Earrrrrrrrn it." The
only problem is that the blessing is a *gift;* you cannot buy
the blessing. You can find some counterfeit blessings that
are for sale—at an incredible price—but they last only as
long as the "showroom shine" on a new car. In real life
travels, such counterfeit blessings rust and corrode once
they leave the showroom floor. Missing their parents'
blessing challenges these driven people to attack a wind-
mill named "accomplishment" in an illusory attempt to
gain love and acceptance.

THE SEDUCED

Many people who have missed out on their parents' blessing look for that lost love in all the wrong
places. As we mentioned in an earlier chapter, unmet
needs for love and acceptance can tempt a person toward
sexual immorality—all in an attempt to try to meet legitimate needs in an illegitimate way. Also in this category
fall substance abusers. All too often, a drink or a pill is
taken initially to try to cover up the hurt from empty relationships in the past or present. Alcoholism or drug abuse
can become a counterfeit way to try to gain the deep emotional warmth that is a part of experiencing the elements
of the blessing.[4]

In a recent study of compulsive gamblers (especially those struck with "lottery fever"), over 90 percent of
the men studied were found to have "dismal childhoods,
characterized by loneliness and rejection."[5] In other words,
missing out on the elements of the blessing in a home can

seduce a child into choosing immoral relationships, alcoholism, or even compulsive gambling as an attempt to fill missing relationship needs.

There is help to leave the ranks of those above and join the ranks of "the blessed." That help begins by discovering the reality of a spiritual family blessing that our Lord holds out to everyone and being willing to courageously face the past.

As we look past these homes that withhold the blessing, we will discover that every one of the elements of the blessing we might have missed out on can be ours. Rather than being locked into repeating the past, we can be free to grow into the people God wants us to be.

We shouldn't look down and lose hope if we grew up without the blessing. We should look up instead to the incredible provision of a blessing for our lives that can leave our lives overflowing, the kind of blessing that can even replace a curse with contentment.

10

$\mathscr{L}$EARNING TO LIVE APART FROM THE BLESSING

Several years ago, I (John) counseled with the parents of a very disturbed twenty-one-year-old named Dean. Even though the problems these parents faced had existed for some time, they had put off coming in for help.

Dean had serious mental problems that had placed a tremendous burden on his family. Often he was angry and belligerent, occasionally becoming violent. Yet life had not always been so damaging for this family.

Dean's problems first began to develop after a car accident when he was eleven years old. The accident occurred soon after the family moved to Texas. Before the accident, when they were living in Michigan, Dean and his family had gotten along beautifully. In fact, they were a model family at the church they attended and in their community.

When Dean's behavior began to change following the accident, his concerned parents took him to specialist after specialist. They always received the same diagnosis: their son's problem had no medical solution. Perhaps time and understanding would work things out.

Dean's mother loved him dearly. Even when he was mad and sullen, she would spend hours trying to reason with him and read him verses of Scripture to make an impression on his life. Always she hoped that his "thorn in the flesh" would be removed and that their lives would be restored to what they were before the accident.

With Dean's brothers and sisters, and even with her husband, Dean's mother would constantly downplay the severity of her son's problems. In an attempt to alleviate the mounting pressure because of Dean's behavior, she would often set up family socials and special holiday events. She wanted to re-create a time when the whole family could be "all together again, just like in Michigan." However, as soon as Dean arrived on the scene, he would ruin the party with his angry words.

This loving mother refused to acknowledge that Dean's problems were as bad as they were. Her husband and the rest of the family could think what they wanted to; she knew that things would get better. Life would once again be just like it was "in Michigan." She even dreamed about this—until one day her dreams turned into a nightmare.

Dean's father was nearing retirement age, and he and his wife were looking forward to his retirement. This couple had been good stewards of the money God had entrusted to them, and they had saved a sizable nest egg to buy that dream retirement property up in the mountains.

Six months before Dad officially retired, Dean's parents called their realtor and said it was time to put their house on the market. They had talked this over with their children, and each of them was excited for their parents—all except Dean. Even though he had been living on his own for several years, he still made his parents' home his headquarters. This was almost a necessity because his violent temper had driven off every roommate and all but the staunchest friends.

When Dean came to his parents' home one night and saw the "For Sale" sign in their yard, he went berserk. He banged on the door repeatedly, but his parents were not at home. Finally, he pulled up the sign from the front yard and used it to bash in the glass in the front door window. Then he proceeded to tear up the house.

Dean's parents returned home several hours later. Chairs were overturned and lamps had been smashed. Dean had even ripped an inside tree out of the planter box and had stuck the "For Sale" sign in its place. Upstairs and down, the house was in a shambles. Yet of all the things that Dean had done, one thing literally broke her mother's heart. In fact, nothing he could have done to her home could have shattered her as much.

In his anger over their plan to move to a retirement home, Dean had gone into the hall where all the family pictures hung and cut every one of them into pieces. From baby pictures on up to their last family portrait with all the grandchildren, each one was torn beyond repair.

Dean's mother, like every parent, had treasured her children's pictures. They were irreplaceable and beyond price to her, especially the pictures of the family before Dean's accident. They had always given her hope that one day things would be just like before, just like "in Michigan."

Dean's mother learned a very painful lesson that night. A lesson that many people have to come to grips with who have missed out on the blessing from their parents, their spouse, a loved one, or a friend.

Dean's mother finally had to recognize and acknowledge that she now lived in Texas and life would never be like it was "in Michigan." Even if Dean made a dramatic recovery, things were not and could not be exactly the way they were. Instead of living with the dreams that Dean's problems would go away, or trying to convince herself that the last ten years of Dean's outbursts "really weren't that bad," she was forced to come to grips with the past and take responsibility for dealing with her problem in the present.

We see this same twofold tendency in person after person who has missed out on his or her parents' blessing. Many will try to explain away and put off admitting the obvious in their lives. Drawing imaginary pictures of their past or denying the real problems that exist can often keep them from honestly facing their past and their parents. By protecting themselves or their parents, they effectively prevent a cure.

If we never face the fact that we missed out on the blessing, we can postpone dealing with the pain of the past, but we can never avoid it. The legitimate pain of honestly dealing with this situation is what leads to healing and life. When we try to avoid this legitimate pain, we are actually laying on top of it layers of illegitimate pain.

Dean's mother refused to make the painful acknowledgment that her son had a serious problem, and she ended up suffering an even worse pain of guilt, anguish, and remorse. People who put off coming to grips with their past often reap the same kind of harvest, a harvest where pain is multiplied and sorrows doubled, all because they did not face the legitimate pain that comes with facing the truth.

In the pages that follow, we want to recommend several things that can help people who are suffering from missing out on the blessing (or help those who work with them). These recommendations are not a simple formula, nor do they guarantee an instant cure. However, in counseling men and women all across the country, we find that many who have applied these principles have received hope and healing.

The road to blessing that we would like to point people toward begins with the very difficult first step we tried to illustrate with Dean's mother. We need to be honest with ourselves.

BEGIN BY BEING HONEST WITH YOURSELF

John 8:32 is a verse in the Scriptures that we require our counselees to memorize. Jesus is talking in this verse, and He says, "And you shall know the truth, and the truth shall make you free." The truth Jesus is talking about in this verse refers to knowing Him in all His purity. Christ offers no cover-ups, no denying there is a problem when there really is one. When we know the truth, we are walking in the light that exposes darkness; and it alone can begin to set us free.

Many of us need to turn on truth's searchlight and shine it on our past. Only then can we be free to walk confidently into the future. Greg was able to do this, and it paid rich dividends in his life.

Greg was four years old when his parents told him that a new little brother or sister was on the way. As with most four-year-olds, nine months seemed like nine years as he waited for his new playmate.

The day finally came when Greg's mother left for the hospital, and he knew he wouldn't have to wait much longer. That next day, Greg went with his father to the hospital to see his new baby sister. However, when Greg came into his mother's hospital room, he had a surprise. He had two baby sisters, two beautiful twin girls who were already becoming the apples of their mother's eye.

Greg was certainly not loved any less when the twins came home, but things had definitely changed. Big brother was now having to share his parents' time and attention with not only one sister, but two. When the twins got older, things became even worse from Greg's perspective. The same people who stopped his mother to comment on how cute the little girls were in their double stroller rarely lifted their eyes to notice an older brother longing for the same affirmation.

Greg's parents loved him deeply. In no way did they intentionally try to overlook Greg or cater to the twins. Also, Greg loved his sisters. He was the perfect big brother, looking out for his charges and showing them the ropes when they got into school. Yet as the years went by, even the special bond between the twin girls became a minor source of jealousy for Greg. He just could not compete with the special closeness between his two look-alike sisters, and it bothered him.

Long after he and his sisters were grown and out of the house, Greg attended one of our seminars where he heard for the first time about the family blessing. In many ways, Greg knew that he was loved and accepted and that his parents had tried hard to provide him the blessing. Yet in his heart of hearts, he questioned whether he had really received it after the twins were born. For years he had had a nagging insecurity in his life that he could trace directly back to this fact.

Greg knew that all his family would soon be gathering at his parents' house to celebrate the holidays. After the conference ended, he also knew that he needed to deal honestly with his feelings of missing out on at least a part of the blessing. With every bit of courage he had, Greg decided he would bring up the subject with his parents.

The first morning he was at their home, the opportunity came up for him to discuss his feelings with his parents. The three of them were alone at the breakfast table; everyone else had gone out shopping for Christmas ornaments or a last-minute present.

Greg began talking with his parents by sharing with them much of what he had learned about the blessing at the seminar. The concept was new to them as well, and they perked up and got right into the discussion.

He then took several minutes to praise his parents and thank them for the way they had put into practice several elements of the blessing.

Finally, he brought up his feelings of missing out on part of the blessing when the twins had come along. In a loving, nonaccusatory fashion, he shared one of the deepest secrets of his heart with his parents.

As soon as Greg began sharing his concern, his mother began to cry. Greg immediately tried to comfort her and told her he wished he had never brought it up. "No!" said his mother. "Please don't be sorry. I've wanted to talk about this for so long. I've always thought it might have bothered you, but I didn't know how to bring it up."

Almost instantly, Greg and his parents were drawn into unity. They cried and laughed and hugged each other as if they had just been introduced after years of being apart, and in fact they had.

That night the now grown children and their parents sat down for a family council, something they hadn't done in years. The topic of conversation at the breakfast table that morning was shared with the twins, and they had their chance to cry, to share, and to reaffirm their love for their brother and their parents. Any nagging guilt they had over the situation was now resolved and turned into gratitude for a courageous older brother.

By Greg's willingness to share his feelings honestly with his parents and his twin sisters, if ever a part of the blessing had been missing in his life, it had certainly been filled up. Greg was even more confident at work in the weeks that followed, something that his employer noticed almost immediately.

We can't stress how important it is to be honest with your feelings regarding missing the blessing. It is the important first step toward healing and restoration.

SEEK TO UNDERSTAND
YOUR PARENTS' BACKGROUND

The next recommendation we make to anyone who has missed out on his or her family's blessing is to understand as much as they can about their parents' background. Following this one bit of advice can free many people from wondering why they never received the blessing, something I (John) discovered firsthand.

For years I felt pain about the relationship I had with my father. It would often be years between our visits, and he never made contact on his own initiative. His silence trapped a layer of hurt in my life that seemed untouchable . . . until I met "Uncle Max."

I transferred from a junior college in Arizona to Texas Christian University in Ft. Worth. I studied hard, and spent a good deal of time in the library. One day a research librarian, who was helping me with a project, asked, "Are you any relation to Max Trent?" In talking with her, and later with my mother, I discovered that I did have a great-uncle named Max Trent. He was living in Dallas, and was the head librarian at a rival college,

Southern Methodist University. It took a good deal of
courage, but I called Uncle Max, and informed him that
he had a nephew in Ft. Worth. Could I come and meet
him? We did meet, and for the first time, I took a step
towards really understanding my father's background.

I discovered what it was like when my father was
born, and what life was like in his home. I learned much
about his war years, and the personal and alcohol-related
problems he'd suffered as a result of those years.

It was like slowly turning on a light in a darkened
room. I often wondered why my father resisted communication; now I saw numerous things that shaped his behavior. I never could understand certain patterns he
developed—and then I discovered that they actually ran
generations deep.

What I learned from Uncle Max was something
that my father wouldn't talk about, but I hope all children
will take into consideration. In the vast majority of cases,
parents who do not give the blessing to a son or daughter
never received it themselves.

Andrea, like me, took this advice to heart, and it
totally changed her perspective on her father. Andrea
heard about the concept of the blessing at a singles retreat
I spoke at. For years she had struggled with how distant
her father seemed to her. He was always cordial to her,
and he never raised his voice with any of the children. But
what was missing left Andrea with nagging questions
about whether she had received the blessing. Besides an
occasional hug, her father had not demonstrated, to her
way of thinking, any of the five elements of the blessing
she had learned about.

Andrea was still living at home, and she took the
first opportunity she could after the retreat to talk to her
father about what she had learned. (What Andrea found
out in that conversation was a key to understanding her
father, the key she had never known before.)

After her father had listened to his daughter talk
about the blessing (he was always a good listener, just not

a good talker), he cleared his throat and shared with Andrea something of his past. Andrea had never met her grandparents on her father's side. They had both died a few years before she was born. And as he had been an only child, her father had no brothers or sisters to become aunts and uncles to pass down family stories.

Andrea's father had grown up in England and his parents were very British. Apparently, they even held claim to a small title of nobility.

When their son, Andrea's father, was born, he was raised with all the dignity and care afforded any English citizen of high birth. During his early years, he had a nanny who helped raise him, while his parents kept the respectable distance proper for teaching children discipline and manners. His relationship with his parents was so formal, anytime he addressed his father it was to be prefaced by "Sir." No using "Dad," "Daddy," "Papa," or anything of the kind in this household. "Sir" was the proper form of address.

In addition to the requirement to formally address his parents, meaningful touching was strictly taboo, and words of praise were as rare as hen's teeth (which, in case you weren't raised on a farm, are quite rare).

In the course of one hour, Andrea learned more about her father's background than she had in the nineteen previous years. As a result of seeing how her father was raised, she gained a new compassion and understanding for his actions toward her and her brothers and sisters. She even found out that compared to his parents, her father felt he was a fanatic in trying to make sure each of his children received the blessing. And all the time she thought he was withholding it!

If we will stop and take the time to look beyond our parents' actions in the present and back at their past, it will be time well spent. As we will see in a later chapter, often we will find out that our parents need the elements of the blessing from us just as much as (or more than) we need these elements from them!

UNDERSTAND THAT EVEN A CURSE CAN BE CHANGED INTO A BLESSING

Some children have a difficult time relating to the concept of a family blessing. From their perspective, they have received a curse from a mother or father in place of a blessing. Can such people ever move past this hurt and pain and feel genuinely loved and accepted?

If you had asked Helen this question four years ago, her answer would have been an emphatic no. In her mind, the pain she had endured from an abusive father had forever trapped her in a cycle of insecurity, fear, and unrest. Many times she thought about a permanent way out of her pain. But she never had the courage to go through with it.

After years of anger, anxiety, and resentment, three years ago Helen discovered a way of escape. She began to understand and apply God's spiritual family blessing, something we will discover more about in this chapter.

No one had to pay Helen's father to curse her. He seemed to enjoy making her life miserable. In fact, Helen would stay at school in the library or at a friend's house as long as she could before she had to go home. At least then maybe her father would have passed out from drinking too much. However, all too often he was awake and propped up in front of the television set when she came home. Then his "fun" would begin.

"Come over and give your father a hug," he would say when Helen tried to sneak past the living room door. She had no place to hide in her home. Her mother worked nights (and often didn't come home during the day), and Helen was left alone much of the time with her father. Without going into the tragic details, Helen was repeatedly subjected to the physical abuse of a sick father. Always careful that he didn't leave "marks that show on the outside," he was daily leaving heart-wrenching scars on Helen's inner life.

Spending so many evenings in the library to avoid her father paid an unexpected dividend to Helen. She graduated near the top of her class in high school and gladly accepted a scholarship to an out-of-state school.

However, physical distance does not equal emotional distance. Even though she was miles away in another state, Helen was still sitting next to her father emotionally.

Only after a number of years was Helen finally able to come to grips with her tragic past. She learned from a caring friend for the first time that God could take a curse from the past and turn it into a blessing.

What Helen learned about God's family blessing is what we would like to share with you now.

THE POWER OF A CURSE

In Biblical times, there was no mistaking the terrible power of a curse. It could freeze people in fear, or drive them from a place of safety.

When David first met Goliath, the army of Israel was paralyzed by this giant's size and cursing. Every day, Goliath stormed out and cursed Israel and the Lord God.

"Am I a dog, that thou comest to me with sticks?" he shouted at the youth. And then for good measure, he "cursed David by his gods." Years later, when the Moabites realized that Israel had come up and camped against them, their King summoned Balaam, a powerful warlock, and hired him to "Curse this people . . . that we may smite them and . . . *drive them out of the land."*

In Old Testament times, people took the power of a curse seriously, and in homes today, people should too. People like Alan.

Alan grew up with a giant in his home. While his father's 6'3" frame might not qualify him as a Goliath, it certainly made him a giant to one small child who faced this man's terrifying anger. Alan would shudder in fear as his father towered over him and cursed him with angry explosions that inevitably left him in tears, often with toys shattered, and always feeling helpless.

Today, Alan is taller than his father, but he still feels mouse-size. The fear, anger, and hurt that were trapped in Alan's life cause him to struggle with truly feeling loved and accepted by God and all others in his life.

In Hebrew, the word *curse* means to consider something of little value or worth. Like mist, or steam, it's something of so little weight that, like a worthless irritation, it's to be brushed aside. In Old Testament times, nothing was as powerful as a curse—with one exception. A more powerful blessing.

Maybe you feel like you received a curse, perhaps you come from one of the homes that withhold the blessing we talked about earlier. In the next few pages, we'll look at what a curse can do to you, how to break its hold on your life, and who holds the only power to truly set you free from the curse.

HOW A CURSE CUTS US OFF FROM A SPECIAL FUTURE

Living under a curse from a parent often leaves three tragic consequences that directly affect a person's future. A brief understanding of these three consequences, and how to move beyond them, is crucial if we're to receive the blessing from others, and give it ourselves.

WHEN WE LEARN TO BE HOPELESS

The first common effect of living under a curse is illustrated in a research study done nearly twenty years ago at the University of Pennsylvania. Researchers made a surprising observation concerning animals.

For several months, researchers conducted two independent studies with laboratory dogs. One group was put in a maze, with various hurdles to climb over to reach their food. The average hungry dog would quickly navigate the set up barriers, and, in under a minute, would be chomping on dog biscuits.

At the same time, another group of dogs were subjected to a pain tolerance test. These dogs were put in immovable, unescapable full-body harnesses, and then given strong electrical shocks. In fact, they would receive sixty-four random shocks in a sixty-minute period. Unable to move, unable to predict when the shocks would come, they were held prisoner in a painful situation, powerless to escape.

With the pain study concluded, researchers decided to use these same animals the next day to run the maze test. The scientists predicted that the dogs would quickly jump the barriers and get their food like the dogs before them, but they were wrong.

When the dogs who had been in a painful, inescapable situation started through the maze and ran into the first barrier they laid down. Even when the dogs were later shocked to "motivate" them to jump over the barrier and move towards the food, they'd simply hunker down, sit still, and endure the pain.

Physically, these dogs had not been harmed by the shocks they'd received. They had both the strength and ability to get over the obstacles. But what had been shocked out of them was the confidence or the willingness to even try.

What were the conclusions drawn from these and a number of other related studies? Namely, that uncontrollable, prolonged, negative experiences can freeze an animal, making him passive, pessimistic, and withdrawn in the face of obstacles.[1]

We know that there is danger in drawing conclusions from animal research and applying them to the more complex reasoning of humans. But the comparisons are striking, especially with those we see in counseling who have received a curse from their parents.

Experiencing a major trauma, like losing a job or losing our parents' blessing, can deeply affect us. And for some of us, it not only marks our past, but immobilizes us as we face the future. Instead of actively trying to solve our problems, we can become passive, dependent, and depressed. And unfortunately, we can also live out two other negative responses to a curse.

SOMEONE HAS STOLEN THE KEY

If we've labored under a curse from our parents, in addition to feeling a deep inner hopelessness when we face later trials, we can also begin to feel that there is absolutely nothing we *can* do to improve our situation!

Take Brian for example. He was the older brother. In his thinking, if Dad had to make a choice, he should have bonded with *him*, not his younger brother! He wore his heart out trying to please his father. But no matter how far he stretched towards him, he could never reach the arms of acceptance he wanted.

In a climate of unfair comparison and favoritism, Brian made a subtle, but terribly damaging, decision. Deep inside, he equated his missing blessing with something he could never become—*younger*. And because he focused on something that could never happen as his key to happiness in the future, he became a committed pessimist in the present—and eventually pushed himself right into clinical depression!

Pessimists persistently look backwards.[2] For example, pessimists look back, wanting to be younger, optimists look forward and wish they were older! By never being able to "forget what lies behind" they stay stuck in their pain, rather than "looking forward" to a positive future.

Listen to a more humorous example of someone who illustrates this point. One man wrote us with the following complaint.

> "I'm thirty-four years old, and I've been married three times. (Not my fault; always seem to pick losers.) My problem is my hair . . . or lack of it.
>
> "I know that many men feel there's nothing wrong with being bald, but I do. I started losing my hair when I was in high school, and have since tried everything I know to stop what's happening to me. I know that my first wife left me because of my hair. My latest wife even told me straight out that I was obsessed with my hair, and that was why she was leaving. *My lack of hair is*

ruining my life! I went to a plastic surgeon recently and offered to pay him, in advance, to transplant whatever skin I needed to fix my head. All he did was to insult me by saying that I shouldn't waste my money on scalp surgery, but should spend the money on a psychiatrist!

I'm sure that doctor wasn't a Christian. That's why I'm writing you to ask your advice . . ."

When it comes to facing the future, this man has a major problem. In his mind (or actually on top of his mind), is something that forever keeps him from finishing first in life—or even coming in a strong second. He can't picture a successful future for himself without thick, curly locks of hair. And by picking out something that he is powerless to change and making it the source of all his problems, he directly affects his future.

If we've labored under a curse that makes us feel powerless, and if we feel that the only key to change is forever out of our reach, there's a final consequence.

I'M ALL ALONE IN MY PAIN

During the experiment we described above, the dogs who had been shocked were verbally, and then physically encouraged to jump the barrier when they ran the maze. But it didn't help. They drew so far into an inner, protective shell that the fear of more pain made them oblivious to outside encouragement.

How many times have we seen this same type of behavior in people we've counseled!

Take just one example. Jim remembers a time when he was nine years old. One Sunday he was sitting next to one of his friends at the back of church. His father was the preacher, and in the midst of his sermon, he saw the two boys whispering to each other. Suddenly his father's voice rang out. He ordered his son to come up front. Before the entire congregation, he laid into him about what a disrespectful and dishonoring son he was. And then he stopped the service, took Jim outside (but in full view of the congregation from the windows), and gave him a whipping he's never forgotten.

Many years later, when his marriage began crumbling, Jim still carried the effects of many episodes like this where he received a curse, not a blessing from his father. As an extension of the pain and powerlessness he felt as a child, whenever his wife would begin to complain or criticize him, he would become almost comatose. When he saw her angry words coming, he beat a hasty, inner retreat. And instead of being open to counsel, or translating what she said as cries for help, he just pulled further inside—which made her even *more* vocal and frustrated.

If all our efforts don't count, if the key to change seems out of reach, and if we feel a deep sense of loneliness and isolation, chances are we're still laboring under a curse from the past. But there is a power stronger than any curse.

THE ONE FORCE MORE POWERFUL THAN A CURSE

There was a power that young David drew on that kept his heart from freezing in fear when cursed by Goliath. When the mighty warlock, Balaam, was hired to curse God's people they were terrified at the time. But someone acted for them to not only frustrate Balaam's words . . . but to turn them completely around. At the dedication of the wall in re-built Jerusalem, Nehemiah told the great story of someone even more powerful than Balaam who could not only stop, but also reverse, the curse: *Almighty God*. We're told that not only did God frustrate Balaam's effort, but, also ". . . our God turned the curse into a blessing."

Turning wrongs around is something God specializes in, particularly for those who have received a curse from their homes. But how? Briefly, here are three crucial elements to see a curse lifted off your life.

A LIFE OF LEARNED HOPEFULNESS
BEGINS WITH COMMITMENT

If some of us have learned to be hopeless through shouldering a curse in the past, then the first step towards reversing the curse and learning to be hopeful comes from making a whole-hearted commitment.

Several years ago, I (John) worked with a man who has carried the curse of hurtful words for years. While it's driven him to succeed, it's never left him with a moment's inner rest or peace. As part of our conversations, I asked him clearly if he had ever truly committed his life to Jesus Christ. "Absolutely," he said. And while he had only recently trusted Christ, he bore a strong, convincing testimony.

"Do you want to be the husband and father God would have you be? And are you willing to do whatever it takes to be the man God wants you to be?" Again, the answers were a resounding "yes." *"Would you put that commitment in writing?"* I asked. And he did.

That day, and now for over two years, that single sheet of paper has hung in his office, becoming for him an important milestone in overcoming the curse he's been under.

Recently, we completed a workbook for this book you're reading, *The Blessing Workbook* (Nashville: Thomas Nelson Publishers, 1993). And guess what is in the first section of the book? A page for you to put in writing your commitment to Christ, to your family, and to personal growth—a milestone to remind you that in Christ, you are "a new creation; old things have passed away; behold, all things have become new" (2 Cor. 5:17).

A key to sorting out the inner confusion that comes with receiving a curse is making clear, definite commitments. Then once we've made those commitments, we begin to gain:

INCREASED ENERGY TO PURSUE SELF-CONTROL

One glaring problem that surfaces for many of those we counsel who have grown up with a curse, is a lack of self-control. And not surprisingly, *the degree of self-control in an individual is directly proportional to their self-worth.*

The *lower* value we have of ourselves (remember, the word for curse literally means, "of little value"), the *less* energy we'll have to discipline our attitudes, appetites, and actions. We'll reward ourselves with junk food instead of consistently exercising; let five hours a night go by before we finally turn off the television and stumble into bed and a fitful sleep; or procrastinate on those things we must do at work.

Out of strong commitments come renewed energy to view ourselves differently, more positively, and to gain more self-discipline and self-worth as a result. And that positive gain is increased as we gain something else.

MOVING TOWARDS A CLEAR CHALLENGE

For those of us who have labored under a curse, our God can break its impact on our lives, renew our commitments, and restore the energy to be self-disciplined. One way He does that is to give us a clear challenge.

Many studies have shown how crucial it is to maintain a clear purpose and challenge in life. In fact, many of these studies center around the fact that the only challenge most men have is their work. That's why the average man in the United States dies within three years of retirement! (Or in Coach Bear Bryant's case, three weeks after spending a quarter century of coaching football.) The Scripture is true, "Without a vision, the people perish." Yet the future painted for many people who have grown up with a curse is anything but clear. How clear is your purpose in life? Do you have a challenge that is big enough to last you a lifetime? To move you forward each day? You do if you are seeking to give the blessing to others. *For one of the most powerful ways of reversing a curse you've received, is to give the blessing to others.*

For the Lord, the opposite of the curse was giving His children the blessing. As His servants, we're called to be a blessing to all the earth. The five elements of the blessing that we've detailed in this book can give you a simple, biblical plan to bless your children, spouse, friends, and others.

Commitment, self-control, and a significant, therapeutic challenge to be a blessing: these are the three things that can help break the negative cycle of the curse. And they're the very thing God desires for your life.

Look at God's Word to see just what kind of future He calls you to. For as He looks at you, He sees a future totally free of a curse.

> "For I know the thoughts that I think toward you, says the LORD, thoughts of peace and not of evil, to give you a future and a hope" (Jer. 29:11).

At Home with God's Family Blessing

Some children will never, in this life, hear words of love or acceptance from their parents. People like Helen. Some will try to break down the door to their parents' hearts to receive this missing blessing, but all too often their attempt fails. For whatever reason, they have to face the fact that their blessing will have to come from another source.

When Helen finally realized this and turned to listen to the voice of her heavenly Father calling her, she discovered an open door of blessing. She found a spiritual family blessing that provided her with every element she had missed in her home.

"God's spiritual family blessing" begins with the fact that when we have a personal relationship with Jesus Christ, our spiritual parentage is secure.

AS BELIEVERS, OUR SPIRITUAL PARENTAGE IS SECURE

Helen was never secure in her relationship with her father. His anger had frozen within her heart a sense of insecurity. Yet when Helen trusted Jesus Christ as her Lord and Savior, she found out that she had a source of blessing that would be with her each day of her life and beyond! Helen discovered verses like these that speak of how stable her heavenly Father is and how permanent her relationship is with Him:

"My sheep hear My voice, and I know them, and
they follow Me. And I give them eternal life, and they
shall never perish; neither shall anyone snatch them out
of My hand" (John 10:27-28).

And Jesus came and spoke to them, saying, . . .
"lo, I am with you always, even to the end of the age"
(Matt. 28:18, 20).

For He Himself has said, "I will never desert you,
nor will I ever forsake you," so that we confidently say,
"The Lord is my helper, I will not be afraid. What shall
man do to me?" (Heb. 13:5-6 NASB).

The Spirit of the Lord GOD is upon me,/Because
the LORD has anointed me/To bring good news to the
afflicted;/He has sent me to bind up the brokenhearted,/
To proclaim liberty to captives,/And freedom to pris-
oners; . . . To comfort all who mourn, . . . Giving them a
garland instead of ashes,/The oil of gladness instead of
mourning,/The mantle of praise instead of a spirit of
fainting./So they will be called oaks of righteousness,/
The planting of the LORD, that He may be glorified (Isa.
61:1-3 NASB).

The first thing Helen had to consider when she
came home at night was what kind of mood her father
would be in. One night it would be anger, the next indifference; and occasionally he could even be very nice. His
vacillations kept her so off balance, it left her insecure and
questioning herself. Now she had a relationship with a
heavenly Father characterized by the words, "Jesus Christ is
the same yesterday and today, yes and forever" (Heb. 13:8
NASB).

Those who have personally believed in Jesus and
trusted their lives to Him have a secure relationship with
their heavenly Father. Yet there is even more to God's spiritual family blessing that they receive when they trust
their lives to Him.

AS BELIEVERS, WE GAIN A SPIRITUAL FAMILY TO BLESS US

In Chapter Three we told the story about a little
girl who was very scared and needed "someone with skin

on" to hug her. As we saw in that chapter, our Lord knows all about our need for meaningful touch. He also knows our need for the physical companionship of others to build up our lives and encourage us.

That is why when we accept Christ, we gain not only a secure relationship with our heavenly Father, but we join an entire family of brothers and sisters in Christ! Men and women "with skin on" who can hug us and hold us and communicate God's love, wisdom, and blessing to us!

In many ways the early church provided a very good model for us to follow. They were often in each other's homes (the earliest churches started in homes) and shared meals together. They were literally a family of the faith, and that is just how Paul expected Timothy to treat the believers he met. Listen to the counsel this noted apostle gave his young charge:

> Do not rebuke an older man, but exhort him as a *father*, younger men as *brothers*, older women as *mothers*, younger women as *sisters*, with all purity (1 Tim. 5:1-2, italics added).

Timothy was not related to these people by physical birth, but Paul points out clearly that he was related to them through spiritual birth. They all shared the same heavenly Father, and they were all necessary members of one another.

For both of the authors, this principle of having a spiritual family has been a tremendous personal help, particularly the way God used an older man in each of our lives to become a spiritual father to us in times of need.

Gary was in college when his father died, leaving a huge vacuum in his life. At this crossroads period in his life, a godly man named Rod Toews stepped in and became a spiritual father. Rod is a nationally prominent speaker and Christian educator. He could have easily let his busy schedule crowd out time for a hurting collegian. However, Rod attached high value to Gary and took him under his wing to shepherd and support. Both verbally and by his presence at a critical time, Rod gave Gary the blessing that was missing in his life now that his natural father had died.

John was a freshman in high school when he met a man who would become his spiritual father. Doug Barram, at the time a Young Life area director, had come to watch a freshman football game. Besides a few parents who were dyed-in-the-wool fans, *nobody* goes to freshman football games. Yet Doug was there, standing along the sidelines every game, offering words of encouragement to a young man who had not yet heard about Christ.

In the years that followed, this man took a fatherly interest in John and his two brothers. In a single-parent home, Doug added spiritual support to three boys who very much needed it. Each brother and even John's mother would come to know Jesus Christ and His heavenly Father personally! All because of this man's deep love for his Savior, a love that was reflected in his fatherly love for us.

To return to Helen's story, she had a similar experience in learning how God's family can become that missing source of blessing she sought. Only hers came with a spiritual sister who blessed her at work.

Helen worked for a major oil company in the accounting department. One day, with the retirement of a woman at the office, Karen came to work. Karen was a committed Christian, who had prayed that God would provide the opportunity for her to share His love with someone who worked in her new office. That someone turned out to be Helen.

Karen was a mystery to Helen at first. She always seemed to have such a positive attitude and such a calm spirit even when there was great pressure at work. Perhaps more than anything Karen's lack of anxiety and inner peace drew Helen to want to be around her.

Soon, Karen and Helen had struck up a friendship and were sharing stories about the "rigors of dating" and their frustrations at work. But Karen also began sharing with Helen the good news about a heavenly Father Helen could come to know. At first, Helen didn't want anything to do with such talk. She had had enough of fathers to last a lifetime. Yet gradually, in spite of herself, the Holy Spirit working through Karen's life drew Helen to a saving knowledge of Christ.

Karen took Helen to church with her for the first time in Helen's adult life. Helen couldn't believe what happened. She was asked to stand up as a visitor, and she was greeted by the pastor. After church a number of people stopped her to say they were glad she had come. One elderly lady even hugged her! Helen went with Karen to the singles Sunday school class. People shared prayer requests before a short message, and they actually held hands and prayed for each other.

Helen found people who had never laid eyes on her treating her like a sister and encouraging her to come back. For the first time, Helen had seen the source of blessing a church family could be, and God used that experience literally to change her life.

Any person who has missed out on all or a part of their parents' blessing can acquire a spiritual family of fathers, mothers, brothers, and sisters who can fill that void. With a personal relationship with a heavenly Father that is secure, and through a spiritual family that can offer warmth, love, and acceptance, every element of the blessing can be ours and overflowing.

FOR BELIEVERS, EACH ELEMENT OF THE BLESSING IS AVAILABLE TODAY

Just in case you have forgotten (or are one of those readers who begin a book in the middle!), let's review the five elements we saw that are a part of the blessing to see how we can give it to each other:

- Meaningful touching
- A spoken message
- Attaching high value
- Picturing a special future
- Active commitment to see the blessing come to pass

Karen provided each element of the blessing to Helen, and it brought Helen to the Savior and to His church. By introducing Helen to a loving group of friends at church, Karen was able to see her blessing multiplied as many people took an interest in Helen's life.

As we will see in more detail in a later chapter, God has equipped the church, the local body of believers, to provide each aspect of the blessing to people in need. Where churches are growing and thriving anywhere in the country, you will find a body of believers who are practicing these five elements of the blessed. These are also the churches that are drawing in the unsaved, not simply luring other believers away from the church down the street.

The past three years had brought tremendous changes for Helen. She had come from feeling isolated and alone to feeling truly blessed for the first time in her life. Helen could retire now in the shelter of her caring friends at church and forget all about the past, right? Not quite. Her life still needed to go full circle.

Helen had received God's blessing from others. Now she would need to become a source of blessing to others around her. People in the office and at her apartment building for the first time could be thought of in terms of what she could give, not just what she needed from them. Because her life was filled with God's blessing through His Spirit and His people, she could love and serve them without needing it to be returned in response.

Helen had eaten fully and had drunk deeply from the feast of life God had provided her in His blessing. However, one final thing was left for Helen to do if she truly wanted to be free from her past. She would need to be a source of blessing not only to her friends at church and work, but to her enemies as well and to one enemy in particular.

GIVING THE BLESSING TO OTHERS—EVEN OUR ENEMIES

As incredible as it may seem, Helen needed to become a source of blessing to her father, the very one who had caused her so much pain and had caused her to begin her search for acceptance in the first place.

"Couldn't I just skip over this part?" Helen asked her pastor when she found out her need to bless her father. Yet in her heart of hearts she knew she would never be truly free of his grip over her life until she could do this.

In a later chapter we will discover the way Helen went about re-establishing contact with her father and how she approached their first meeting in years. Suffice it to say that in spite of her change in attitude about blessing her father (which went from adamant refusal, to quiet aquiescence, to firm resolve, to wanting to chicken out at the last minute and not get on the plane to go see him), it was the second most meaningful day in her life.

Her most meaningful day was when she met the Lord Jesus, the One who changed her life by meeting her missing need for the blessing. He gave her a spiritual family to bless her in the present and provided her the power to be truly free from the yoke of the past.

Jesus is the Person who can change our life, or the life of loved ones who are struggling without the blessing, by providing us and them with God's spiritual family blessing. A blessing that not only parents need to give to their children, and vice versa, but also one that can enrich your relationship with your spouse, intimate friends, and church family.

11

WHEN YOU KNOW YOU WILL NEVER RECEIVE A PARENT'S BLESSING

*O*ver the years, we have received literally hundreds of letters telling us about dramatic turnarounds with a parent. At seminars, we have heard countless stories of men and women who went back to a father or mother who hadn't blessed them. They gave that parent the blessing, and saw their life radically transformed. Many were "deathbed" conversions, where in the last days, weeks, or months of their life, parents not only turned around and gave their children the blessing, but also asked forgiveness from them, and sought salvation from Christ.

That was the kind of happy ending I always pictured for my own father. For years, I prayed for him, and tried to give him each element of this blessing you've read about. I felt sure that one day, he would return it to my brothers and me. We would talk about the hurt and loneliness, and close the loop on any painful memories with caring words. Even more important, I just knew that with all my prayers and sharing, with all the prayers *others* around the country had made for him, he would come to know Christ as well.

This chapter is for those of us who live with less than happy endings.

WHEN HEARTACHE DIALS YOUR NUMBER . . .

"He's in bad shape, John . . . Really bad. You'd better come down right now."

It was August 9, 1992. The call came from my older brother, Joe, and it was one I'd been dreading.

It was a crystal clear Sunday morning, with the promise of yet another scorching day in Phoenix. Cindy and I had just gotten the kids ready for church. Even two minutes later, and I'd have missed the call. But with everyone heading towards the car, I stopped and picked up the phone.

On a day that would hit 111 degrees, Joe's words shook me like a blast of cold air. There had been several times over the past two years when I'd received similar calls, on those occasions I'd always known Dad would pull through. Somehow on this day, I knew deep inside: This was my father's last day on earth.

Cindy, Kari, and Laura all gathered around me, and we knelt in a little circle and prayed for Grandpa. Then I urged them to go on to church, and I drove the short distance to the hospice where my father was dying.

I can't describe to you the feelings I had as I sat in the car before I went in. Sadness, hopefulness, anger, and compassion, all jumbled together. I just knew that something positive was going to happen . . . *that it had to happen.*

I arrived at 8:10 in the morning and found my father sitting on the edge of the hospital bed. Even then he was fighting for breath, his chest heaving as he sought to bring in enough air to fill his collapsing lungs. He was losing his life to lung cancer, complicated by congestive heart failure. A terrible reward for chain-smoking over the years, and a horrible way to die.

For the next eight hours, my brother and I would take turns sitting beside him, holding his hand, praying for him when he'd let us, shifting his pillows, trying to help him be more comfortable. And time after time, when I'd look at him, pictures would pop into my mind . . .

PRESS THE BAR . . . FEEL THE PAIN

One picture was of meeting my father for the first time since my childhood. My parents divorced when I was three months old, and while my father always lived within a few miles of us, it wasn't until my teenage years that he called and finally made contact with us. When he did, it was to come and see my twin brother, Jeff, and me play in one of our high-school football games.

You can imagine how hard we played that game. For the first time, our *father* was coming to watch us! He hadn't come down on the field before the game like we'd hoped, but we were sure he was somewhere up in the stands, cheering like crazy, proud of his sons. But we were wrong. He had gotten sidetracked at his work, and didn't show up at the game.

What happened to me emotionally that day reminded me of a study I would read about years later by animal researchers who trained mice to press a bar in a cage—and out would drop a pellet of food. Mice are extremely motivated by food: they quickly learn to press the bar to get it.

But then, while the mice slept, the experimenters would link up an automobile battery to the back of the metal bar. The next time the little mouse got hungry—he'd walk over, press the bar, and *zzzzaaaap!* He received his food pellet all right, along with a tremendous shock!

Reeling and disoriented, the mouse would move far away . . . but eventually his hunger pangs would overcome his confusion. Finally, he'd come close and gingerly reach out and press the bar a second time to get his second pellet—*and* a second shock.

The researchers kept plenty of water in the cage for these mice, but the only way to get a pellet of food was to press that bar. Something a mouse would do a third time . . . and a fourth . . . and occasionally a fifth. . . . But there it ended. They wouldn't take the shock a sixth time. In fact, they would die in the cage, rather than go back and press that bar.

As I watched my father dying before me, I kept reliving picture after picture of times I had pressed the "bar" with him. Only I wasn't looking for physical food.

I was looking for his blessing.

Going to Father and Son banquets with a neighbor's dad was like pressing the bar—and getting a shock. Having him not show up at a major holiday, never getting a birthday card, or later, his forgetting the names of my children were like pressing the bar—and getting a shock. And over the years, there were times when my feelings toward him died. I'd rather walk away, than be shocked again.

And there were other times when I thought the shock had been turned off . . . I remember an afternoon, a year before his death, when I sat in a different hospital room, waiting for him to wake up from yet another heart surgery. We talked for a short while after he was awake. Having been there for several hours, I needed to go home, and I told him, as I always did in leaving, "I love you, Dad."

As I turned, I heard him say, "I love you, too, John."

I stopped and turned around, in shock at what I'd heard. I had never heard those words from my father.

"What did you say?"

"I love you, too, John," he repeated.

As you can imagine, I walked out of that hospital on cloud nine. That night, I did a national radio program with Gary. On "Life Perspectives," an outstanding radio program we're on with our good friend, Don Hawkins, I told the entire nation that for the first time in forty years, I heard my father say he loved me!

The next morning, I went back to the hospital to see my father, and to ask him if he would call my brothers (one in California and one in Michigan at the time) and tell them what he had told me the previous night. Perhaps his words would turn off the shock for them as well.

"Tell them what?" he said suspiciously.

"Tell them what you told me. You know . . . before I left . . . that you loved me."

My father not only refused to make the call, he denied that he'd ever said those words at all. "It must have been the drugs they have me on!" he joked. But I wasn't laughing. In retrospect, I'm sure his words of love were buried beneath the surface, like most parents. But at the time, it was another example of pressing of the bar—and feeling the shock.

THE END OF THE BATTLE . . . THE BEGINNING OF THE WAR

And now, I was pressing the bar for the last time.

As the day unfolded, it became clear that years of praying and hoping weren't leading to an ending I would have chosen. My father was the first person, besides Cindy, I gave a copy of *The Blessing* to—and it remained unopened to that day. So too had the Bible I had given him years before. He had resisted talking with me about the blessing and about his personal faith, and now as his breathing became more labored, I realized that even any last words he might have spoken were being stolen along with his breath.

It was a hard battle for an old warrior that day. The hospice nurse occasionally came in to administer pain medication, and she told us his struggle could go on for hours, even days. For weeks thereafter, I would wake with the horrible sounds and sights of his struggle in my mind. After staying by his side faithfully all day, my older brother had to leave for a short time to run an important errand.

Before he came back, I sat holding my father's hand and praying for him. It had been eight hours since I had arrived. Eight hours of being next to the man who helped give me life, and whom I didn't even know. Eight hours of wishing there were some way I could help him, some way I could reach him even now.

At 4:40 P.M., his condition finally changed. God

mercifully allowed him to fall into a fitful sleep. As I watched him, his breathing gradually began to slow. His worn out body began to relax. At last his battle was ending. In the quiet space of only a few minutes, I could tell that his life was slipping away.

It was like reaching out and trying to catch the wind. I didn't want him to go. Not with words of love left unsaid. Not without his coming to know Christ. Not without his laying his hands on my children's heads and blessing them, *even once*. His breathing stopped, and I buried my head on his shoulder, and cried my heart out in an empty, sun-splashed room.

WHEN THE BLESSING IS FOREVER OUT OF REACH

Some of you have felt that same pain of reaching out for the blessing, and receiving a shock instead. Others, like me, have lost a parent without words of love or forgiveness ever being spoken. Yet, as I've sought to pick up the pieces of a shattered dream these past few months, God has encouraged me in four specific ways. It's my prayer that if you've lost that chance to receive the blessing these will be helpful principles for you as well.

HAVING DONE ALL . . .

As I have reflected on my father's death, there have been times when I've felt tremendous guilt. Often, I've caught myself thinking, *Maybe you could have been clearer in presenting the Gospel . . .* or *John, How can you talk about giving the blessing to so many people, and yet you never received it yourself? Maybe if you'd spent more time with him,* or at rock bottom, there've been the cutting words, *Maybe if you'd have been a better son . . .*

Guilt, piled upon guilt. Reinforced by so many stories of people whose parents *did* turn around. What was wrong with my prayers? With my love? Why couldn't I have broken through his hard, outer shell, and drawn out the love and softness that I knew were there? Like a broken gumball machine, I felt like my father's blessing was always just beneath the surface. I could see it! But I never could get to it, no matter how many emotional coins I put in the slot.

Perhaps you've felt an aching failure at not turning your parents around as well. Perhaps you've felt that all your efforts ended up slipping out of your hands. If so, the apostle Paul's words in the book of Ephesians can be an encouragement to you as well: *"Having done all . . . stand"* firm in the faith (Eph. 6:13, italics added).

For many of us, it isn't that we haven't done enough . . . in fact, we may have done *more* than enough. We may have paid for their hospital bills, kept up their medications, helped move them into our home, or from there to care center after care center. We may have listened to endless complaints. We did our best. We prayed hard. We sought their forgiveness for things we did wrong. We tried to give them an example, to give them the blessing in practical, tangible ways.

Yet effort doesn't always equal a desired response. There are times when we've done it all, and our all isn't enough. But that's another tremendous advantage of being a Christian. The apostle Paul who had labored long and well didn't have to measure his efforts in human terms. He could rest on the fact that he had "done all." He could stand on the fact that his faith and acceptance rested in a God who would rather have us give Him our hearts than our sacrifice.

Recently, I sat down with a large company that was looking for some consulting work. Several of their top managers had been promoted to significant positions, only to be served divorce papers by their wives, and their performance at work had come crashing down.

"We're thinking of adding a new employee benefit," they shared. "Perhaps marriage and family counseling would help head off what's happened to our executives." But as I listened to them, I was struck by the words of their corporate head. "You understand, Dr. Trent, we measure everything here by one standard—*results*. If we're going to put money into counseling, we want to see results—and fast."

In pure, unvarnished language, that's the way the world measures success. Not in how a life is lived, or by the sincerity of our efforts. But in the bottom line, in measurable success or failure according to worldly standards.

Isn't it great to know that when it comes to our acceptance from Christ, we're not on the performance track? Certainly, He calls us to do our best. To lay down our lives if need be. But Christ's bottom line is love, not results.

No matter how many voices tell me I failed, I don't have to feel shame that my father didn't receive Christ; and neither do you. I can stand firm in the faith, knowing I faithfully laid the Gospel before him. While the world may measure our efforts in terms of a balance sheet, God looks at our hearts, and His love covers us no matter what.

And yet, even armed with this fact, there is something else I had to learn.

YOU CAN'T GUARD AGAINST THE UNGUARDED MOMENT

Four weeks had passed since my family assembled at the National Veterans Cemetery to pay last respects to my father. Because of his combat experience and decorations during World War II, he received a full honor guard, a 12-gun salute, and a clear-as-a-bell salvation message from a retired Army chaplain (that I wish he could have heard).

I was up early one morning, coming in from jogging, when I ran right into our seven-year-old daughter, Kari, just walking out of her room. She was sobbing.

I dropped to my knees, and she fell into my arms, her little shoulders shaking.

"What's the matter, Honey?" I asked in confusion. My mind was racing, trying to think what could have upset her so much from the happy night before.

"It's Grandpa," she said. "He's gone now . . . *and I never got to hug him.*"

I can't tell you how much that "unguarded moment" cut my heart. I had Scriptures memorized to re-

mind me of my wholeness in Christ (Col. 2:10). I had
God's word that I was His child, and a much loved son
(Hebrews 12:7; John 3:16). I knew that He would never
leave me or forsake me (Hebrews 13:5). Yet I also discovered that I wasn't quick enough to out-logic an
emotion.

Let me repeat that. We'll never be fast enough to
out-logic an emotion.

To illustrate this, think about being at church or at
work last week. A dear friend you haven't seen in ages
rushes up to hug you, and they accidentally step right on
the top of your foot with the tip of their high heels! And
to top it off, you're wearing sandals!

What is your instantaneous, *emotional* reaction?

Pain!

And then what?

Anger at being stepped on by a clumsy friend!

But when you stop hopping around, hear their
profuse apology, and slowly begin to be able to put
weight back on your aching foot, your emotions die
down. After possibly wanting to chant a Lithuanian curse
over the person, you can even begin to laugh at the situation and assure them, "Oh, . . . It's all right!"

God made us with emotions. Jesus felt them.
We're told in Scripture, "Be angry, and do not sin" (Eph.
4:26). And no matter how many verses we memorize, we
may still run into an unguarded moment that stomps on
an emotional weak spot like a size 14 boot.

That's what happened to me that day in the hallway. All the hurt, all the pain, all the memories of empty
arms, and even more painfully empty arms for my children, spilled out. Both Kari and I cried in the hallway. We
grieved his loss all over again.

It's important to realize that while we may be
grounded in God's truth, we often aren't, nor should we
be, cut off from our emotions. David grieved and cried at
the loss of his sons. The nation of Israel mourned the loss
of Moses. Jesus wept at the death of a friend.

It's been almost a year now since my father died,

and still I run into those unguarded moments. Perhaps it's at a movie that pictures a father/son relationship I never had. Or it comes when hearing someone else's story in counseling or at a conference. It was C. S. Lewis who observed that the only place we are truly safe from the pain love can bring is in hell. Here on earth, we shouldn't feel defeated, or fail to honestly grieve the loss of our parents.

Yet we should commit ourselves to a third, important principle.

AFTER A SEASON OF GRIEVING . . .

When David's child by Bathsheba fell ill, we're told that David "fasted and went in and lay all night on the ground" (2 Sam. 12:16). Yet once news reached him of his son's death, he "arose from the ground, washed and anointed himself, and changed his clothes; and he went into the house of the LORD and worshiped. Then he went to his own house; and when he requested, they set food before him, and he ate" (2 Sam. 12:20).

A calloused response to a painful time? Not at all. David honestly grieved, and prayed before the Lord for days. But he also worshiped the God whose ways were higher than his own. After a season of pain, he began the difficult process of moving on in daily life. He didn't allow "sackcloth and ashes" to become a permanent garment.

We live in a society where victims abound. While the recovery movement has done many tremendous things in many people's lives, it can also leave others stuck in recovery. Let's face it, under an intense enough spotlight of parental faultfinding, we can all find someone who will classify us as co-dependent, addicted, or somehow "victims."

I am no way discounting the genuine pain that many parents have caused, nor am I negating the very real time (sometimes years) where healthy grieving can and should take place. However, like David, there must also be a time when we worship a mighty God, wash and eat, and get back into life.

The fact that we are forever victims is something

that is not true for the Christian. Because we're related to a mighty God who's worthy of our worship, we can even sing again. There may be sadness in the night, but "joy comes in the morning" (Ps. 30:5).

These three things God has taught me after losing my father, and also a fourth.

A LIFELONG COMMITMENT . . .

There is nothing more precious than watching your children sleep. Returning from a trip, I often get home after Cindy and the kids are in bed. Without fail, I'll walk down the hallway and stop first in Laura's room. Her beautiful brown hair all a tumble, she melts my heart even when she's asleep. Then there's Kari, our precious first-born, the one who always kicks off her covers—and who always knows that Dad or Mom will put them back on.

Even watching Cindy sleep, I'm reminded of how much I love her, and how much I want each of them to know they're loved. And believe it or not, that has been a powerful, positive legacy from my father's death.

I know the heartache of missing out on loving words—and of having them denied if they were once spoken. And that's one pain I'm determined that my own family won't have to face. I can't protect them from every problem. I can't ensure that they won't experience sorrow. But I can ensure that they'll hear my blessing on a daily basis. Something that Kari taught us is extremely important, even for a young child.

Since Kari and Laura were born, Cindy and I have made the decision that every morning, we'd wake them up with a blessing song. While it sounds much better when Cindy sings it than me, it's the words, not the talent behind them, that we want to communicate. The little rhyme put to music goes like this:

Good morning, good morning, how are you today?
The Lord bless you and keep you throughout the day.
We love you. We love you. We love you, (Kari, or
    Laura).

The Lord bless you and keep you throughout the day.

As Kari has gotten older, she even comes in and sings it to Laura as well.

Nearly four years ago, when Kari was not yet three, we were putting her to bed. We had brought in water, her favorite stuffed animals, and even a puzzle she loved, and arranged them all "just so" on her bed. Then we prayed with her, and left the room. But before we'd gotten very far down the hall, she yelled out, "Night, Mom. Night, Dad. And don't forget to *bless* me in the morning!"

Not even three, and still she knew her blessing was waiting for her in the morning!

Is it time you washed your face and hands of the long road of hardship, worshiped the King of kings, and got on with life? Is it time you made a commitment to blessing your own family each day? I can't think of anything that has helped me more in these last several months than that powerful combination of worship and reaching out to give others the blessing, beginning with my own family.

May God indeed heal all your hurts, as He is healing mine. As I pray for you who read this book, I would ask for your prayers for our family as well. And may each of us never leave a doubt in a loved one's mind, that each time they wake up, our blessing will be there in the morning.

12

*G*IVING THE BLESSING TO YOUR SPOUSE AND FRIENDS

*E*arly in our research on this book, I (John) went through this material with several couples in a Bible study group. I asked for the participants' honest evaluation of the material during the sessions, and then had them fill out an evaluation at the end.

One of my favorite comments was written by a wife in the group. Commenting on what her husband had learned during the class, she wrote:

> Dennis has learned so much about how to "bless" the children. It has made a real difference in his relationship with them. How about teaching him how to bless me!!!

This woman's request was right on target. The elements of the blessing are not just limited to the parent/child relationship. We feel strongly that they can be found at the heart of *any* healthy relationship.

Let's continue to discover just how valuable applying the five elements of the blessing can be to three important relationships besides those with our children. First we will look at how the blessing can and should be given to a spouse and the relationship gains that can happen as a result. Then we will look at how friendships can be strengthened and developed through applying these same elements. Finally, in the next chapter, we will look at what can happen when a church family begins to apply these blessing principles to reach out to those beyond the church and especially to those within.

BEING A SOURCE OF BLESSING TO YOUR SPOUSE

Laura was fed up with her husband and with all the upheaval in their lives. He often traveled out of town, and when he was home, he drank and made life miserable for her.

In her frustration, Laura came within an eyelash of throwing in the towel and filing for divorce, but her good friend Gayle talked her into going to see her pastor who she felt might be able to help. Even though Laura was reluctant at first, she was at the end of her rope. Against her better judgment, she made an appointment and went to see him.

For nearly forty minutes this wise pastor simply listened to her story. After Laura had shared her nonstop description of every one of her husband's faults, she finally sat back with a loud "Humph." Smugly she waited to hear an "Amen" from the pastor or at least a hearty confirmation that hers was the worst husband he had ever heard about.

At first the pastor didn't say a word. Deeply engrossed in thought, he literally waited several minutes before he spoke. Finally he sat up, looked her in the eye, and said gently, "Laura, have you ever forgiven your husband for all his many faults?"

You could have heard a pin drop. Laura had not expected to receive this kind of advice. ("No wonder his counseling is free," she thought.) Of course she had not forgiven her husband! He had never asked her to, and she wasn't about to bring it up. He had caused her to suffer, and she wasn't going to let him off the hook that easily.

"Laura, would you think about what I've said today, and would you promise to come back and see me next week?" As she grabbed her purse and headed for the door, she heard herself mutter something like "That would be fine, Pastor"; but she never thought she would be seeing him again. Yet something happened that week that began to change Laura's perspective on her marriage. Something drew her back to this man's office the next week.

In spite of telling herself repeatedly that she should simply forget what he had said, Laura did a great deal of thinking during the week. While it didn't all make sense, it began to dawn on her that it wasn't her husband who was on the hook—she was! He didn't lose any sleep about his behavior; she was the one getting ulcers.

Laura was still confused and had a great many questions for the pastor the next time they met. However, God had already begun to do some miraculous things in Laura's life. That afternoon, in the quietness of the pastor's study, she surrendered her life to Christ. She also decided to give up her need for revenge, to forgive her husband for all he had done, and to learn to love him unconditionally.

Laura's husband was a truck driver, and almost a week went by before he returned home. When he came into the house, he could have sworn he was at the wrong address. He couldn't believe how peaceful things were. Just a week ago everything he did made his wife mad; now she was going out of her way to do things for him.

When this rowdy truck driver found out Laura's change of heart had something to do with religion, he tossed her behavior aside as though it were another diet his wife had discovered. While it made things a lot nicer in the short run, soon her willpower would fade and they would be back at each other's throats.

After five months, Laura's *husband* made an appointment to see the same pastor she had seen. "You've got to tell me about what happened to Laura," the truck driver said. "She's changed so much. It's made me realize what a rotten husband I've been these past years. Pastor, I have a drinking problem, and I need help with it."

What made all the difference for this couple was

that Laura, in spite of the fact her husband didn't "deserve" it, decided to give him the blessing. For years she had made just the opposite decision. She had devalued him and even cursed him to his face. She hated his occupation that took him out of town and filled his clothes with the smell of diesel fuel.

When Laura's life was changed by the Source of blessing Himself, she was able out of the overflow of her life to attach high value to her husband and bless him. Instead of riding him about getting another job, she found ways to build him up and encourage him. Where once she had gone days without speaking to him when she was angry, now she told him her feeling, but without anger and hate. Meaningful touching even began to come back into their relationship, something that Laura had withheld from her husband when her spirit was unforgiving and bitter. As a result, her husband became so convicted about his behavior at home that he also made an appointment to see the pastor.

Granted, this is a dramatic example of what can happen when one spouse decides to be a source of blessing to the other. Their problems were of the major league variety and they needed to make a great deal of changes. However, in everyday households all across the country, with everyday problems and tensions, providing the elements of the blessing to a spouse can revive, encourage, and rejuvenate a marriage.

Let's look briefly at each element of the blessing and see just how important they can be to a healthy marriage. In fact, show us a couple that is growing together, and we'll show you two people practicing these principles of blessing.

MEANINGFUL TOUCH IN MARRIAGE

The same need for meaningful touching we saw with our children is equally important in a marriage. One wise husband realized the importance of this need during a difficult time for his wife, and it did more to minister to her than anything else he could have done.

When Marilyn was getting dressed one morning, she noticed something that didn't seem quite right. She noticed a small lump on her breast that she had not been aware of before.

Marilyn wasn't overly concerned, but she knew enough from reading magazines and watching television to know that she needed to get it checked. She told her husband, Art, what she intended to do, and then called the doctor for an appointment.

Two weeks later, Marilyn went to the doctor to have a biopsy done on the lump. Three days after her appointment, she was lying in a hospital bed facing a radical mastectomy. Besides coming to the hospital twice to deliver their two boys, this was the first time in her forty-seven years Marilyn had had to undergo an operation.

For Marilyn, the hardest thing she faced after the surgery wasn't her recovery, but what Art would think of her now. Would she still be attractive to him? How would he feel about touching her? Questions like these ran over and over in her mind.

The morning she was to be released from the hospital, Marilyn and Art were alone in her room. Her husband sat on her bed and took her hands in his. "Sugar," he said. "I want you to know something. You're as beautiful to me now as you were on our wedding night. Don't you ever forget that." Then Art looked over to make sure the door was shut, winked at her, and said, "After you get home and get rested up, we're going to have to get the lock fixed on the door."

Marilyn hugged her husband, and tears came to her eyes. She knew exactly what he meant by that last statement. Early in their marriage, when someone had forgotten to lock the door, one of the boys had walked into their room at a most inappropriate time. The result was that a new lock was installed on the door the next day, and a new saying began for them. "We're going to have to get the lock fixed on the door" became their private password to an intimate evening.

What had concerned Marilyn was not only how her

operation would affect their sexual relationship, but also whether it would keep Art from touching her outside the bedroom. His words and actions that morning assured her that this important element of the blessing would still be a part of their relationship.

Sexual touching is important in any growing relationship; however, it should not be the only time a couple touches. Our friend, Dr. Kevin Leman, notes this in his book, *Sex Begins in the Kitchen*. He points out that genuine intimacy is developed in the small acts of touching in the kitchen, or walking through a mall together hand in hand, or sitting close together on the sofa watching television.

Speaking of "sex beginning in the kitchen," we heard a true story from a recent participant in a seminar who tried to apply the concept of meaningful touching with his wife, and it left him in an embarrassing situation!

After hearing the concept of meaningful touching talked about over and over, it really stuck with this man. One afternoon after cutting the grass, he came in to take a shower and clean up. He had left the bedroom door open and when he finished his shower he walked over to the rack to get a towel. From where he stood, he could see his wife standing in the kitchen preparing their dinner.

What a time for meaningful touching, he thought to himself. Without a moment's thought, he ran down the hall in his birthday suit and burst into the kitchen to give his wife a big hug. What he couldn't see from the bedroom or as he raced down the hall was his neighbor's wife who had come over to visit. That shocked neighbor saw a great deal more of this husband than she had ever expected! His timing was terrible, but no one could fault his commitment to meaningfully touch his wife!

Meaningful touch can enrich your relationships in many ways. Studies show that regardless of gender, people who were comfortable with touching were also more talkative, cheerful, socially dominant, and nonconforming; those uncomfortable with touch tended to be more emotionally unstable and socially withdrawn. Those more comfortable with touch were less afraid and suspicious of

other people's motives and intentions, and had less anxiety and tension in their everyday lives.[1]

Yet as powerful as touch is, it is not enough to sustain, alone, a growing marriage. Researchers at the University of Illinois used three measures of intimacy to
assess marital satisfaction and happiness. They found that
each form of intimacy made its own important contribution. However conflict and divorce potential were most
closely linked with a lack of the next two elements of the
blessing—emotional and *verbal* intimacy.[2]

A SPOKEN MESSAGE ATTACHING
HIGH VALUE TO A SPOUSE

Let's combine the next two elements of the blessing
into one way of making sure your spouse receives the
blessing. When we decide to place high value on our
spouse, and then back that up with spoken words to that
effect, it can do wonders for a relationship.

Using a word picture to praise a character trait of
our children or our spouse is something we spent several
pages discussing in Chapter Five. Like that royal couple
we looked at in the Song of Solomon, husbands and
wives can take on that look of royalty when they hear how
highly we value them with our words.

A popular bumper sticker slogan reads, "Have you
hugged your kids today?" Another, equally important
phrase that you can copy and paste to your refrigerator,
bathroom mirror, or forehead is:

---

*Have You
Praised Your
Mate Today?*

An everyday dose of praise, whether in the form of a word picture or just a statement like "Great dinner, Honey" or a "You are so kind to other people" or even a "You make me so proud the way you handle the children" can do wonders in a relationship.

Spoken words that attach high value to our spouse are so powerful that they can enrich almost any marriage. Why not try a project in your home to discover just how true this statement can be.

For one month, thirty days, praise at least one thing you appreciate about your spouse each day. Be sure you point out things about his or her character (being kind, generous, thoughtful, punctual, organized, and so on), as well as what they accomplish. Don't tell your husband or wife you're doing this. We give this assignment to many couples in counseling, and it in itself has caused positive changes in relationships.

While we have talked exclusively about using word pictures to praise a husband or wife, they can also be used to help discuss an important issue or avoid a heated argument. By using a word picture to convey a concern we have, instead of lashing out with damaging words, we can often motivate our mate to change and get across a message we can't seem to get across with only words.

One woman at a conference Gary was leading had a concern she had unsuccessfully tried to communicate to her husband for years. Yet by using a single word picture, she so affected him that he was willing to write her a $150,000 check right on the spot to build her dream house!

When we were talking through this story for the book, we kiddingly talked about asking people to mail in a dollar with a stamped self-addressed envelope to find out the word picture she used. We'd be rich in no time! We're sure every wife in America would like to know what she did to motivate her husband to respond the way he did.

You'll be glad to know that at absolutely no extra charge, we have decided to go ahead and tell you the word picture she used. Actually this story is not just about how one woman got her dream house. It is a beautiful example of how attaching high value to a spouse (in this case, not wanting to devalue a spouse in any way) can be powerfully communicated through a word picture.

Don and Bee are dear friends who have attended several relationship seminars that our ministry, Today's Family, has put on. As part of these seminars, Gary teaches couples and singles how to use word pictures with their spouse, their children, or in any meaningful relationship.

Bee had been struggling with something in her marriage for quite a long time. Something that ate away at her self-confidence and caused her constant embarrassment over the years. She was bothered about the condition of their house.

The Lord had greatly prospered Don's business, and much of their resources went into supporting their church and various ministries. They were both generous with their time as well. Don especially was always inviting a new couple at church home to dinner or offering to put up this missionary or that speaker.

Bee was every bit as hospitable, but she was the one having to struggle in an undersized kitchen to feed all the guests, or skip taking a shower because the hot-water heater allowed only three hot showers, or somehow finding a place for six or even ten people to sleep when there were only two beds in the house.

It was not a question of finances that held Don back from moving into a larger home; rather it was his desire not to be ostentatious and flaunt what God had given them. Bee understood her husband's motives and made do with the situation as best she could.

When Gary came back to their city for a second time, they signed up immediately for the seminar as a "refresher" course. After listening again to Gary share about using word pictures to communicate a concern with her spouse, Bee decided she would share one with her husband to describe her feelings toward the home she was living in. That night, she did share with her husband, and here is the word picture she used.

"Don, I feel like you're the game warden who takes such good care of the trout in the waterways around our house. You help keep the streams and ponds clean, and even make sure that when the trout are spawning, they have help getting upstream.

"When we were first married, I felt like I was one of those trout in the stream. I could see you standing on the bank, and I longed for you to scoop me up in a net and take me to the stream by your house. Then one day you did come for me with a net and gently picked me out of the water. It was the happiest time of my life; but instead of ending up in the little stream, you put me in an old, rusty barrel filled with fresh water.

"For twenty-two years you've made sure I had plenty of food and you've kept the water clean, but I long for the day when you will pick me up in your net and put me in that little stream by your house. Don, that's the way I feel about living in this house. I feel like we're living in a rusty barrel, and it makes it hard on me and the people we have over to the house."

Bee's years of longing came to an end that night. She had talked to her husband numerous times about this subject and had even tried to share her feelings with him about their living situation. Yet Don had never seemed to understand how important it was to her, until she shared this word picture with him.

Don loved his wife deeply and had attached high value to her throughout their marriage. He did not want to devalue her in any way, so when he finally understood through this story how she really felt about their house, he responded immediately. Don wrote her a check that night to hire an architect to draw up the plans for a new home, a home where she could enjoy having people over, serve them better, and have a comfortable place for them to stay.

We were so convinced of the benefits of using word pictures that we wrote an entire book on the subject,

Language of Love (Focus on the Family, 1989). And we hope by this story you can see their usefulness in a marriage. Whether you use a word picture in praising your spouse or in sharing a concern, it can be a helpful tool to communicate words of high value to your mate.

PROVIDING A SPECIAL FUTURE FOR YOUR SPOUSE

The other night my (John's) wife and I were watching part of a comedy show on television that we thought was funny. The scene was a forest meadow where an outdoor wedding was taking place.

There in the clearing were the bride and her attendant, and the best man alongside the bridegroom, who looked worried and out of place. The minister asked the bride to say her vows, which she had made up especially for this occasion. Unhesitatingly, she launched into goal after goal, commitment after commitment, and dream after dream she had for herself, her husband, and their marriage. In fact, she went on so long night fell in the forest.

When she finally finished, the exhausted minister turned to the groom and asked him to repeat the vows *he* made up. Looking around nervously, his only words to the minister were, "Well, I hope this works out!"

His vows were not the kind of words that a new bride could build a secure future on. They were funny all right, but they did not provide the kind of security a wife needs to know that she has a special future ahead of her.

In a marriage, our mate needs to know that he or she is a special part of our future. What's more, our spouse needs to know that the way we look at him or her today leaves room for positive change and growth in the future. Tod learned this lesson the hard way with his wife, Betty.

Betty was not the world's best house cleaner. Her home was not what you would call neat and clean before they had children, and with three little ones running around, she had nearly given up on their home ever being clean. Like what happens in many marriages, her husband, Tod, had a different temperament. He was incredibly neat and clean. Tod even kept his workshop, where he spent time on his hobbies, so clean a person could safely eat off the floor.

Tod was so frustrated with his wife's sloppy ways, he spent much of his time berating her for being a poor house cleaner. She would *always* be messy and could *never* change. Tod told her stories about how, in the future, their house would become so dirty that their grandchildren would catch incurable diseases and the County Health Department would come out and shut them down.

Not only was Tod not placing high value on his wife, he was helping to see that the very thing he sought to change became a lasting part of their future! By painting a picture of his wife with no window of hope or door for change, he literally boxed her in to viewing herself as the "world's messiest housekeeper" that he thought she was.

In a Sunday school class, Tod saw for the first time how his words of a negative future had hurt his wife, not helped her. He learned that he was effectively killing any motivation his wife did have to change. His words of a negative future were telling his wife that it was impossible for her ever to please him. So why should she bother trying?

Tod thought back on what he had said to his wife. The times she had tried to make a dent in the house cleaning chores, he had met her with a "Finally!" or a "Why can't you keep things like that all the time?" But then he began to change.

Tod started to praise small things Betty did and to put aside the criticism of her poor performance. He even began to change his picture of her future and their house to a positive one. Change is always slow to take root, but it can grow ten times faster in the soil of encouragement than in the hard, rocky soil of criticism.

By picturing a special future for his wife in this area and encouraging her for small accomplishments, a miracle began to happen. Even though the house is not up to Tod's workshop standards, no longer does he have to fight his way through the laundry in the washroom or fear going into a shower that has things growing in it.

Whether it is the fear of entertaining, the need to go on a diet, failing to discipline the children promptly, or keeping a messy house, we do not motivate our mate to change by picturing a negative future. Our mate needs to hear words that picture a special future in the same way our children do, positive words that provide our spouse the room to become all that God can help him or her to become.

ACTIVE COMMITMENT TO YOUR MATE

As we have discovered in earlier chapters, providing the individual elements of the blessing without the glue to hold them all together is not enough. That glue is our active commitment. In fact, this final element of the blessing is at the heart of "cleaving" in a marriage.

When the Scriptures tell us we are to "cleave" to our spouse (Gen. 2:24), the root word in Hebrew means "to cling, to be firmly attached."[3] It takes a firm decision to be committed to blessing your spouse, a decision that will not remain intact if you don't make room for your mate's fallibility.

In the 1929 Rose Bowl game, Georgia Tech came to California to meet the mighty football team from the University of California. In that game, something happened that demonstrated how fallible even a star could be.

Roy Riegels was a starter and star athlete for California. He had performed admirably during the regular season and was expected to make a great contribution to the team that day. What actually happened was that Roy made a winning contribution to the *other* team!

In a brilliant defensive play late in the first half, Roy intercepted a pass, fought off several would-be tacklers, and headed for the end zone and a touchdown. What he didn't know was that in fighting off the tacklers, he had gotten turned around and he actually scored a safety for the other team! When the half ended, Georgia Tech had gone ahead of California because of Roy's safety, and they hung on to win by that margin.

At halftime, everyone was wondering the same thing. Would Roy's coach, Nibbs Price, yank him out of the game? When it came time to announce the starting lineup for the second half, Price called out Roy's name! This coach had watched Roy work hard all season, and he remained committed to him even when he made a major mistake.

Another football coach, at the University of Texas, made famous an old country saying. Darryl Royal was like Coach Price; he remained committed to his starters in the game, even if they were fumbling the ball or missing a tackle. The press constantly asked him about this, and his reply was always the same, "You dance with the one who brung ya"—not good English, but an excellent example of active commitment.

What these two coaches had, and what every man or woman owes his or her spouse, is the willingness to stay committed, even if the other person fumbles the ball. Amy did this, and it was the very thing her husband credits with saving his life.

Grant owned a manufacturing business that had done quite well. His business was small, but it found its niche in the marketplace and was growing by leaps and bounds. Borrowing against the property and expecting his profits to continue, Grant took out a large loan to expand the facilities. No sooner had construction begun on his new plant than a multinational manufacturing concern decided to go into competition with Grant's product.

With cash flow tight because of the huge interest payments on the loan, Grant did not have the resources to put more salesmen on the street. Neither could Grant lower the price on his product because of the profit margin needed to keep the business afloat.

In less than a year, Grant had literally gone from riches to rags. His competitor had undercut his prices drastically to get into the marketplace, and it literally drove Grant out of business. Saddled with unpaid employees, lawsuits from suppliers, and with the bank breathing down his neck, Grant had to shut down his plant and liquidate his equipment at a fraction of its actual worth. He even lost his home that had been collateral for the note and had to move into a small apartment. Perhaps the crowning blow came when he had to explain to his children at midyear that they would have to change from the private school they loved to public school.

Grant was not a believer at the time of his business's collapse, and he was devastated as he had never been before. He even contemplated suicide, but one thing held him back:

"I didn't know the Lord at the time my business went under, and my whole world seemed to end. I would like to say it was the thought of my children that kept me from ending it all, but that wouldn't be true.

"The one thing that kept me from it was Amy and the way she constantly believed in me and blessed me with her love. Listening to her pray for me at night and having her hold me and let me cry were what pulled me through. I tell everybody she saved my life "twice." The first time was when the business failed; the second was when she led me to Jesus Christ!"

Grant could no longer provide for his wife and family "in the manner to which they had become accustomed." Yet because of this loving wife, who based her blessing for her husband on active commitment instead of material possessions, their relationship remained strong and secure.

Every husband and wife will drop the ball and prove themselves fallible time and again. If we are to be people of blessing, our commitment will rest on our decision to love our spouse "in spite of." Our love must be the kind of love that motivated our heavenly Father to bless us with His Son, in spite of the fact we didn't deserve it and because He knew we needed that blessing so much in our lives.

The blessing can make a tremendous difference in marriage, but it takes work to pull these principles off the page and apply them with our spouse. Even so, we know you won't regret a minute of time you spend cultivating each of the elements in your home, especially when you see the harvest of love and happiness that can result.

BEING A SOURCE OF BLESSING TO YOUR FRIENDS

We constantly meet people who "wish they had a close friend." Many of those same people would not have to make that comment if they knew how to be a "close friend." We discovered in studying the blessing in the Scriptures that an important part of becoming a close friend is to apply each element of the blessing in a friendship.

In all the Scriptures, perhaps the most universally acknowledged model of a close friend is Jonathan. His relationship with David is a graduate course in what makes a lasting relationship. These two young men were not a likely pair to strike up a friendship.

Jonathan was the heir apparent to his father's throne. He was also a mighty warrior in his own right. He led Israel's armies in battle and even attacked twenty Philistines with only his armor carrier to back him up and defeated them all (1 Sam. 14:6–14).

David and Jonathan first met just after David had slain Goliath. With all the attention David was getting, Jonathan could have looked at David as an arch rival and enemy. Yet we are told in the Scriptures that "the soul of Jonathan was knit to the soul of David, and Jonathan loved him as his own soul" (1 Sam. 18:1).

One reason that their friendship was unique is that it was a friend-to-friend relationship that included, and models for us, every aspect of the blessing.

Without the fear that exists today among men of appearing like homosexuals, David and Jonathan demonstrated meaningful touching in their friendship. In their last meeting, Jonathan had to tell David it was no longer safe for him to be around his father, Saul. We read that they "kissed one another; and they wept together, but David more so" (1 Sam. 20:41).

While men giving each other a kiss and crying in each other's arms is almost taboo in our culture, it was not considered strange in ancient Israel nor is it unusual in many foreign countries today. Friends in these cultures demonstrate their love for each other with a kiss or a hug.

A friend today will include meaningful touching in blessing his or her friend. Withholding a hug or even a handshake from a friend can freeze that relationship at a surface level.

In giving us another picture of what it means to be a close friend, Jonathan spoke of his appreciation for David and placed high value on him. Let's look back on Jonathan's actions toward David when they first met.

David certainly stole the spotlight on that day. Yet we are told that "Jonathan took off the robe that was on him and gave it to David, with his armor" (1 Sam. 18:4). A warrior only lays down his weapons in front of someone he considers his better. Jonathan placed such high value on David that he was willing to sacrifice his symbols of authority (his armor and his robes) in order to honor his friend.

Jonathan also made a verbal covenant with David that he would be his close companion for life (1 Sam. 20:13). He said to David, "The LORD be with you as He has been with my father." No words of blessing were spared in what Jonathan said to David.

The last words Jonathan spoke to David illustrate his active commitment to David and his desire that God bless David in the future. "May the LORD be between you and me, and between your descendants and my descendants, forever" (1 Sam. 20:42).

Who are your true friends? Just think a moment about someone in your life who has been an intimate friend. Almost without exception, a close friend will be someone like Jonathan, a man or woman who has demonstrated each aspect of the blessing in his or her relationship with you. A close friend will be someone like Larry, who decided to provide each element of the blessing to his boss, Glenn.

Glenn was not an easy person to befriend. For one thing, Glenn didn't seem to *need* any friends. He was a tremendously successful businessman who always seemed on top of everything. Also, Glenn had been trained in the old tradition of maintaining professional distance from his employees and competitors. "Don't let anyone get close" was the unspoken motto Glenn lived by, that is, until the day his teenage son was picked up for selling illegal drugs to his classmates.

In order not to be taken advantage of by others, Glenn had built a wall around himself at work and at his church. He was constantly around people, yet he had no close friends. Glenn didn't even know how to be a friend to his wife or children, and the rebelliousness of his son and Glenn's total ignorance of his son's drug problem graphically pointed that out to him.

Now, in a time of dire need, Glenn needed the emotional support of a man he could pour his heart out to; and no one was there. No one was there until Larry noticed that something seemed wrong with his boss and decided that Glenn needed a friend, in spite of his non-verbal language that said just the opposite.

Larry was already an accomplished "Jonathan." He knew the importance of supplying another person with the elements of the blessing, and he had a number of close friends. But befriending Glenn was a different matter. He was his boss, and besides, Glenn certainly did not look as if he wanted any company.

Day by day, watching Glenn suffer in silence, Larry became convinced that he needed to befriend him. Their friendship began one Tuesday morning when Larry gathered up his courage, walked into Glenn's office, and laid his hand on Glenn's shoulder.

"Hey, old buddy," Larry said, "you just don't seem to have been yourself for a while. I may be way out of line, and you can tell me so if you want, but you seem to be really hurting. I just want you to know that if you ever need somebody to talk to, I'm around." Larry expected to be dismissed with a curt rebuff, but instead Glenn didn't say a word. Finally, after a long pause, he looked up at Larry, close to tears, and said, "I'll remember that, Larry. Thanks a lot."

Larry thought that was the end of things when a few days went by without hearing from Glenn. However on Friday, his secretary gave him the message that Glenn wanted to have breakfast with him one day that next week.

During that meeting, Larry listened, and listened, and *listened* to Glenn pour out a heart full of hurt. Larry didn't try to lecture Glenn, nor did Larry try to lessen the emotions that were present by saying, "Well, it's not all that bad" or "You're a Christian, Glenn, just pray about it." When Larry heard Glenn share the heartbreak that only comes when dealing with a rebellious child, he cried with him. The only time Larry remembered saying more than a sentence or two was when he prayed a short prayer with Glenn in his car after their breakfast.

Over the next several months, Larry met every week with Glenn to listen, talk, and pray about Glenn's relationship with his son. Larry couldn't directly relate to Glenn's hurt (Larry's children were just entering grade school), but he could still shake Glenn's hand and let him know that day or night, he had a friend he could turn to.

An interesting thing began to happen around the office as a result of Larry and Glenn's meeting. Glenn actually began to soften a little in his strict rule of professional distance. For the first time in years, Glenn had a friend who cared about him, and the result was that he was rediscovering how to be friends with others again.

Through Larry's providing each element of the blessing to his boss—by shaking his hand or patting Glenn on the back (meaningful touch); in speaking encouraging words to Glenn (spoken message); through pointing out the positive character traits that Glenn did have and the way he was trying to make a fresh start with his wife and the other children at home (attaching high value); by providing him with the hope of a special future that God could bring to pass regardless of how his son responded (special future); and by committing himself to be available to his friend when he needed someone to talk to (active commitment)—these two men's hearts began to be knitted together.

Things finally did get better with Glenn's son and as a result Glenn had *two* things to thank the Lord for. One was the new way his son responded to him as he began to become a better friend to him, and the other was an employee named Larry who had taught Glenn about genuine friendship by modeling for him the elements of the blessing.

Understanding the relationship elements of the blessing can communicate parental acceptance to a child, enrich a marriage, and deepen a friendship. But that is not all. The blessing can also provide helpful guidelines for a church family to use in remaining or becoming a place of blessing. Both to those outside the church and especially to those within.

13

*G*IVING THE BLESSING TO YOUR PARENTS

*O*ur portrait of the blessing is almost complete. In past chapters we have used broad strokes to illustrate how the blessing was viewed down through the centuries. We have also used the fine strokes of the literal meaning of the word *blessing* to bring out the subtle nuances of this concept. Five predominant patterns run throughout the painting, each an important element of the blessing, and together they provide the viewer with a sense of structure and balance. Stories of people, past and present, have been used to bring color and depth to the picture. Some of these colors are dark and subdued and stir our compassion. These are the stories of Esau and others like him who never received their family's blessing. Yet we have also tried to paint the brilliant colors of joy, happiness, and security from the lives of those who have received the blessing.

However, before we lay down our brush and move away from this portrait of the blessing, we need to paint one final corner. In fact, this corner is a key to completing our picture and truly capturing its total scope.

In our final strokes to complete this portrait of the

blessing, we need to illustrate the importance of seeing the blessing go full circle. We began painting in a corner of the canvas that showed how parents need to give their children the blessing; we will end by seeing how these same children need to return the blessing to their parents. Helen returned the blessing, even though it was the most difficult thing she had ever done in her life.

A Story of Blessing

Let's look back at the story of Helen. Helen had been physically abused by her father the entire time she was growing up. He was an alcoholic whose changing moods left her insecure, fearful, and distressed. The first chance Helen had to leave home, she was out the door. From her perspective, she didn't care if she ever saw her father again, an attitude that was confirmed when he and her mother were divorced while she was in college. Helen had absolutely no reason to go home now and refused even to consider the thought.

Then Helen met a coworker named Karen, and her whole life began to change. For the first time, she heard about and received God's blessing of salvation and His provision of a spiritual family at church to help meet her needs. With spiritual fathers galore at her church, Helen felt even less of a need to make peace with her natural father.

Gradually, Helen began to notice that some areas of her spiritual life were lagging behind. She had grown by leaps and bounds, but still had a tendency to criticize others. She had come a long way, but her temper still needed control. For a long time, Helen thought these nagging tendencies did not disappear because of a lack of faith or knowledge of God's Word. Countless times she had committed herself afresh to study God's Word. Yet her struggles continued.

Then one day Helen discovered what was at the heart of her problem. She did not lack faith; she was not willing to honor her father. The deep bitterness and resentment she felt still had an iron grip on part of her life, an area she had not opened up to God's leadership, healing, and love.

When Helen looked closely at her life, she found she was becoming more and more like the person she hated most in life—her father. Until and unless she dealt with the stranglehold he still held on her life, she would find a continuing struggle in her spiritual life and possible destruction in her personal relationships.

At first, Helen tried to push away the growing conviction that she needed to deal with her relationship with her father. Even thinking about him again hurt her. This is always the case when we remember something painful from the past. Memories bring back with them feelings, and sometimes those feelings are the things we don't want to face. However Helen knew what was right. While her emotions didn't agree, she knew that God honored those who honored their parents. By remaining at enmity with her father, she was doing what was wrong and was draining herself of life.

Helen went to see her pastor and explained what God had been showing her over the past several months. After several sessions of prayer and counsel, Helen decided to visit her father. Whether he would respond or not, she was determined to bless and honor him.

On June 14, sitting in the pastor's study, Helen made the most difficult call of her life. She had found out her father's phone number from an old family friend and, after praying with her pastor, picked up the phone and dialed the out-of-state number.

She made the call at 3:00 P.M., and secretly Helen hoped her father would be at work and not be there to answer the phone. But on the fifth ring, her father answered the phone. God gave Helen the strength to choke out, "Hello, Dad?" After a long silence on the other end, he replied, "Helen?"

In a short conversation, Helen told her father she was going to be flying to his city and asked if she could see him. "Please do, Helen," her father said. She got directions to his apartment and hung up the phone.

The first skirmish had been won, but the battle still lay before her. A hundred times in the four days before her flight Helen talked herself in and out of going to see her father. Yet each time she decided to back out, that still, small voice within her convicted her of what was right. If she received nothing from her father except the pain she had gotten in the past, she knew she still needed to go for *her* sake and do what was right.

Helen did board the plane, and her pastor and several friends came with her to the airport to encourage her and see her off. The flight was both the shortest and longest airplane fight of her life. Helen rented a car when she arrived at the airport and drove the thirty minutes to her father's home. With a deep sigh and a short prayer, Helen walked to his apartment and knocked on the door.

An old, tired-looking man opened the door. (Why had she remembered him as being such a giant?) Sitting on the couch with her father, Helen poured out her heart to him. She told about becoming a Christian and the difference it had made in her life. Then, hardest of all, she admitted the anger and hatred she had carried toward him for years and asked his forgiveness.

By the time Helen finished talking, they were both in tears. For fifteen years Helen's father had denied the burning conviction of his wrongs against his daughter. He asked her to forgive him for being such a terrible father and lamented over all the pain he had caused in her life.

After four hours that seemed like only four minutes, Helen left. At the door she put her arms around her father and heard herself say the words that she never thought she could say: "I love you, Daddy." All the hurt he had caused in her life had not stopped her from loving him. Even during the times when she hated him the most, she still felt an attachment to him and a love for the man who had brought her into the world. Where once she could not express that love or even feel it, now she felt compassion, pity, and warmth for a man who had shattered his own life when he shattered hers.

Helen went back to her home, her office, and her church a new person. Not looking different on the outside, but knowing that on the inside she was more free than she had ever been in her life.

When she had come to know Christ, He had freed her from the guilt of every sin and unlocked the shackles that kept her chained to the past. By having the courage to face her father, to honor and bless him, Helen finally took off the shackles Christ had unlocked. She walked away from her father's house that day free to truly live in the present, because she was at last unchained from the past.

THE FIRST COMMANDMENT WITH A PROMISE

What Helen was willing to do in facing her father took a tremendous amount of courage. However, Helen had a God who understood her fears and gave her the strength to face them.

Is it only those like Helen, who have such a hurtful past, who need to bless their parents? Certainly not. In fact, the Scriptures direct every child to give the blessing to his or her parents.

In the book of Ephesians, Paul goes into detail about what it means to have healthy family relationships. In the fifth chapter of this book he gives a beautiful picture of God's design for the husband/wife relationship. With the man as a loving leader and the woman as a highly valued partner and responder, the stage is set for children to come into a loving home.

Paul's next instructions are for those children. While under the roof and protection of one's parents, children are to "obey your parents in the Lord" (Eph. 6:1). Then Paul gives a general admonition for children of all ages: "'Honor your father and mother,' which is the first commandment with promise: 'that it may be well with you and you may live long on the earth'" (Eph. 6:2–3).

What does it mean to honor your parents? We can

see that if we will look at the word *honor* in the Scriptures. In Hebrew, the word for "honor" is *kabed*. This word literally means, "to be heavy, weighty, to honor."[1] Even today, we still link the idea of being heavy with honoring a person.

When the President of the United States or some other important person speaks, people often say that his words "carry a lot of weight." Someone whose words are weighty is someone worthy of honor and respect. However, we can learn even more about what it means to honor someone by looking at its opposite in the Scriptures.

In Chapter Ten, we discovered that the literal meaning of the word *curse (qalal)* was "to make light, of little weight, to dishonor."[2] If we go back to our example above, if we dishonor a person we would say, "Their words carry little weight." The contrast is striking!

When Paul tells us to honor our parents, he is telling us that they are worthy of high value and respect. In modern-day terms, we could call them a heavyweight in our lives! Just the opposite is true if we choose to dishonor our parents.

Some people treat their parents as if they are a layer of dust on a table. Dust weighs almost nothing and can be swept away with a brush of the hand. Dust is a nuisance and an eyesore that clouds any real beauty the table might have. Paul tells us that such an attitude should not be a part of how any child views his or her parents, and for good reason. If we fail to honor our parents, we not only do what is wrong and dishonor God, but we also literally drain ourselves of life!

WHAT HAPPENS WHEN YOU HONOR (OR DISHONOR) YOUR PARENTS?

Paul goes on to remind us in this passage in Ephesians that a promise is available to all those who will keep the commandment to honor their parents. However, we need to understand something about the promises of God before we look any further. The first thing to remember is

that God's promises are always fulfilled. What God promises, He will see come to pass.

The second striking reality we need to see about
this promise is that it is conditional. If you fulfill the con-
ditions of the promise, God will honor that in your life.
God's promise to you cuts both ways. If you will honor
your parents, this promise will apply. But if you dishonor
them, you will have to live life apart from God's promise.

Paul tells us that two aspects to this promise relate
to those who would honor their parents. The first reflects
on our relationship with God.

"THAT IT MAY GO WELL WITH YOU"

In New Testament Greek, this entire phrase is captured in the tiny word, *eu*. In ancient Greece, this word
was used to salute someone with the words, "Well done!
Excellent."[3] When you honor your parents, the first thing
you can know for sure is that God is saying to you, "Well
done! Excellent!"

For God's people, doing what was right before
God has always included doing what was right by their
parents. In Leviticus 19:3, Moses commands the people,
"Every one of you shall revere his mother and his father,
and keep My Sabbaths: I am the LORD your God." Linked
with the importance of setting aside a special Sabbath day
each week to honor God is the command to be consistent
in revering and honoring your parents.

Jesus felt just as strongly that the actions you take
toward your parents reflect your heart toward God. If you
are dishonoring your parents, you are following the tradition of your times, not the Word of God. Listen to the
strong rebuke Jesus gave the Pharisees and scribes who
willfully chose to dishonor their parents:

> "Why do you also transgress the commandment of God
> because of your tradition? For God commanded, saying,
> 'Honor your father and your mother.' . . . But you say,
> 'Whoever says to his father or mother, "Whatever profit
> you might have received from me is a gift to God"

then he need not honor his father or mother.' . . .
Hypocrites! Well did Isaiah prophesy about you,
saying:

> 'These people draw near to Me
>   with their mouth,
> And honor Me with their lips,
> But their heart is far from Me'"
> (Matt. 15:3–8).

For Jesus, doing what was wrong in dishonoring
your parents could never be linked with what was right in
God's eyes. Anyone who urges you to dishonor your parents speaks words of hypocrisy and falsehood. You will
only hear a "well done" from your heavenly Father when
you honor your parents, not if you dishonor them by
treating them as a speck of dust.

Not only does it affect your relationship with the
Lord when you follow what is right in honoring your parents, God promises that it will affect your own life in a
positive way as well!

"THAT YOU MAY LIVE LONG ON THE EARTH"

God promises that those who will honor their parents actually receive life! How can this be? Just ask many
physicians, counselors, or pastors. They have seen in their
offices the shattered lives of those who dishonor their parents, with their strength drained away as a result.

Each of you has only so much emotional and physical energy, and you choose how you will spend it. What
physicians and researchers are finding out more and more
clearly today is that a close link exists between what we
think and how we physically react.

Positive attitudes have been linked with positive
physiological changes while negative attitudes can open
the door for illness or disease.[4] When persons choose to
hate or dishonor their parents because of anger, bitterness,
or resentment, they pay a spiritual, emotional, and physical price.

The Scriptures have shown the strong connection between the words we speak and how they affect us physically. In Proverbs 16:24 we read, "Pleasant words are like a honeycomb,/Sweetness to the soul and health to the bones," and in a later passage, "A merry heart does good, like medicine,/But a broken spirit dries the bones" (Prov. 17:22).

When you decide to honor your parents, you are placing high value on them. God says such actions will increase your life on the earth. However, if you decide to see your life dried up by holding on to bitterness or resentment toward your parents (attitudes of dishonor), you eat up your strength and shorten your very life.

Some people have been dishonoring their parents for years. If that is something you have been doing through your actions or attitudes, you need to deal with it as soon as possible and begin the process of making things right. Otherwise the words of King David can ring true in your life, "When I kept silent about my sin, my body wasted away/ Through my groaning all day long./For day and night Thy hand was heavy upon me;/My vitality was drained away as with the fever-heat of summer" (Ps. 32:3–4 NASB).

Paul's words have clearly demonstrated to us that we need to honor our parents. Yet, practically, how do we do this? Once again, we find ourselves at the doorstep of the blessing.

HOW DO YOU HONOR YOUR PARENTS?

The book of Proverbs was written to teach us the skill of right living. We have already seen that honoring your parents is the right thing to do, but how is it done? You honor your parents by acting as wise people, not as fools.

Many of the Proverbs talk about and illustrate different kinds of fools. All are people who are not applying God's principles for right living. One vivid description of a destructive fool is found near the end of the book. Look at this description of a worthless, treacherous man. Then go back and see what heads the list of things that characterize him:

> There is a kind of man who curses his father,
> And does not bless his mother.
> There is a kind who is pure in his own eyes,
> Yet is not washed from his filthiness.
> There is a kind—oh how lofty are his eyes!
> And his eyelids are raised in arrogance.
> There is a kind of man whose teeth are like swords,
> And his jaw teeth like knives (Prov. 30:11–14 NASB).

The man pictured above brings pain to those at home and those outside the home. As we have already seen, he also robs himself of life by cursing his parents. However, he is not only being rebuked in this passage for cursing them, he is also being scolded because he did not bless them.

If you want to be a person who honors your parents, you will be a person who blesses them. In providing the blessing to your parents, you truly honor them, do what is right in God's eyes, and even prolong your life.

We have talked at length in earlier chapters about the five elements of the blessing. We have seen these elements applied to our children, our spouse, our friends, and our church family. Yet where these elements can be of tremendous importance is in providing a blessing for our parents. Each one can be a useful tool in honoring them.

To begin with, your parents need you to *meaningfully touch* them. Even if they have struggled with hugging and touching you when you were young, as they grow older they need the reassurance that comes from being touched.

They also need *spoken words* from their children. Isn't it interesting that Mother's Day is the busiest day of the year for interstate phone calls! For many mothers, these will be the only encouraging words they hear from their children until the next year. Unfortunately, many fathers will hear fewer words of praise. You need to be consistent in your contact with your parents. They need to hear your voice and the spoken words of blessing they carry.

It is common for a parent to think back in guilt on the past. The things that often seem to stand out to a parent are not the many positive things they did, but the times they spoke out in anger or did something that accidentally hurt their child. When you bless your parents with words that *attach high value* to them, you can be a tremendous encouragement in their lives. You do not have to pretend a wrong was never committed, but you can forgive them and keep them from self-pity. You can decide to value them highly, to honor them because of the great worth they have to you and to God.

Parents need words that picture a *special future* for them. In fact, for many parents the reason they can only look back to times past is because they do not feel a sense of a future in their lives. You can point out useful and beneficial aspects to your parents' lives, even if those useful qualities are different from when they were younger. You can also point them to the Scriptures and the encouragement that their future with their heavenly Father and spiritual family does not end when this life does.

Something that can help is assuring your parents of their important place in the family as the years go by. In some homes with older parents, the grown children will take over the finances and all major decisions and toss aside an older parent's advice or input. Nothing is wrong with providing a helpful service to your parents, but you should be sure you still honor them in the process. By continuing to ask for their wisdom and advice, you can provide them with a picture of a special future.

One last thing that can encourage a special future for your parents is letting them be a part of your future, the future wrapped up in your children. Providing the time for grandparents and grandchildren to meet and interact can be a tremendous tool for providing your parents with a special future. If you will let them know how they can be and have been a blessing to your children, you honor them in a very valuable way.

Of all the ways you can bless your parents, the genuine commitment to walk with your parents through each step in life is particularly important at the end of their lives. Particularly when one parent dies, the other will need an extra measure of your love and commitment to lean on in his or her journey through life.

BLESSING OUR PARENTS WHILE MAINTAINING HEALTHY BOUNDARIES

Thus far, we've talked about giving the blessing to our parents in a positive, honoring way. But it's important to state that honoring a parent does not mean that we have to drop all healthy boundaries.

For example, my (John's) father had an explosive temper that came out many times when I was with him. In fact, the very first time I ate dinner with him at a nice restaurant nearly turned into a brawl!

My father had re-established a relationship with us, and after closing a large business deal, took us out to a nice restaurant to celebrate. While World War II had ended twenty years before, in many ways my father had never left the battlefield. And one evidence of that was his thinly veiled hatred for anyone of oriental descent.

It didn't matter that our waiter was of Chinese, not Japanese origin. With each round of drinks he ordered, he became more upset with his "slanty eyes," his "poor" service, and "smart #@$#" attitude.

Finally, when the waiter was slow getting us our check, my father blew up in anger. He stood up, challenged the man to fight and started towards him. I feel sure that if my older brother Joe hadn't grabbed him and forced him outside (even then Joe was 6' and 220 lbs.), we'd have witnessed the battle of the Pacific all over again.

Keeping his explosive nature in mind, I put strict boundaries around his behavior when he was in my home. He could say or do anything he liked when I was at his home. But like everyone else who came over to my house, if he chose to smoke it would have to be outside. If he chose to drink before he came over, he should hold off on coming that night. And at all times, his words should be civil and without profanity in front of the children.

As you might imagine, the first time I sat down with my father at a Denny's restaurant and explained these family "rules" was an invitation to an explosion. However, we had just moved back from Texas to Arizona, and I knew the time to set loving boundaries was then.

Without judgment, and without a doubt, I wanted to make sure he knew that I loved him. I didn't preach, or condemn him in any way. But I also had a wife and little ones to consider, and a home where I didn't want anyone, even my father, to cross the line into dishonor.

Healthy boundaries with a difficult parent aren't incompatible with giving them the blessing. I'll have to admit that were times when our family boundaries acted like a wall to him. But every stone was built from his side of the fence.

If you have a parent who consistently "crosses the line" into dishonor, you too may have to establish clear boundaries with them, and have the strength to enforce them despite their reactions.

COMING FULL CIRCLE WITH THE BLESSING

In honoring our parents as very valuable, we have come full circle in our look at how the blessing in the Scriptures can enrich and encourage healthy relationships. Many of us have never thought in terms of providing our parents with the blessing. But if we will, we can leave them a tangible gift of love that they can carry throughout their lives, just as Don and his brother and sisters did for their parents.

Cindy and I (John) have been to some very creative parties over the years. From "re"gressive dinners to "Roaring Twenties" nights, we thought we had seen them all. Then an invitation came that really caught our attention. We were being asked to attend a surprise, "This Is Your Life" party for an older couple in our church.

The party had been planned by the children in this family specifically to honor their parents for years of loving care and sacrifice. It wasn't anybody's birthday, nor was it tied in with an anniversary. It was simply an evening to remember and say thank you for years of commitment to friends and family.

There was not a dry eye in the place by the time the evening was finished. Thanks to the oldest son's, Don's, initiative, their parents had received an evening of blessing from their children. As we left this older couple's house, you could see in their eyes that their hearts were bursting with pride, appreciation, and love. These children had provided their parents with an evening that was worth far more to them than any department store gift from their children ever could be.

Please don't assume that "my parents would never let us do something like that for them." If Don's parents had known what was coming, they would have probably tried to talk their children out of the evening. Yet regardless of how difficult it can be for some parents to let their children give back to them, we need to make an effort to bless them. In Appendix A at the end of this book, we have included suggestions on how to plan a special evening of blessing for those you love. Has it been too long since you honored your parents with words of blessing? All you need is an active commitment to give back to them what God has already richly given you.

14

GIVING THE BLESSING TO YOUR OLDER CHILDREN

When our children were young, Norma and I (Gary) made a commitment to give our children the blessing. We knew that simple acts of unconditional love could make a major difference in their lives. We have seen the fruits of the blessing by watching them mature, leave home, and increase their desire to enrich the lives of others. *But what I never realized, or ever dreamed, was how powerful—and how necessary—the blessing would become to my older children.*

Kari, Greg, and Michael have now grown up and left the house, Kari and Greg to spouses and homes of their own, and Michael to college at an out-of-state school. Our home is much quieter, but not empty. Their laughter, voices, pictures, and love still echo from each wall in our house. And what's more, instead of their growing out of their need for our blessing, they've grown to appreciate it even more. So if you have older children who have moved away from home, they're never out-of-reach of the blessing you can continue to give them. Here are eight important ways you can bless your children to show them your love and appreciation for who they have become as adults.

OLDER CHILDREN FALL BACK ON OUR PRAISE

While we've spoken at length about the need to verbally praise our younger children, I've seen with my own grown children how important affirmation continues to be. In fact, as the decisions they make become more serious, and the trials they face become more real, praise is a tremendous source of security and strength for them.

Children of all ages have an "affirmation bank," that requires constant deposits. When we do verbalize our love, we continue to give them a foundation that operates apart from any trying circumstances they might face.

Recently, I saw two examples of how important words of praise are for older children. First, I met a bright, energetic young woman in her early twenties who, already, is building an outstanding career. She is poised, confident, and always wears a smile. And that's someone who only gets paid commission sales in a highly competitive field, and who faces rejection every work day of the week! What keeps her going as she faces so many closed doors? What is the main thing she credits for her top honors as a sales rep?

"Without a doubt, it's my parents," she told me.

"I deal with rejection from people every day, but I've never gotten anything but acceptance from my parents. For example, I can't think of a single time when I've been alone with my father—and I mean since I was a child—that he didn't verbally affirm me about something. Let me tell you, there are a lot of days that I draw on his praise, and it keeps me going." Now as an adult, facing criticism and stiff competition, her parents' words of praise for who she is, and what she does, are like a lighthouse on a stormy night.

The second example of the power of praise came from my son, Greg. In fact, he taught me a lesson I'll never forget about this important aspect of the blessing.

Last May, Greg married a wonderful young woman named Erin. After their honeymoon, Norma and I had the

privilege of traveling a good part of the summer with
them before they headed to graduate school and their new
home in Colorado.

In my own life, I'm always looking for ways to
strengthen my marriage and parenting skills. Perhaps
that's why, without realizing it, I began pointing out
things that I noticed in Greg's interaction with his new
bride.

If he did something I felt was somewhat insensitive, or not completely loving, I found myself taking up
Erin's defense. Without meaning to, I made him feel uncomfortable around me, even defensive.

I had no idea how deeply this affected Greg until
one night after we'd been traveling for almost four weeks.
My son pulled me aside when Norma and Erin were out
of the room and we had a "son-to-father" talk.

"Dad," he said, in a serious tone. "I need to have a
talk with you."

He outlined his feelings and concerns in a very
loving way. But sandwiched in between his words of appreciation for me, was the clear message that my "helpful" pointers were being taken as criticism of him as a
brand new husband.

As we talked, Greg reminded me of a crucial lesson. "Dad," he told me. "I'm not perfect, but I'm *trying*.
This is all new to me. Do you think that for the first year
or so, instead of concentrating on the negative things I'm
doing, you could praise me for what you see me doing
correctly? I think that would help me a lot more than what
you're doing now."

Greg's words made an immediate impact on me.
He gave me a reminder that praise is one of the most positive reinforcing tools God has given us as parents!

Since that conversation, Greg hasn't had to come
to me one time about my "help." But what he has heard
from me is consistent encouragement and praise for the
many things he is doing right.

Look for anything your children are doing, saying,
acting, or experiencing that you believe is valuable and

healthy for them, and that honors God and others. Like the fourth chapter of Philippians says, "Whatever is honorable," these are the things we should think on, and praise in our children.

Remember that even the smallest act of praise can be an encouragement to our children. Michael, our youngest, has even expressed how he appreciates seeing bumper stickers on our cars that read, "Our son and our money go to Baylor University!" I have two other smaller Baylor logos stuck on my car windows as well. Small thing, but to him they say, "I'm proud of you, I'm proud of your college and of the way you're working so hard at school."

Without question, praise inhabits the best of homes. And as our children grow older, their need for our affirmation becomes even greater, not less.

OLDER CHILDREN NEED A WRITTEN RECORD OF OUR WORDS

Written words become a lifelong legacy for a child to keep. In a letter, you can express your pride in them, or share what you're learning from the Scriptures, or what you're doing that fills them in on your life. Whether they're waiting in the mail-line in the military, reaching into their mailbox at school, or thumbing through their letters in their own home or apartment, written words of blessing from a parent are incredibly powerful.

How powerful? John was involved in a wedding several years ago where a young woman graphically demonstrated the power of written words.

At some reception dinners, words of love and blessing are easily spoken from both sets of parents. But in Angie's case, her father was a very quiet, extremely shy person. He did manage to stand up and share briefly—and nervously—how much he approved of the marriage. But then his daughter did something that expressed his love better than any speech he could have given.

Without his realizing it, since she was a young child, she had kept *every* card and note he had ever written her. Somewhat awkward with his spoken words, he eloquently expressed his love for her through written words. And she treasured and kept every one. Even recent letters that expressed how proud he was of her, and how much he looked forward to her marriage.

In front of the entire crowd (whose eyes were all filled with tears), she had her dad come up and stand beside her as she talked about how much he loved her; how meaningful his support had been over the years. And his love for her was all recorded in written blessings, captured in the several thick scrapbooks she had brought to the dinner.

With the kids out of the house, do you find yourself with a little more time? Then why not take some of that extra time and put your blessing for your children into written words. Even if they don't keep every card or letter you write in an album, they'll keep your words of love in their hearts forever. Often, our written words of love become priceless treasures when we're gone—a paper trail of love! a written memorial to our blessing to them.

If you're reading this chapter as a son or daughter, let me tell you how this same principle can be a tremendous encouragement to your parents. For years, I've greatly appreciated my daughter, Kari's, thoughtfulness in leaving Norma and me little notes around the house. Sometimes on a door, sometimes on the sink or refrigerator we'll find the words, "Mom and Dad, I was just thinking about you and wanted you to know how much I love you and look forward to the fun times we'll have in the future!" In many ways, Kari has taught the rest of us the power of written words of encouragement.

WE BLESS OLDER CHILDREN BY HELPING DRAIN ANGER OUT OF THEIR LIVES

I began my book *The Key to Your Child's Heart* by stating that the single most important factor in maintaining harmony in any home is to resolve anger as soon as possible. Even today, the single greatest problem I observe

in homes across the world is the epidemic of broken relationships, most destroyed by unchecked, unresolved anger.

Too many people are simply not aware of how
much damage anger heaps on any family or friendship. I
label this unresolved anger as "closing a person's spirit."
The more a family member "closes the spirit" of another,
the greater the disharmony and distance in the relationship, and the less interest in spiritual things you'll see.
Prolonged anger can lead to depression, ulcers, or high
blood pressure. These are just a *few* of the emotional and
physical problems that can accompany anger!

Most of us can recognize a closed spirit in another
family member. They usually won't talk with us openly or
cheerfully, and they dislike our reaching out to hug or
touch them. They tend to argue more, and we can sense
their subtle (or obvious) avoidance of us. With older children who have a great deal of anger, they may move away
at the earliest opportunity, or even deliberately choose any
path to take, except the one we've pointed them towards.

For anyone serious about reducing family friction,
blessing older children, and dealing with anger in a
healthy way, here are five brief, practical suggestions on
opening another person's closed spirit. For greater detail,
see *The Key to Your Child's Heart*.

FIVE STEPS TO REOPEN A CHILD'S SPIRIT

Years ago, I disciplined my son Greg in anger after
he was screaming while I was on the telephone. Without
finding out the reason why he was yelling, I spanked him
and watched his little spirit "close" towards me.

When I realized what I'd done, I applied the five
principles (not steps) I'll share with you, and in a matter
of minutes I witnessed his spirit reopen.

Today, almost twenty years later, I *still* use these
same principles if I see I've done something to put anger
in Greg's heart. What's more, I've even used these guidelines to help him deal with the anger others may have
placed there over the years.

1. Become tenderhearted

The first step that I needed to take to open Greg's spirit was to reflect tenderness and softness in my words. "A soft word turns away anger," the proverb says, and gentleness has a way of always melting anger.

We communicate several things to the person whom we have offended when we soften our tone. First it says, "You're valuable and important." Second, it shows that we are willing to slow down long enough to correct what has happened. Finally, by adopting gentleness we communicate that we are open to listen, that it is safe for him or her to share what has happened, and that we don't want anyone to maintain a "closed spirit" in our home.

2. Increase understanding

The second step to open a person's spirit is to increase our understanding of the pain he or she feels.

As Greg has grown older, when I have stopped to listen and softly ask Greg why he was hurting, I've found his resistance to talking begin to drain away. As my spirit became even softer, I had deeper understanding and could feel his pain. Many times just these two factors—being soft and then understanding a person's pain—will open a person's spirit.

This is particularly important as children get older. The gift of listening with understanding to an older child is often all they need to make the connection between what they're hurt or frustrated about, and dealing with that hurt in a positive way. Avoiding lectures, and increasing careful, honoring listening can be very helpful for a child of any age.

3. Recognize the offense

The third step to opening a person's spirit is admitting that we were wrong. One of the hardest things for many parents to do is to admit when they are wrong. I find it is especially hard for fathers. I do not necessarily like to find out when I am wrong, and it's not always easy to admit when I am. But I must remember that a hardened, resistant attitude is extremely detrimental to children.

One of my favorite Christian camps is Kamp Kanakuk, in beautiful Branson, Missouri. Jim Brawner was for years one of the directors of the camp (now our National Homes of Honor Director!), and one summer, he made an incredible discovery.

He asked each of the several thousand teenagers who came to camp during the summer, "What is the one thing you wish your parents would do more often?" The answer wasn't, "Say, 'I love you,'" more often, or even, "Spend more time with me." They didn't even say, "Send more money!" The overwhelming number of teenagers said the very same thing: *"I wish my mother and father would admit when they're wrong."*

There is tremendous bonding power when we become strong enough to admit our mistakes to our children. While some children may use our apology as ammunition to shoot back at us, most will be moved to a level of closeness—and a freedom from anger—that would shock you.

Softness, listening, and admitting we're wrong. These three factors are crucial, but there are two more actions that are equally important to making sure the spirit has reopened.

4. Attempt to touch

The fourth factor is attempting to touch the offended person. Why? First of all, he needs to be touched. If he reaches out and responds to our touching, then we know his spirit is opening or the anger is draining out. This is an extremely important time to take his hand, put an arm around him, or otherwise touch him in a meaningful way. Even with an older child, that touch lets him know that we care, that we love him, and that he is very important.

Second, touching often allows us to find out if the child's spirit is *not* opening. If my child pulls back or moves away when I try to touch her, it is commonly an indication that she isn't ready to open her spirit. She may need more time or greater understanding from the one who offended her.

For all the reasons we listed in the chapter on meaningful touch, we encourage you to practice appropriate hugs, handshakes, and kisses with your older children.

5. And finally, seek forgiveness when warranted

The final step we need to take is to seek forgiveness from the one we offended. When we have offended someone, we must not only be willing to admit we're wrong, but also to give that child a chance to respond. For me, the best way is to say something like, "Could you find it in your heart to forgive me?" When Greg was young, this is when I knew I had reopened Greg's spirit, for when I asked for his forgiveness, he would rush into my arms.

Once they're talking to us again, allowing us to hug them, and speaking to us in honoring tones, we can say at this point that true restoration and forgiveness has been gained. And usually, most of the anger is gone.

Praising our older children; leaving them a written legacy of our love for them; and helping to drain anger out of their life. All three are powerful ways of giving the blessing. And a fourth way is equally powerful.

GIVE THEM THE INHERITANCE OF A GOOD NAME

Not everyone can leave a $100,000 inheritance to their children, even if they want to. I remember when Norma and I were first married, her father took us out to dinner and told us we were going to receive a $100,000+ inheritance very soon. In our minds, that very night we began to spend that inheritance in one hundred different ways! Thank the Lord, we never actually went out and bought things based on his words, because the economy went into a deep slump. Her father lost all the money he had verbally promised (and far more) nearly overnight.

So, while not everyone can leave a monetary inheritance to their child, and we shouldn't always count on that kind of inheritance anyway, every one of us can leave our children the inheritance of a good name.

In Proverbs, we're told that a "good name" is better than jewels. It's a priceless gift that we can pass down to our children, and they can pass down to their children in turn. Our name is something that, no matter what, we will pass down to our kids, and it can either be a blessing to them, or a curse.

Take Darwin Smith, and his son, Darwin, Jr. While this is an extreme example, it illustrates the importance of looking ahead two, and even three generations, on the impact we have on future family members. Darwin, Sr. came from an abusive home, and the home he made for his son was incredibly unstable. He was fired from over a dozen jobs all because every boss he had was terrible. But what his instability led him to do one winter day was even more terrible still.

After being dismissed from yet another job, Darwin, Sr., took a rifle, a handgun, and pockets full of ammunition and killed four people at his former plant, and then killed himself as the police moved in. His father left a name to remember all right, only Darwin, Jr. had to carry it as well. Every day at school, and every time his name was spoken in their small community, the name his father left him became a curse, not a blessing.

How different when we see a person whose parents have loved God and spent a lifetime helping others. The name these people have leaves a sweet fragrance for those who hear it and a powerful blessing to the children and grandchildren who carry it. How is your character today? From truthfulness, to consistency, to Christlikeness, we need to leave our older children a name they can be proud of, not ashamed of.

WE BLESS OUR OLDER CHILDREN BY TAKING CARE OF OUR OWN HEALTH

While it may sound unimportant, one of the most important ways we can bless our older children is to maintain our own physical, mental, and spiritual health! When we pay attention to what we eat, the vitamins and prescription medications we take, and even exercise regularly, it's bound to help us live longer. And in my case, hopefully, it's extending my ability to be around to bless my children and their children even longer.

In my family, my father died of a massive heart attack at the age of fifty-eight. My oldest brother had a similar heart attack at age fifty-one and has had by-pass surgery since then. My next oldest brother died of a heart attack at age fifty-one.

I have the same genetic tendencies that the other Smalley men do and have had for generations—high cholesterol.

Yet instead of my health's becoming a cloud that my children have to worry about, I've done all I can to maintain a healthy life-style. Through the help of my doctors, diet, and regular exercise, I've seen my cholesterol move to a level below even the average risk factor.

For almost twenty years, I've vigorously exercised one half-hour each day—walking, tread-milling, stair climbing, bicycling, and occasionally jogging. And there's a reason. Whether we realize it or not, our children do worry about our health as we get older, even at times, more than we do. That's why actively taking care of ourselves not only blesses us physically—it's a way of giving our children the blessing as well.

Recently, I just went through a procedure, angioplasty, where a camera was literally inserted into my heart arteries, allowing a doctor to see if the Smalley "curse" of high cholesterol had caused any heart damage. The result? To my amazement, and the doctors', all the efforts and prayers I've made over the years seemed to pay off one hundredfold. I was told by the doctor when I finally awoke from the procedure,

"Smalley, get out of here and go home! You've got a 'baby' heart, it looks so good. Yours is the best looking heart I'll see in here all year."

Many supportive friends celebrated with me about how positive my health has become, but none celebrated as much as my own spouse and children. Our daughter, Kari, called me in the hospital and said, "Dad, call me the minute you get out of the operating room and tell me everything's OK. Because if it isn't, I'm jumping on a plane and coming out right now!" It's natural for our children to worry about us. However, they've seen me take an active role in doing all I can, not to become a burden on them through ill-health, and to avoid being any kind of burden to them for years to come.

While the previous five blessings for our children involve who they are in their relationships, this sixth blessing can become a tremendous, personal help to them.

TEACH THEM FINANCIAL RESPONSIBILITY

When our children were young, we were responsible for them financially. But in the years that follow, we need to teach them financial independence and responsibility.

There is a tremendous temptation to try and rush in and provide financial help, resources, or even luxuries that a grown child needs. However, at times, this can lead to over-controlling, and even short-circuiting the learning process when it comes to being financially responsible. Rather, like Sam Walton, the founder of Wal-Mart stores, we need to help our children see the value of hard work, savings, and thrift.

Norma and I see each of our children learning to work hard and plan financially for themselves and their own families. We've tried to instill within them an understanding of three important financial guidelines:

1. What do they believe God wants them to do in serving other people? The highest calling for each of us is serving people in love.

2. Once they decided on what area of serving others is best for them, anything from medicine to selling

a helpful service, they then need to commit to gain the best knowledge and practical skills possible to become an expert in that field.

3. They must continually practice and increase their skills in their chosen area of service.

I've watched God honor and reward people all over our world who have held to these three guidelines. You'll notice that the focus isn't on money. It's on serving others with an expertise that leads to their efforts being recognized and rewarded.

My children know that they can't depend on others to take care of them forever. They have to find their own plan for satisfying service, knowing that "the greatest among you is the servant of all."

AVOID OVER-CONTROLLING

As we've visited Michael, our youngest son, at college, he's mentioned many times a major problem of parenting—and blessing—older children. Namely, well-meaning children can find themselves with a parent who is far too controlling for their good.

Mike has actually told us that instead of these parents' being appreciated by their children, they look at them as actually withholding the blessing from them. One example he gave was of a junior in college who still has to call her mother every time she plans to do anything significant, either in-town or out-of-town. Instead of communicating concern, this checking-in has become a control device that her mother uses to live her own life through her daughter.

When our children are young, it's important that we remain in control as their parents. But as they grow older, there's a balance that must come into play. Namely, that we lead them by example and love, encourage them always, and support them with a listening ear or personal counsel—but not control. Rather, we should bless our children out of a desire that they take *positive control* of their own lives as they grow older.

GIVE YOUR CHILDREN THE CHANCE TO RETURN
THE BLESSING TO YOU

For me, it's easier to give a gift than to receive it. But as I've learned over the years, it's important that the blessing become a two-way street. While we need to travel the road first and give our children the blessing in every way, they also need to be able to express their blessing back to you.

Without question, one of the greatest rewards of giving your children the blessing is having them grow up one day and return it to you. That's what happened to me a few years ago, when I received something incredibly meaningful from my son.

While it might not catch your eye, if you were to walk into my (Gary's) office, you'd see something hanging on my wall that's priceless. It's not an oil painting, or a bronze sculpture. It's a small plaque that my son Greg created and gave me that carries a picture of the two of us, a father's day card, and his words of blessing returned to me.

All of us have tough, discouraging days at times. But not everyone has the words of love and appreciation I have hanging behind me. Words of blessing returned to me from my oldest son, Greg, that brighten the darkest day.

The Father's Day card that I can't read without mist gathering in my eyes says,

This Is for You

This is for you, Dad, for the father I love,
For the one who has cared all these years,
but has never heard enough about how much I care.
So this is for you,
For the one who has helped me through,

all my childhood fears and failures,
And turned all that he could,
into successes and dreams.
For the man who is a wonderful example,
of what more men should be.
For the person whose devotion to his family,
is marked by gentle strength and guidance
And whose love of life, sense of direction,
and down to earth wisdom,
make more sense to me now,
than nearly any other thing I learned.
If you never knew how much I respected you,
I want you to know it now, Dad,
and if you never knew how much I admire you,
let me just say that I think you're the best father
that any child ever had.
This is a card filled with love,
and it's all for you . . . Dad.

And then added to Adrian Rodgers' beautiful poem are my own son's words of blessing.

"Father, my wish and prayer on this special day, is that we can share another fifty years of friendship together. To the molder of my dreams, yet still, to my best friend. I love you."

Gregory T.

Greg's words are precious to me because they come out of a commitment Norma and I made years ago to provide our children with the blessing. We've looked at it as our gift to give our children to help them have a wonderful, meaningful life. But it is so humbling and encouraging when they return the blessing to us, it can make our hearts want to burst.

While I've spoken and given Greg numerous examples of my love and commitment (and Kari and Michael as well), I need to be able to receive the blessing from them, too. Not look for it. Demand it. Or pout if we don't get it. But be open to receiving it should they complete the loop by blessing us as well.

*E*ight Ways to Bless Your Older Child

1. *Praise*
2. *Written words of blessing*
3. *Drain anger from their lives*
4. *Leave a positive inheritance*
5. *Teach financial responsibility*
6. *Take care of your own health*
7. *Avoid being over-controlling*
8. *Let your children return the blessing to you*

While the applications of the blessing may change when they're older, their hearts don't change. Even grown children are waiting for words of love to be spoken and heard.

15

A CHURCH THAT GIVES THE BLESSING

Jim had struggled in his marriage, in his job as a mechanic, and in his life in general for many years. The only time he went to church was when he and his wife attended a wedding or when he was forced to attend an occasional Christmas or Easter service.

From Jim's perspective, the most encouraging place of fellowship he knew was at the bowling alley with his Wednesday night bowling league. Jim lived for Wednesday nights when he and some of the guys from work would arrive early, have a few beers, and then bowl in league play.

From the slaps on the back for making a strike, to the closeness and camaraderie of being on a team, Jim looked at bowling as a shelter to get away from the storm clouds at work and the problems with his family. Unfortunately, after an evening at the lanes, Jim still had to go back home that night and to work the next day and face the reality that his life was falling apart all around him.

During the next year, through the example and loving commitment of a new mechanic at work, Jim heard the gospel for the first time. The new mechanic's name was Ed, and he was a deeply committed Christian. Jim quickly grew to respect Ed's skill in repairing engines, but it was his personal life that Jim envied even more. Ed was not perfect, but he had an inner peace and a growing marriage that Jim longed to have. Ed did not force his belief on Jim; rather he did something much more powerful. Ed lived a positive Christian life in front of his coworker, which was like giving salt to a thirsty man.

With Jim's marriage on the rocks and with his bordering on having a drinking problem, one afternoon Jim asked Ed why his life was so different from his (Jim's). Over the next several months, Ed met regularly with Jim and taught him about his need for the Savior and the new life he could have in Christ. On a cold day just before Christmas, Jim prayed with his friend Ed to receive Christ. After thirty-seven years of failing at life on his own, Jim finally turned to the Source of life Himself to lead him and guide him.

Like Jonathan in the Old Testament, Ed was a source of blessing to his friend. His personal caring helped Jim feel secure. Jim's personal life and his marriage began to change for the better as a result of God's working in his life. Ed also encouraged Jim to attend a church where he could learn more about God's Word.

Jim and his wife did begin to attend a fairly large church near their house. This church had an outstanding reputation as a Bible-believing church. However, they never seemed to feel comfortable and accepted there. The preaching didn't bother Jim; in fact, he loved to learn from the pastor who was an excellent communicator. What hurt and confused him was the lack of personal relationships or warmth once the preaching was over.

Everyone was polite to Jim and his wife, but no one with bright eyes gave them a warm greeting, and dinner invitations after church were nonexistent. To try and develop some deeper friendships with other people at the church, they began attending a Sunday school class. However, after several months of attending the class, they were little closer to the people in the class than they were on the first Sunday they attended.

When Jim's friend Ed took a job at another auto shop out of state, Jim was crushed. He particularly ached over the lack of personal relationships with other men at the church. Since Jim had become a Christian, he had given up his Wednesday night bowling league to attend midweek services. Yet without any committed Christian friends, he was getting lonelier and lonelier. Even when he tried to initiate a conversation with someone else at church, after an initial "Hi, how are you doing?" the strain to find topics to talk about would become uncomfortable. Finally Jim gave up trying at all. There were pockets of friendly people, but Jim noticed that they were friendly to the same people week after week.

This was Jim's first experience at a church and he began to feel that somehow Christians didn't need friends. He tried to immerse himself in studying the Bible and hoped that would take away his need for meaningful relationships. However, as time went by, Jim felt more alone when he was surrounded by the people at his church than he ever had at the bowling alley. The thought of switching churches never really occurred to Jim. This was the only church he had ever gone to and he felt certain this must be what they were all like.

With his only Christian friend gone and with no one at church who took a personal interest in his life, Jim began to spend more and more time with his old friends at work. As a result, he began to slip back into the old patterns he had before he became a Christian. Unfortunately, that included beginning to drink again.

Jim stopped attending Sunday school and attended only the church service. As the weeks went by, no one in his Sunday school class called to ask why he was no longer attending or even stopped him after church to say more than "Hello." While their lack of concern may have been from a feeling of "I didn't want to pry" or "We don't want to put pressure on him," in Jim's mind their indifference confirmed to him that they didn't care. Soon his attendance at the church service was sporadic.

With all the people at this growing church, no one

seemed to miss one man who began drifting away from the fellowship; that is, until the pastor unexpectedly ran into Jim's wife one Saturday at the market.

"Hi," said the pastor. "How are you and Jim doing?" It was only an innocent question, but it was met with tears and sobs right in the middle of a supermarket aisle. "Pastor, Jim won't come back to church with me. He said that he has better friends at the bowling alley than he ever did at church."

Jim had been searching for closeness in relationships and a blessing from his church family, but he never found it. In less than ten months, Jim had gone from sitting at the midweek service at church to drinking beer again with his buddies back at the bowling alley. Perhaps Jim should have been mature enough to stay in the church and to concentrate on giving to others, never receiving love back himself, but he wasn't. And neither are many new believers just like Jim.

Is this simply the story of one man who had too little faith? We wish it were. Unfortunately this story can be told of many churches today that talk about the blessings of genuine fellowship (*koinonia*) in a sermon or in a Sunday school class, but do not practice it with people within the church. While we may not like to admit it in the evangelical community, many people who come to our churches find more of the elements of the blessing in a bowling alley than they do inside the church walls.

Instead of letting this discourage those of us inside the church, it should encourage us to learn how to be a people of blessing. We need to learn how to make significant relationships within the church, not superficial ones. From the first time God called a special people to be His own until today, we as believers have always been called to be a blessing to others.

OUR CALLING IS TO BE A PEOPLE OF BLESSING
From earliest times, God's people have been called to be a blessing. When God first came to Abraham, He gave him a very specific promise. We read: "I will bless you/And

make your name great;/And you shall be a blessing. . . .
In you all the families of the earth shall be blessed" (Gen.
12:2–3).

Centuries later, in the book of Acts, Peter tells us
what form this blessing took for all nations. The blessing
came in the body of the suffering servant, Jesus, a descen-
dant of Abraham's who has the power to bless our lives
by freeing us from sin. Peter said:

> "God . . . says to Abraham, 'Through your offspring all
> peoples on earth will be blessed.' When God raised up
> his servant, he sent him first to you to bless you by turn-
> ing each of you from your wicked ways" (3:25–26 NIV).

Introducing people to Jesus Christ is the first and
foremost way a church can bless others. When men and
women are introduced to the Source of blessing, they
come face to face with Someone who can be their best
friend and their very source of life.

If we have been called to provide people with the
blessing of knowing Christ, what is the best way to see
that happen? Let's let our Lord answer that question. "A
new commandment I give to you, that you love one another; . . . All [people] will know that you are My disciples, if you have love for one another" (John 13:34–35).
What does that mean to us?

People outside the church will never care how
much we know about Christ until they know how much
we care for each other. When a body of believers becomes
committed to loving each other, then they can truly be
called a church that is serious about winning others to
Christ.

THE BLESSING: A CHURCHWIDE GUIDELINE FOR LOVING OTHERS

If Jesus commanded us to be people who deeply love each
other, why do so many churches struggle with being
warm and sensitive to the needs of others? Is it a lack of
loving people in the church?

We fully believe that it is not the lack of caring believers in the church that results in people like Jim going away unblessed. Rather, these people lack the knowledge about how they can practically meet the relational needs other people have once they come to know Christ.

The church needs to be first and foremost a place where the gospel is preached and where Christ is honored as our Lord and Savior. But God designed the church to be a caring community as well. We can't escape the fact that when we fail to bless and love our brothers and sisters in Christ, we are failing in our duties as a family of God. When one member of the body rejoices, we should all rejoice. When one member weeps, we should all weep (1 Cor. 12:26).

The exciting thing about the concept of the blessing is that it can be a guideline for all kinds of loving relationships. Obviously it can provide a tangible way for parents to bless their children. We have also seen how a marriage and even an intimate friendship can be built up by the elements of the blessing. However, it doesn't stop there. Some churches today train and encourage their people to provide each aspect of the blessing to others. And thankfully more and more churches are learning to do this training.

In fact, show us a church anywhere in the world that is meeting the genuine needs of its members and drawing others to Christ, and we'll show you a church where God's Word is being taught and where the relationship elements of the blessing are being applied.

What happens when a church, or even a department within a church, gets hold of the concept of the blessing? Let's look at how the principles of the blessing, applied in one church's singles department, literally turned their ministry around.

A CASE STUDY OF APPLYING THE BLESSING WITH GOD'S PEOPLE

Mark was the leader of a large singles Sunday school class. In fact, on any given Sunday, they could have more than 150 young men and women in attendance. Like many church groups, Mark's class struggled with the problems of turnover and building deep relationships. They had the heart for ministry to others, but that caring desire never seemed to move out of their class leaders' meetings and into their class.

Almost two years ago, we shared the principles in this book at a conference Mark attended. He jumped on every bit of information we could give him about the blessing and asked us to speak at a class retreat he had coming up. God used that conference Mark attended and the ensuing class retreat to plant the biblical principles of the blessing within the hearts of the people in the class.

We found out only a few months ago that after the retreat, Mark formed a group of people within the class called the Blessing Bunch. Their goal was to identify people in the class who particularly needed one or more elements of the blessing and then actively to commit themselves to be the person who provided that need.

With one young lady in the class who had broken an engagement, providing the blessing meant simply taking her hands and crying with her. For a man, it involved a brother in Christ picturing a special future for him that gave him the confidence to tackle a difficult new assignment. Still another woman needed to know she was of high value to her friend and to the Lord after a week of listening to her employer say she was worthless.

Having a strategy for meeting needs within the group by teaching and applying the elements of the blessing became a real help to this leader. In fact, Mark talked about the principles of blessing so much, many of the class members would say to each other in fun, "Have you had your blessing this week?"

"Have you had your blessing this week?" These people meant this as a joke, yet making the people in that class aware of the elements of the blessing opended many doors of ministry, doors to a number of men's and women's lives that had once been tightly closed. But what happened in this singles group did not stay confined to their classroom. Giving the blessing began to spread throughout the entire church.

Several of the members of the class became convicted about their relationships with their parents as they learned about the concept of the blessing. One young man in particular walked out of the classroom one Sunday morning and right to a pay phone where he called his father for the first time in more than four years. Other people began to share the principles of the blessing with their family members at the church and it, too, led to a time of healing.

The singles class even talked about the concept of the blessing at a Sunday evening service a few weeks following their retreat. One thing Mark shared was that the married people in the church could bless the singles by not expecting them to get married tomorrow and by inviting them into their homes. This began an "adopt a single" program that helped bring a once nearly isolated group into the mainstream of church life.

This story is of just one department that decided to get serious about blessing other people in their lives. The results spread throughout the entire church and helped bring a new sense of warmth and caring to many people.

Imagine what would happen if an entire church decided to bless those in their fellowship and were trained how to do it! We would have a church where relationship needs were actively being met by a welcoming handshake or hug (meaningful touch); where appreciation for a fine sermon, working in the children's department, or simply listening to a hurting brother or sister was verbally acknowledged (spoken message). We would have groups of believers who acknowledged every member's true worth (attaching high value) and who gave them words of hope and encouragement to reach their God-given potential (a special future). All these elements would be wrapped in the willingness to let people fail and not let them walk away unnoticed, because a decision had been made already that they were valuable (an active commitment).

This church sounds like the kind of church most of us would like to belong to, and it can be. All it takes is one person to start a Blessing Bunch to begin to meet the needs of those around them. Even more than that, this kind of church can become the kind of place that those outside the church long to be a part of, a true place of blessing.

A church that is committed to applying the principles of the blessing can make a tremendous impact on the unsaved. Once church members learn about this concept and experience it within the church, they can begin to transport it outside the church walls. Monday through Saturday they can provide the elements of God's blessing to a non-Christian society desperately in search of genuine security and acceptance.

An employer can evaluate how well he or she is doing in being a blessing to his or her employees. A school teacher can learn about the blessing and recognize the telltale signs of a child's growing up without parental acceptance. A student can befriend a fellow classmate and point him or her toward a secure source of blessing through Christ.

HITTING THE TARGET WHEN IT COMES TO LOVING EACH OTHER

Aristotle once observed, "You stand a far greater chance of hitting the target if you can see it." At first glance, this statement might not sound too profound, but it really is. Churches, parents, spouses, and friends stand a far better chance of hitting the target of loving each other if they can see how to do it.

Following the guidelines provided in the blessing can help our words and actions score a bull's-eye when we want to communicate God's love and acceptance to our loved ones. Coupled with sound teaching from the Word of God, the elements of the blessing can also provide a tremendous tool for evangelism. The blessing can even help us fulfill the Great Commission to "Go therefore and make disciples of all the nations" (Matt. 28:19). If the mark of disciples is that they "love one another" (John 13:34), applying the principles of the blessing can help God's love radiate to a needy world.

As we end our look at how the blessing applies to our church family, we are nearing the end of our journey in this book. However, we have one more important stop to make. There are two people in our lives who can especially profit from a blessing we can give them—our parents.

Before we look at how we as children can give back a blessing to our parents, let's listen to the words of a song that capture the kind of place the church needs to be: a shelter for those who have faced the storms of life, and a place where God's love radiates to a needy world; a place where the blessing is given to others and where authenticity is a password to fellowship. A place Ken Medema pictures in these haunting words:[1]

If This Is Not a Place . . .

If this is not a place, where tears are understood,
then where shall I go to cry?
And if this is not a place, where my spirit can take
wings, then where shall I go to fly?
I don't need another place, for trying to impress you,
with just how good and virtuous I am,
No, no, no, I don't need another place, for always
being on top of things. Everybody knows that it's a
sham, it's a sham.
I don't need another place for always wearing smiles,
even when it's not the way I feel,
I don't need another place, to mouth the same old
platitudes; everybody knows that it's not real.
So if this is not a place, where my questions can be
asked, then where shall I go to seek?

And if this is not a place, where my heart cry can be
heard, where, tell me where, shall I go to speak?
So if this is not a place, where tears are understood,
*where shall I go, where shall I go to fly?**

16

A FINAL BLESSING

We hope that discovering more about the blessing in the Scriptures has challenged each of you to have a new reason and a new way to honor your parents, your children, your spouse, your friends, and your church family. Our prayer for each reader is that your life will be one where each element of the blessing is given and received.

Remember, we build the blessing into a person's life on a daily basis. You never know what small act of love and encouragement will be the one that your children, spouse, or friends remember as a key way in which you blessed them. How do we know this? In seminars throughout the country and in numerous counseling sessions with couples and individuals, we asked people this question: "What is one specific way you knew that you had received your parents' blessing?" Let's look at how one hundred people responded to this question. Through their responses we can discover how powerful a parent's everyday actions and attitudes are in communicating the blessing to their children.

One Hundred Homes That Gave the Blessing to Children

1. My parents would take the time to really listen to me when I talked to them by looking directly into my eyes.

2. We were often spontaneously getting hugged even apart from completing a task or chore.

3. They would let me explain my side of the story.

4. We went camping as a family. (This response was repeated often.)

5. They would take each of us out individually for a special breakfast with Mom and Dad.

6. My father would put his arm around me at church and let me lay my head on his shoulder.

7. I got to spend one day at Dad's office, seeing where he worked and meeting the people he worked with.

8. My mother always carried pictures of each of us in her purse.

9. They would watch their tone of voice when they argued.

10. My parents made sure that each one of us kids appeared in the family photos.

11. My parents would make a special Christmas ornament for each child that represented a character trait we had worked on that year.

12. They were willing to admit when they were wrong and say "I'm sorry."

13. They had a "king or queen for a day meal" for us that would focus individual attention on each child.

14. As a family we often read and discussed the book *The Velveteen Rabbit*, which talks about how valuable we are.

15. I saw my parents praying for me even when I didn't feel I deserved it.

16. My folks wrote up a special "story of my birth" that they read to me every year.

17. We read Psalm 139 as a family and discussed how God had uniquely and specially designed each of us children.

18. They attended all of my open houses at school.

19. My father loved me by loving my mother.

20. They would tell us character traits we possessed that would help us be good marriage partners when we grew up and got married.

21. My mother would tell us "make believe" bedtime stories that illustrated positive character traits she felt we had.

22. They tried to be consistent in disciplining me.

23. My mom was always willing to help me with my math homework.

24. My folks really tried to help me think through where I should go to college.

25. My dad would constantly tell me that whoever I married, he'd be committed to him and our children for life.

26. My parents openly discussed and helped me set limits in the sexual area.

27. My mother and father would ask us children our opinions on important family decisions.

28. When my father was facing being transferred at work, he purposely took another job so that I could finish my senior year in high school at the same school.

29. My mom had a great sense of humor, but she never made us kids the brunt of her jokes.

30. My parents wouldn't change things in my bedroom without asking me if it was OK with me.

31. My folks pursued resolving conflict with me instead of letting issues build up.

32. When I wrecked my parents' car, my father's first reaction was to hug me and let me cry instead of yelling at me.

33. My dad could correct me without getting all emotional or lecturing me.

34. My parents were patient with me when I went through my long hair stage in high school.

35. My mother tried really hard to keep her promises to me.

36. My dad would ask me all the time, "What would it take for this to be a 'great year' for you?" and then try to see that it was.

37. Even though my dad had played football in college, he never forced me to go out for sports when I didn't want to.

38. At least once a year around my birthday, my dad would take me out of school for a special lunch where he would let me know I was special to him.

39. My parents would tell me over and over that I was a good friend to my friends.

40. Even when I was in high school, my father sometimes would tuck me into bed like when I was little.

41. My mother would pray with me about important decisions I was facing, or even that I would have a good day at school.

42. When I was thirteen, my dad trusted me to use his favorite hunting rifle when I was invited to go hunting with a friend and his father.

43. We would have "family meetings" every two weeks where everyone would share their goals and problems.

44. If it was really cold, my mom would get up early and drive me on my paper route.

45. When I had my appendix out, my parents were right there with me before and after the operation.

46. Sometimes when I would get home from school, my mother would have left a plate of cookies on the counter with a special note saying she loved me.

47. My parents used to take me and a friend out for a special dinner sometimes.

48. When I had a teacher that didn't like me, my parents defended me and stood up for me.

49. My mother got interested in computers just because I was interested in them.

50. They could have just shipped my stuff, but my parents drove a U-Haul trailer over 1,800 miles when I went off to college.

51. My dad gave up smoking because he knew how much it bothered Mom and us kids.

52. My father taught me how to budget my money.

53. Even though I didn't like it at the time, the chores my parents made me do helped me learn responsibility.

54. My parents would always make sure I knew why I was being disciplined.

55. My father let me go with him on some of his business trips.

56. I realize now how hard my mother worked to take care of us all.

57. My parents were good examples to me of how a Christian marriage should function.

58. When I was down about my boyfriend breaking up with me, my father took extra time just to listen to me and cry with me.

59. My parents never acted like they were perfect, and they never expected us to be perfect either.

60. Now that I'm an adult, I really appreciate how my father taught me to communicate with him. That has helped me know how to talk to my husband now that I'm married.

61. My mother would let me explain my point of view on issues—even when she disagreed with me. She always made me feel that my opinion was important.

62. My parents didn't compare my abilities with those of my older brother or the other kids at school, but helped me see my own unique value.

63. My parents allowed me to give back to them when I got older, like picking up the tab at dinner.

64. I appreciated my father working to keep a good relationship with me when I was a teenager. I can see now that helped keep me from some really bad dating relationships.

65. When I asked for it, my mother would give me advice on dating and other areas of my life.

66. I always had the best sack lunch at school of anybody in my class.

67. My folks were always willing to hang in there with me and help me work through conflicts with my friends.

68. My father went with me when I had to take back an ugly dress a saleswoman had talked me into buying.

69. My mother was always interested in what I was doing at school, but she wasn't interfering.

70. My father acted more excited about getting to spend time with us kids than he did about working at the office.

71. My father helped me buy an old Mustang that had been wrecked and worked with me to rebuild it into a beautiful car.

72. I never felt like I had to perform to gain my father's approval.

73. My father worked with me for hours on my soap-box derby racer.

74. Some people's parents criticize them behind their backs, but I was always hearing something positive from my parents' friends that my parents had said about me.

75. My mother had a Bible study with me every Monday morning before I went to school.

76. Even though I didn't appreciate it at the time, I know that my parents were protecting me by putting a curfew on when I had to be in on a date.

77. When I first started wearing make-up, my mother never made fun of how much time I spent in front of the mirror.

78. Even when I was very overweight in high school, my parents still made me feel I was attractive.

79. My mom took on a part-time job to help me earn enough money to go to a Christian summer camp.

80. My parents paid for me to take several vocational tests when I was struggling to find out what I wanted to do for a living.

81. My father would reward me for a job well done on the yard by taking me to Dairy Queen where we would both get a sundae.

82. My father let me share in his failures as well as his successes.

83. My father went with me to six different used car dealers to help me find my first car.

84. My parents would always make sure that each of us children was introduced to their friends when they came over to our house.

85. My parents quit using a "nickname" that really hurt me.

86. My mom used to rub my legs after cheerleader practice.

87. My father would always point out my good table manners to others.

88. My mother would see to it that I had the necessary tools to complete a project (crayons, ruler, and so on).

89. My father would put a special note on our pillows when he had to go out of town on business.

90. My parents would involve the whole family in planning family vacations.

91. My father took me and my sisters out on a very special date on our sixteenth birthdays.

92. They would always go to my piano recitals and act interested.

93. My father would let me practice pitching to him for a long time when he got home from work.

94. We used a special red plate at dinner to designate birthdays or outstanding achievements.

95. Every Saturday morning, my father would get up before anybody else and cook us all pancakes and bacon.

96. We always went out to eat as a family after church and discussed what we had learned at Sunday school.

97. My father would ask to talk to each of us kids personally when he called in from a trip.

98. We would all hold hands together when we said grace; then when we finished, we would squeeze the person's hand next to us three times, which stood for the three words, "I love you."

99. My mother would slow down when I helped her cook to let us accomplish the task together.

100. Even though I had never seen him cry before, my father cried during my wedding because he was going to miss me no longer being at home.

Sounds like a lot of small things, doesn't it? Yet these small acts of love and acceptance left a lasting impression on these people's hearts. Each act was actually a decision a parent made to provide an element of the blessing to a child. A blessing that even now, years later, is remembered and cherished.

We could have included a list of "one hundred ways to bless your spouse, friends, or church family," but we're sure you get the idea. Providing the blessing to those we love can encourage and enrich their lives. It also does wonders for the one giving the blessing as well. We have looked at the children of one hundred families who provided the elements of the blessing to their children. Our prayer is that your family will become number one hundred and one.

A PERSONAL MESSAGE

As we close this book and our look at the blessing, we hope you've been encouraged and challenged to be a person of blessing. But we don't want to leave you with just our thoughts on these pages. We would also like to leave you with our blessing for your life.

If we could reach out to each of you reading this book right now, and place our hands on your shoulder, our final blessing to you would be the words of Aaron, in the Old Testament (Num. 6:24–26).

May God enable you to become a mighty source of blessing, and may these words always ring true in your life:

"The LORD bless you and keep you;

The LORD make His face to shine upon you,

And be gracious to you;

The LORD lift up His countenance upon you,

And give you peace."

Gary Smalley   John Trent

Appendix A

*I*t's good to talk or read about the blessing, but putting its elements into practice is even better. That's why we want to give you four sample "Evenings of Blessing" that you can adapt and use with your loved ones.

What follows are suggestions we have either tried ourselves or know have been successful with other people or groups. The best way to use them is to take ideas from the sample evenings that follow and add your own special touches. (Then write us at Today's Family, Route 4, P.O. Box 2211, Branson, MO 65616, and tell us the ways of blessing you've come up with and how your evening went. We're always looking for new ways to bless people and would love to hear yours.)

None of these ideas is sacred. One husband actually had a "Morning of Blessing" instead of an "Evening of Blessing" for his wife that included breakfast in bed. Be creative and have fun. Most of all, know that you can waste precious time on a thousand different things, but you will never waste one minute in blessing your loved ones.

AN EVENING OF BLESSING FOR YOUR CHILDREN

Goal: That your children will know and experience your love for them in a special setting and in a unique way.

Basic Idea: Whether this evening happens once or several times a year, each child in the family would have a time when he or she experiences the elements of the blessing from his or her parents (or parent in a single-parent home).

Possible Program: We know several people who have tied their time of blessing in with a birthday celebration. Again, feel free to vary these suggestions so that they bless your uniquely special child.

1. Give your child(ren) several days' notice that this evening is coming. Half the fun for children is anticipating an event, particularly when it involves a special time for them!

2. Ask your child ahead of time what his or her favorite meal would be and use that as your guide for a festive dinner to begin the evening. Be prepared for peanut butter and hot dogs as a main course, topped off with chocolate cake for dessert (and then Rolaids on the side). Remember, this is your opportunity to honor them. That doesn't mean that you can't sneak in a vegetable or something nutritious, but it should be a meal your child feels is fit for that "king" or "queen" in your household.

3. Beginning with holding hands when you say grace at the meal, meaningful touching or hugging should be part of this time of blessing.

4. You can bless your children with a spoken message in several ways, attaching high value to them and providing them with the picture of a special future. Here are a few things you could try after dinner.

- Put together a slide show or picture album showing each year of the child's life that you have on film.
- Each parent can list five to ten things about that child that the parent has appreciated over the

past year. (Try to pick character traits as well as accomplishments.)

- Each parent could also say a word about how these character traits will help the son or daughter be a godly, helpful, or loving person in the years to come.
- Pick out an everyday object and use it as a word picture to share praise with your child, or to point out a talent God could use in the future. One dad we know used a sponge to picture his son! "Henry," he said, "this past year you've reminded me of a sponge. You've soaked up your Sunday school lessons like a sponge and then squeezed out big drops of love all over your little brothers and sister and your mom and me."
- Present your child with a homemade gift. This isn't the time for an early Christmas present. Make sure if you do give a gift it's something that your fingerprints are all over. One mother we know gave her daughter a beautiful afghan she had spent months working on that became the beginning of her daughter's hope chest.
- Some parents like to write out a "story of their child's birth" and read it to their child. This story talks about the special events of the nine months before birth, their mad dash to the hospital, and the indescribable joy of seeing their little one for the first time. It blesses children to know that they were planned and looked forward to (regardless of whether they came in our timing or not).

5. While it can be short, take the time to formally bless and pray for your child. (Be sure to look at Appendix B to see several sample blessings based on scriptural passages you may want to use.)

- Sing a hymn or a familiar chorus as a way of transition from slides or a fun story.

- Candles fascinate children (and many adults).
  The lighting of candles is an important part of
  blessing children in orthodox Jewish homes, and
  it's something you might want to try. This act
  can also be a good way to get the other children
  in the family involved.
- If your denomination permits, sharing Communion with older children is especially meaningful.
  This can also be a time to ask forgiveness if we
  have offended anyone in the family and a chance
  to focus together on the cup of the blessing that
  represents Christ's love for us.
- Write out a few short sentences for you to read
  that express your love and appreciation for your
  child. This would be a special time to lay your
  hand on the child's shoulder or head while you
  bless him or her. Whether as a prayer, or with
  eyes open, your words can be something like the
  simple blessing below. Here's an example of a
  blessing for a boy named Joseph. (Again, look in
  Appendix B for other examples based on scriptural passages.)

"Thank You, Lord, for our son, Joseph. We ask that
You be the source of his joy and the Source of his life.
Help us as parents to love Joseph as You would have us
love him. Thank You for the way he is already growing
into the unique person You designed him to be. Lord, we
know how special Joseph is to You, and tonight may he
realize how valuable he is to us now and forever. May he
become all You intend him to be, and we are honored that
we are his parents. Bless us all now, for it's in Jesus' name
we pray."

Closing comments: Again, these are just a few suggestions on how you could design an evening of blessing
for your children. For some children, ending the evening
with a special family activity or even a VCR movie they
have picked out would be a "10" to them. Others may
just want to talk to you or have a hug. However you de-

sign this evening, it can be a special and meaningful time for you and your children.

AN EVENING OF BLESSING FOR YOUR SPOUSE

Goal: To set aside a meaningful time to provide your husband or wife with each of the elements of the blessing.

Basic Idea: Plan an evening for your spouse that will be a memorable time as he or she experiences your love and high value for him or her. While this evening can adopt some of the same elements that were a part of blessing a child, you can personalize this time for a husband or wife in several ways.

Possible Program: An anniversary is always a good time to provide a spouse with an evening of blessing. However, any evening apart from the children and away from the phone will do.

1. If there is money available, you might want to consider going to a hotel room for the night. Many nice hotels and resorts have special weekend rates when their weekday business guests are gone. If money is tight, why not try swapping houses with a close friend for one night. This means that you trade houses with another couple for one night (leaving your kids for them to babysit) and agree to swap with them at some future date. Swapping houses cuts the cost way down and still lets you have the privacy to really focus on each other.

2. As with the times of blessing in the Scriptures, a special meal is always a great way to start things off. Remember to include your spouse's favorite dish. Even if you have a coupon for a steak dinner, if he or she would rather have fish, honor that request.

3. You can communicate your love to your spouse by expressing your commitment to your marriage and by pointing out several of your spouse's endearing qualities. Here are some practical ways to do that:

- Write a "story of our marriage" where you recapture some of the drama and excitement of your courtship and of each season of your marriage. If you're not a writer, try making a tape recording of your fond memories. While talking into a microphone may seem a little awkward at first, this can leave a lasting record for your spouse of some of the things you appreciate about him or her.

- Photographs of special times together can be very endearing. Pictures bring back memories and memories bring back feelings. Just looking again at a few happy times you have shared together (without going overboard and showing ten trays of slides of your one fishing trip together) can do wonders to set a positive tone for the evening.

- Select one or several everyday objects to use as a word picture to communicate things you appreciate about your spouse. One husband used a bottle of "White Out" correcting fluid as a word picture to praise his wife. "Sweetheart," he said, "you remind me of this little bottle of 'White Out.' Every time I make a mistake or do something to hurt you, you cover over my faults with your love like covering mistakes on a page. Every day with you, I get to start with a clean sheet of paper." Don't underestimate the power of such pictures! As we have stressed before, word pictures can leave a lasting positive impression on your spouse.

- One way to picture a special future for your spouse is to dig out your original wedding vows and repeat them. Something else that is special is to write a new set of vows that expresses your love and commitment. If you did not memorize and repeat your own set of vows during your wedding, here's your chance to do it!

Appendix B can give you some good ideas that you can apply to blessing your spouse.

- If your denomination permits, partaking in Communion as you re-commit your life to your

spouse can be a beautiful and meaningful part of
an evening of blessing.
- List ten reasons why, of all the guys or girls in
the world, you would choose your spouse again
to be your life-partner.
- Take an extended time to pray together, thanking
God for each other and asking God to keep your
love as fresh and refreshing as spring.

4. Since you've gone to all the trouble to get away
for the weekend, meaningful touching as a married couple
can take on a whole new meaning after a special evening
of sharing words of love and commitment.

AN EVENING FOR CHILDREN
TO BLESS THEIR PARENTS

Goal: For children who have now grown up to take a special time to provide the elements of the blessing to their
parents.

Basic Idea: Many parents are used to giving the elements of the blessing to their children, but they may not
be as used to receiving them in return. In this evening,
children have a chance to give back words of love and acceptance that they have received as a way of honoring
their parents.

(If one parent has died or if your parents are divorced, do not avoid such an evening simply because it
might remind the parent too much of the departed loved
one. While we need to be sensitive, we can still honor the
memory of a parent who has died and provide needed
words of love and encouragement to the parent who remains behind. If your parents are divorced, at another
private time you could share a time of blessing with your
other parent.)

Possible Program: You might want to turn to the end
of Chapter Thirteen to see some of the ways Don and his
brother and sisters designed a special evening of blessing
for their parents. Each set of parents is different, and it
can be difficult for some parents to receive these words of

love from their children. However, time and time again we have heard that embarrassed or uncomfortable parents have warmed up to their children's words of blessing and then treasured them for the rest of their lives.

PLEASE NOTE: While grandchildren are special in and of themselves to their grandparents, for this one evening they should be left at home with a babysitter. Children are wonderful and delightful, but they can also be distracting. The children should have their special time of blessing. This should be a time to focus all our attention on our parents.

1. If possible, try to gather each brother and sister together for this time of blessing. If someone absolutely can't make it for some reason, get them to send a tape recording of some words of blessing they can share with their parents. Why a tape? Listening to a person's voice has a way of putting them right in the room with you. Also, like taping the entire evening, it can give a parent a record of this missing child's thoughts.

2. What would an evening of blessing be without a special dinner! Parents like to eat, too—especially if you cook some of their favorite items, and then forbid them to help clean up the dishes.

3. Slides or old family photo albums can be a tremendous tool for remembering fun times in the past as a family. Again, don't overdo it. Remember the words Jack Benny once said to a reporter who asked him, "What do you want to be remembered for?" Benny replied, "I would like to have carved on my tombstone, 'Here lies a man who never bored his friends with home movies!'" Pictures won't be boring to your parents, but be sensitive about how many you show.

4. Each child can then share five positive character traits that their parents built into their life. In other words, how are you a different person today because of the parents God has given you? Don and his brother and sisters shared in this way and it had an incredible impact. As you can tell, this activity will take some advance planning

and careful thought on the part of each child. But the results will be well worth it.

5. Homemade gifts or a special portrait of the children might make a special gift for your parents at an evening of blessing.

6. Let's not forget how an everyday object used as a word picture can bring encouragement to your parents' hearts. One person we know told her mother, "Mom, when we were growing up, you reminded me of a fork. Your eyes were always sharp enough to catch us when we were doing something wrong, and you had more than one good point!" While you may not want to use a fork, we're sure at least twenty objects in the very room you're sitting in could be used to point out the high value of your parents.

7. A special time of prayer for our parents, with everyone gathered around them arm in arm, can be a memorable way to close such an evening. Don't expect this to be an emotionless time. While we can share love with each other by laughing together, it is also healing to cry together. This is not to say we should try to force any emotions, but rather allow both tears and laughter to be a part of the evening.

Closing Comments: Many people wait too long to share words of blessing with their parents, or they simply don't know how to do it. Armed with all the suggestions above, what's stopping you from honoring your parents with an evening of blessing? Forget about giving them an all-expense-paid trip to the Bahamas as a way of showing you love them. Expressing your love and appreciation for them is the best present you could ever give them. (But don't let them know you substituted their trip to the Bahamas for this time of blessing!)

AN EVENING OF BLESSING WITH YOUR CHURCH FAMILY

You say it has been too long since you had a church pot-luck dinner? Here's a special evening with your church family that can help you get to know new people, honor those who have served the Lord in a special way, and learn more about blessing God all in one!

Goal: To provide an evening when our church family can come together to bless each other and bless the Lord.

Basic Idea: Invite church families to a potluck dinner that centers around the theme of "blessing."

Possible Program: Talk about having fun while you're doing something meaningful. Watching a popular television program can't hold a candle to the excitement and light of God's love that can flow through a time when the church family is gathered to bless each other.

1. Ask each family to bring a main course to feed their own family, and then a dish to share that says something about their roots. For example, one family's origins might be Swedish and they could bring Swedish meatballs. Another family might be French and they could bring pastries or even French onion soup. If they are all-American they can bring hot dogs or even apple pie. If they're not up on their ethnic roots, they could bring a dish that represents their geographical roots. For example, if one family is from Washington State, they could bring baked apples. Each family should label their dish as to its origins. Sharing a meal like this is a great way to get to know a little bit about the background of people in the church.

2. As an admission ticket to get into the dinner, each adult should be required to bring a verse from the Bible that has been a blessing in his or her life. Just before grace is said, or later in the program, the pastor or program leader can randomly call on a table and have someone there share his or her favorite verse. Or each person could share his or her verse with the others at the table as a way to encourage each other and get to know each other better.

3. You will bless the children and parents who attend by providing child care for the little ones before the more serious part of the evening begins. After the meal

would be a good time to have the little ones march out to a movie or to special games.

4. We are told in the Scriptures to bless the Lord. What better way to do so than with our church family and friends. Here are some ways this can happen during the evening program:

- Sing several songs in your hymnal that focus on the theme of God's blessing us or our blessing Him. Hymns or choruses like "Make Me a Blessing" and "Bless the Lord, O My Soul" can be a meaningful way to bless our Lord with song.
- We are told to bless God's holy name. Ask the pastor or a church leader to talk briefly about the names of God in the Scriptures and how each name gives us a new reason to praise Him.
- Communion is a tremendous way for us to come face to face with God's priceless blessing in sacrificing His Son for our sins. Even the Scriptures tell us that Communion is a "blessing." In 1 Corinthians 10:16 we read, "The cup of blessing which we bless, is it not the communion of the blood of Christ?" In keeping with preparation for Communion, perhaps if someone in the congregation has dishonored someone else in some way, he or she can be encouraged to go to that person and ask his or her forgiveness to set things right.
- In some churches, a foot-washing service could be another way to bow the knee to our brother or sister in Christ by humbling ourselves to wash another's feet.
- One church had a large, blank poster at the front of the room. Each table had pencils, paper, and straight pins. After a short message on how faithful God had been in blessing the congregation over the years, the pastor asked people to write down one way in which God had blessed them over the past year. Then anyone who

wanted could come up to the front, read or share
how God had blessed them, and pin their paper
on the blank poster. By the end of the evening,
dozens of testimonies to God's gracious blessings
were pinned to that poster.

- This time can even be used to bless other people
in the church for a job well done or simply for
being a good friend or godly example. You might
even want to ask people to come prepared to
share word pictures that illustrate traits they appreciate about another member of the congregation.

- Close the ceremony of blessing by holding hands
and singing a closing chorus or benediction. If
the early church could greet each other with a
holy hug and kiss, we should at least be able to
take each other's hands as we close this time of
blessing.

Can you imagine what would happen if parents,
spouses, adult children, and even entire churches put
these evenings of blessing into practice? So many people's
lives would change for the better that it would drive us
out of a job when it comes to marriage and family counseling. And we'd love it! We hope you'll adopt even one
evening of blessing described above as a model for design-
ing one of your own and that it will prove to be one of the
most encouraging times in your loved one's and your own
life.

Appendix B

SAMPLE BLESSINGS BASED ON THE SCRIPTURES

*These are some ways that you can bless your children or even
your mate by inserting his or her name where
the blank is on each passage.*

How blessed _____ will be because you do
not walk in the counsel of the wicked, nor stand in the
path of sinners, nor do you sit in the seat of scoffers. But
as your parents we have seen you delight in the law of the
Lord. You have been thinking about His law day and
night. May God make you, _____, like a tree
firmly planted by streams of water. May God allow you to
grow and bear His fruit in His season and your life will
not wither and whatever you shall do, it will prosper!"
(Psalm 1)

"O Lord may _____ always abide in
Thy love. May [he] dwell in Your holy presence. May [he]
walk with integrity and do works of righteousness. May
[he] speak truth in [his] heart and not slander with [his]

tongue nor do evil to [his] friends, nor get revenge on [his] friends.

"May _____ despise being a reprobate and value those who honor You. May [he] always keep [his] word for the good of others and not cheat [his] friends or use their misfortune for [his] benefit, nor take bribes against the innocent. Consequently You Lord, have promised that _____ will never be shaken." (Psalm 15)

"O Lord, may _____ come to know Your wisdom and instruction. May [he] discern the sayings of understanding, may [he] receive the instruction in wise behavior, righteousness, justice, and equity. May You Lord give [him] prudence, knowledge, and discretion. May [he] truly listen and increase in learning, always seeking wise counsel. May [he] come to understand the greatest of all Your instructions, to love and value You with all [his] heart. Then will [he] begin to know knowledge." (Proverbs 1)

"Lord, may _____ trust in You with all [his] heart and may [he] not lean on [his] own understanding. But may [he] seek to know what You would want [him] to do in all [he] does. Then You have promised to make [his] paths straight." (Proverbs 3:5–6)

"May _____ never try to be wise in [his] own eyes, but may [he] learn to value You above all else and keep turning away from evil ways and thinking.

"Then You have promised to heal [his] body and refresh [his] bones." (Proverbs 3:7–8)

"Lord, may _____ never lose the willingness to turn from reproof. Behold then You have promised to pour out Your spirit on [him] and to make Your words known to [him]! If [he] does not turn to Your ways You have also promised to refuse to listen to [his] cry or grab [his] hand in distress.

"May _____ never neglect Your counsel nor turn from Your counsel nor turn from Your reproof." (Proverbs 1:23–25)

"My [son or daughter] _____:
If you will:

- Receive and believe what God says
- Treasure with high value His commandments
- Listen attentively to His wisdom
- Draw your heart to understanding Him
- Cry out for discernment
- Raise your voice for understanding
- Seek Him more than silver or hidden treasures

"Then you, _____, will understand how to honor God.
"God will give you knowledge and wisdom. From Him you will receive understanding for God has been storing up wisdom for you because you have sought Him above all else.
"He will be your shield, your bodyguard, and He will preserve your way." (Proverbs 2:1–8)

"Oh Lord, may _____ never forget Your teaching. Let [his] heart keep Your commandments. Then, Lord, You will give _____ many more days and years to [his] life and You will add peace to [his] life.
"May kindness and truth never leave [him]. Lord, may [he] bind them around [his] neck and write them on [his] heart.
"Then, Lord, You will give [him] favor and a good reputation both with You and man." (Proverbs 3:1–4)

Notes

Chapter Two

1. Gerhard Kittel & Geoffrey W. Bromiley, *Theological Dictionary of the New Testament, Vol.II* (Grand Rapids, MI: W. B. Eerdmans Publishing Co., 1964), p. 755.

2. Francis Brown, S. R. Driver, and Charles A. Briggs, *A Hebrew and English Lexicon of the Old Testament* (Oxford: Clarendon Press, reprinted edition, 1974), p. 139.

3. David Hunt & T. A. McMahon, *The Seduction of Christianity* (Eugene, Ore.: Harvest House, 1985), pp. 28–29.

4. Nathan Ausbubel, *The Book of Jewish Knowledge* (New York: Crown Publishers, 1964), p. 98.

5. J. A. Thompson, *The Bible and Archaeology* (Grand Rapids: Wm. B. Eerdmans Publishing, 1972 edition), p. 26.

6. K. A. Kitchen, *Ancient Orient and Old Testament* (Chicago: Inter-Varsity Press, 1966), p. 154.

7. C. H. Gordon, "Illustrations from Pre-Nuzi Data on Biblical Archaeology," *The Biblical Archaeologist*, vol. 3, 1940, p. 5.

8. Changing the blessing between children was indeed quite common in the Ancient Near East during Biblical times. For example, a father named Tupkitilla of Nuzi sold one son's blessing to another for three sheep! C. H. Gordon, *Tyndale House Bulletin*, vol. 17, (1966), p. 71.

9. Ausbubel, *Book of Jewish Knowledge*, p. 355.

10. A. Cohen, *Everyman's Talmud* (New York: Schocken Books, 1975), p. 171.

11. Ibid.

12. How do we know that this group of children was both boys and girls? The Greek word used for *young children* in Mark

10:13 is *paidion*. (See William F. Arndt and R. Wilbur Gingrich, eds., *A Greek-English Lexicon of the New Testament and other Early Christian Literature* [Chicago: University of Chicago Press, 1957, p. 609].) This was a general word used for little children of both sexes. There are specific Greek words that could have been used if the group was of all boys or all girls.

Chapter Three

1. Robert Salt, "Affectionate Touch between Fathers and Preadolescent Sons," *Journal of Marriage and the Family,* vol. 53, August 1991, p. 545.

2. Job 41:15–17; also see Brown, Driver, and Briggs, p. 621.

3. Robert Salt, "Affectionate Touch Between Fathers and Preadolescent Sons," p. 545.

4. Ibid.

5. Ibid.

6. As we mentioned in Chapter Two, the blessing of Ephraim and Manasseh also had a unique spiritual message. When Jacob "crossed" his hands and blessed the younger with the older son's blessing, it was a picture of God's election.

7. Charles F. Pfeiffer, Howard F. Vos, and John Rea, editors, *Wycliffe Bible Encyclopedia* (Chicago: Moody Press, 1975), p. 750.

8. Harvey Richard Schiffman, *Sensation and Perception: An Integrated Approach* (New York: John Wiley & Sons, 1982), p. 107.

9. Frank A. Geldard, "Body English," *Psychology Today,* December 1968, p. 44.

10. Dolores Krieger, "Therapeutic Touch: The Imprimatur of Nursing," *American Journal of Nursing,* May 1975, p. 784.

11. *UCLA Monthly,* Alumni Association News, March–April 1981, p. 1.

12. *Reader's Digest,* vol. 140, January 1992, p. 21.

13. *Current Health,* vol. 13, no. 2, 1986, p. 13.

14. *Parents,* vol. 64, no. 2, 1989.

15. L. W. Linkous & R. M. Stutts, "Passive Tactile Stimulation Effects on the Muscle Tone of Hypotonic Developmentally Delayed Young Children," *Perceptual and Motor Skills,* vol. 1, no. 3, December 1990, pp. 951–954.

16. F. B. Dresslar, "The Psychology of Touch," *American Journal of Psychology,* vol. 6, 1984, p. 316.

17. Marcia Mark & Perla Werner, "Agitation and Touch in the Nursing Home," *Psychological Reports,* vol. 64, no. 3, part 2, 1989, p. 1020.

18. Ibid., p. 1023.

19. *Health,* vol. 21, no. 10, October 1989, p. 73.

20. James Hardison, *Let's Touch* (New Jersey: Prentice-Hall, 1980).

21. Helen Colton, *The Gift of Touch* (New York: Seaview/ Putnam, 1983), p. 102.

22. *Reader's Digest,* p. 21.

23. Edgar Wycoff & Jill Holley, "Effects of Flight Attendant's Touch upon Airline Passenger's Perceptions of the Attendant and the Airline," *Perceptual and Motor Skills,* vol. 1, no. 3, part 1, December 1990, pp. 932–934.

24. Colton, *The Gift of Touch,* p. 49.

25. Arthur Janov, "For Control, Cults Must Ease the Most Profound Pains," *Los Angeles Times,* Dec. 10, 1978, part 6, p. 3.

26. Marc H. Hollender, "The Wish to Be Held," *Archives of General Psychiatry,* vol. 22, 1970, p. 445.

27. Ibid., p. 446.

28. Ross Campbell, *How to Really Love Your Child* (Wheaton, Ill.: Victor Books, 1977), p. 73.

29. Alfred Edersheim, *The Life and Times of Jesus the Messiah, Part Two* (Grand Rapids: Wm. B. Eerdmans Publishing Co., 1972), p. 329.

30. Sidney Jourand, *Psychology Today,* vol. 22, no. 3, March 1988, p. 31.

Chapter Four

1. Gary Smalley, *The Key to Your Child's Heart* (Waco, TX: Word Books, Inc., 1984). See the chapter on "Balancing Loving Support Through Contracts," pp. 77–107.

2. Jack Burton, "Goodbye . . . Be good to each other." Article in *USA Today,* August 19, 1985, p. 1.

Chapter Five

1. To "value" something in the Scriptures is captured in the word *honor* that we looked at in Chapter Two. See also, Arndt and Gingrich, editors, *A Greek-English Lexicon of the New Testament and other Early Christian Literature* (Chicago: The University of Chicago Press, 1957), p. 825.

2. Brown, Driver, and Briggs, *Hebrew Lexicon,* p. 139.

3. Ibid.

4. That is why Psalm 95:6 translates the word *bless* as "to bow the knee" when it says, "Come let us worship the Lord and *bow before Him*" (literally *bless* Him).

5. J. D. Douglas, "Lion of Judah," *New Bible Dictionary*

(Grand Rapids: Wm. B. Eerdmans Publishing, 1971 edition),
p. 742.

6. Some circles dispute how Solomon, with all his many
wives, could be a model for a godly marriage. One can see a com-
mentary on the Song of Solomon for a fuller explanation, but in
brief here are two reasons why we feel Solomon's story can still
help any married couple today. First, Solomon did not begin to
take foreign wives and concubines until later in life, after his visit
by the Queen of Sheba. This book is dated by most scholars as
being written early in his reign as king. Most importantly, *any
person* including Solomon could leave their first love when they
stop walking with God. During Solomon's later years when he
took many wives, his fellowship with God was certainly not
where it was when he asked for the gift of wisdom.

7. S. Craig Glickman, *A Song for Lovers* (Downers Grove, IL:
Inter-Varsity Press, 1974), p. 48.

Chapter Six

1. M. J. Cohen, *The Jewish Celebration Book* (Philadelphia: The
Jewish Publication Society of America, 1946), p. 108.

2. Jay Stifler, *The Epistle to the Romans* (Chicago: Moody
Press, 1983), p. 119.

3. While we do not recommend the book because of its secular bent and conclusions, William S. Appleton's *Fathers and
Daughters* (New York: Berkley Books, 1984) has a number of chill-
ing studies that have been done on the destruction that happens
when a father has a poor relationship with his daughter.

4. We would like to extend our special thanks to Dr. Jeffry
M. Trent, Associate Professor of Medicine, University of Arizona,
for putting this example into "everyday English" for us.

Chapter Seven

1. For a helpful discussion on this point, see Charles Swin-
doll, *You and Your Child* (Nashville: Thomas Nelson Publishers,
1977), pp. 27–32.

2. Gary Smalley, *The Key to Your Child's Heart* (Word, 1984),
Chapter Two, "Expressing Loving Support—The Most Important
Aspect of Raising Children."

3. Smalley, *The Key to Your Child's Heart*, Chapter Seven,
"The Secret of a Close Knit Family."

4. Dewey Roussel, "Message of the White Dove," published
in *Reader's Digest*, September 1984, p. 29.

Chapter Eight

1. For an excellent discussion of our need today for a time of

"Sabbath rest," see Gordon MacDonald's *Ordering Your Private World* (Nashville: Thomas Nelson, 1984), the chapter titled "Rest Beyond Leisure."

2. Quoted by Roger Hawley, "The Family Blessing: Implications for Counseling." Unpublished paper presented at the Texas Council of Family Relations Conference, 1983.

Chapter Nine

1. H. Norman Schwarzkopf with Peter Petre, *It Doesn't Take a Hero* (New York: Bantam Books, 1992), p. 19.

2. Quotation by Rev. Steven Lyon in "Loving Your Children God's Way," unpublished message given in Dallas, Texas, 1983.

3. Robert Barnes, *You're Not My Daddy! Winning the Heart of Your Stepchild* (Dallas: Word Books, 1992).

4. An excellent book we would recommend that deals with the impact family influences can have on both the creation and cure of substance abuse is entitled *Good News for the Chemically Dependent* by Jeffery VanVonderen (Nashville: Thomas Nelson, 1985).

5. Richard A. McCormick, "Affective Disorders Among Pathological Gamblers Seeking Treatment," *American Journal of Psychiatry,* vol. 141, no. 2, p. 215.

Chapter Ten

1. See the book by Martin Seligman, *Learned Optimism* (New York: Pocket Books, 1990).

2. Christopher Peterson & Lisa M. Bossio, *Health and Optimism* (New York: The Free Press, 1991), p. 81.

Chapter Twelve

1. Stephen Thayer, "Close Encounters," *Psychology Today,* vol. 22, no. 3, March 1988, p. 33.

2. Ibid., p. 34.

3. *Hebrew Lexicon,* p. 174.

Chapter Thirteen

1. *Hebrew Lexicon,* p. 457.

2. Ibid., p. 866.

3. Arndt & Gingrich, *Greek-English Lexicon,* p. 317.

4. Gerald C. Davison & John M. Neale, *Abnormal Psychology* (New York: John Wiley & Sons, 1978), pp. 135ff.

Chapter Fifteen

1. Ken Medema, sound recording, *Through the Eyes of Love,* Word Records.

If you would like more information on Dr. Trent's ministry or "Blessing" seminars held in churches across the country, please write to:

John Trent, Ph.D.
Encouraging Words
12629 North Tatum Boulevard
Suite 420
Phoenix, AZ 85032

For information on Gary and John's "Love is a Decision" seminars, please write to:

Today's Family
Route 4, P.O. Box 2211
Lakeshore Drive
Branson, MO 65616

Additional Blessing Resources from Gary and John

The Blessing Workbook
The Blessing video
Daily Devotionals:
In Search of the Blessing
Giving the Blessing
A Dad's Blessing: Devotions for Fathers
The Legacy of the Blessing: Devotions for Mothers
Itty Bitty *Moments of Blessing*